Mastering Elasticsearch 5.x

Third Edition

Master the intricacies of Elasticsearch 5 and use it to create flexible and scalable search solutions

Bharvi Dixit

BIRMINGHAM - MUMBAI

Mastering Elasticsearch 5.x

Third Edition

First published: October 2013

Second edition: February 2015

Third edition: February 2017

Production reference: 1160217

Published by Packt Publishing Ltd.
Livery Place
35 Livery Street
Birmingham
B3 2PB, UK.
ISBN 978-1-78646-018-9

www.packtpub.com

Credits

Author

Bharvi Dixit

Reviewer

Marcelo Ochoa

Commissioning Editor

Amey Varangaonkar

Acquisition Editor

Divya Poojari

Content Development Editor

Cheryl Dsa

Technical Editor

Prasad Ramesh

Copy Editor

Safis Editing

Project Coordinator

Nidhi Joshi

Proofreader

Safis Editing

Indexer

Tejal Daruwale Soni

Graphics

Tania Dutta

Production Coordinator

Nilesh Mohite

About the Author

Bharvi Dixit is an IT professional with extensive experience of working on search servers, NoSQL databases, and cloud services. He holds a master's degree in computer science and is currently working with Sentieo, a USA-based financial data and equity research platform, where he leads the overall platform and architecture of the company spanning across hundreds of servers. At Sentieo, he also plays a key role in the search and data team.

He is also the organizer of Delhi's Elasticsearch Meetup Group, where he speaks about Elasticsearch and Lucene and is continuously building the community around these technologies.

Bharvi also works as a freelance Elasticsearch consultant and has helped more than half a dozen organizations adapt Elasticsearch to solve their complex search problems around different use cases, such as creating search solutions for big data-automated intelligence platforms in the area of counter-terrorism and risk management, as well as in other domains, such as recruitment, e-commerce, finance, social search, and log monitoring.

He has a keen interest in creating scalable backend platforms. His other areas of interests are search engineering, data analytics, and distributed computing. Java and Python are the primary languages in which he loves to write code. He has also built a proprietary software for consultancy firms.

In 2013, he started working on Lucene and Elasticsearch, and in 2016, he authored his first book, *Elasticsearch Essentials*, which was published by Packt. He has also worked as a technical reviewer for the book *Learning Kibana 5.0* by Packt.

You can connect with him on LinkedIn at `https://in.linkedin.com/in/bharvidixit` or can follow him on Twitter `@d_bharvi`.

Acknowledgements

This is my second book on Elasticsearch, and I am really fascinated by the love and feedback I got from the readers of my first book, *Elasticsearch Essentials*. The book you are holding covers Elasticsearch 5.x, the release of Elasticsearch that brings a whole lot of features and improvements to this great search server. Hopefully, after reading this book, you will not only get to know the underlying architecture of Lucene and Elasticsearch, but also posses a command over many advanced concepts, such as scripting, improving cluster performance, writing custom Java-based plugins, and many more.

Now it is time to say thank you.

I would like to thank my family for their continuous support, especially my brother, Patanjali Dixit, who has been a pillar of strength for me at each step throughout my career. I extend my big thanks to Lavleen for the love, support, and encouragement she gave during all those days when I was busy writing this book or solving complex problems at work.

I would like to extend my thanks to the Packt team working on this book, including our technical reviewer. Without their incredible support, the book wouldn't have been as great as it is now.

I would also like to thank all the people I'm working with at Sentieo for all their love and for creating a culture that helps make work more fun. At Sentieo, I extend my special thanks to Atul Shah, who always inspired me to go into the intricacies of Lucene and Elasticsearch and solve some really complex problems using these technologies.

Finally, thanks to Shay Banon for creating Elasticsearch and to all the people who contributed to the libraries and modules published around this project.

Once again, thank you.

About the Reviewer

Marcelo Ochoa works at the system laboratory of Facultad de Ciencias Exactas of the Universidad Nacional del Centro de la Provincia de Buenos Aires and is the CTO at scotas, a company that specializes in near real-time search solutions using Apache Solr and Oracle. He divides his time between university jobs and external projects related to Oracle and big data technologies. He has worked on several Oracle-related projects, such as the translation of Oracle manuals and multimedia CBTs. His background is in database, network, web, and Java technologies. In the XML world, he is known as the developer of the DB Generator for the Apache Cocoon project. He has worked on open source projects such as DBPrism and DBPrism CMS, the Lucene-Oracle integration using the Oracle JVM Directory implementation, and the Restlet.org project, where he worked on the Oracle XDB Restlet Adapter, which is an alternative to writing native REST web services inside a database resident JVM. Since 2006, he has been part of an Oracle ACE program. Oracle ACEs are known for their strong credentials as Oracle community enthusiasts and advocates, with candidates nominated by ACEs in the Oracle technology and applications communities. He has coauthored *Oracle Database Programming using Java and Web Services* by Digital Press and *Professional XML Databases* by Wrox Press, and has worked as a technical reviewer for several Packt books, such as *Apache Solr 4 Cookbook*, *ElasticSearch Server*, and others.

www.PacktPub.com

For support files and downloads related to your book, please visit www.PacktPub.com.

Did you know that Packt offers eBook versions of every book published, with PDF and ePub files available? You can upgrade to the eBook version at www.PacktPub.com and as a print book customer, you are entitled to a discount on the eBook copy. Get in touch with us at service@packtpub.com for more details.

At www.PacktPub.com, you can also read a collection of free technical articles, sign up for a range of free newsletters and receive exclusive discounts and offers on Packt books and eBooks.

https://www.packtpub.com/mapt

Get the most in-demand software skills with Mapt. Mapt gives you full access to all Packt books and video courses, as well as industry-leading tools to help you plan your personal development and advance your career.

Why subscribe?

- Fully searchable across every book published by Packt
- Copy and paste, print, and bookmark content
- On demand and accessible via a web browser

Customer Feedback

Thanks for purchasing this Packt book. At Packt, quality is at the heart of our editorial process. To help us improve, please leave us an honest review on this book's Amazon page at `https://www.amazon.com/dp/1786460181`.

If you'd like to join our team of regular reviewers, you can e-mail us at `customerreviews@packtpub.com`. We award our regular reviewers with free eBooks and videos in exchange for their valuable feedback. Help us be relentless in improving our products!

Table of Contents

Preface

Welcome to the world of Elasticsearch and *Mastering Elasticsearch 5.x, Third Edition*. While reading the book, you'll be taken through different topics—all connected to Elasticsearch. Please remember though that this book is not meant for beginners, and we really treat the book as a follow-up to *Mastering Elasticsearch 5.x, Second Edition*, which was based on Elasticsearch version 1.4.x. There is a lot of new content in the book since Elasticsearch has gone through many changes between versions 1.x and 5.x.

Throughout the book, we will discuss different topics related to Elasticsearch and Lucene. We start with an introduction to the world of Lucene and Elasticsearch to introduce you to the world of queries provided by Elasticsearch, where we discuss different topics related to queries, such as filtering and which query to choose in a particular situation. Of course, querying is not everything, and because of that, the book you are holding in your hands provides information on newly introduced aggregations and features that will help you give meaning to the data you have indexed in Elasticsearch indices and provide a better search experience for your users.

We have also decided to cover the approaches of data modeling and handling relational data in Elasticsearch along with taking you through the scripting module of Elasticsearch and show some examples of using the latest default scripting language, Painless.

Even though, for most users, querying and data analysis are the most interesting parts of Elasticsearch, they are not all that we need to discuss. Because of this, the book tries to bring you additional information when it comes to index architecture, such as choosing the right number of shards and replicas, adjusting the shard allocation behavior, and so on. We will also get into places where Elasticsearch meets Lucene, and we will discuss topics such as different scoring algorithms, choosing the right store mechanism, what the differences between them are, and why choosing the proper one matters.

Last but not least, we touch on the administration part of Elasticsearch by discussing discovery and recovery modules and the human-friendly cat API, which allows us to very quickly get relevant administrative information in a form that most humans should be able to read without parsing JSON responses. We also talk about ingest nodes, which allow you to preprocess data within Elasticsearch before indexing takes place and use tribe nodes, giving the ability to create federated searches across many nodes.

Because of the title of the book, we couldn't omit performance-related topics, and we decided to dedicate a whole chapter to it.

Just as with the second edition of the book, we decided to include a chapter dedicated to development of Elasticsearch plugins, showing you how to set up the Apache Maven project and develop two types of plugins—custom REST action and custom analysis.

At the end, we have included one chapter discussing the components of the complete Elastic Stack, and you should get a great overview of how to start with tools such as Logstash, Kibana, and Beats after reading the chapter.

If you think that you are interested in these topics after reading about them, we think this is a book for you, and hopefully, you will like the book after reading the last words of the summary in Chapter 12, *Introducing Elastic Stack 5.0*.

What this book covers

Chapter 1, *Revisiting Elasticsearch and the Changes*, guides you through how Apache Lucene works and will introduce you to Elasticsearch 5.x, describing the basic concepts and showing you the important changes in Elasticsearch from version 1.x to 5.x.

Chapter 2, *The Improved Query DSL*, describes the new default scoring algorithm, BM25, and how it would be better than the previous TF-IDF algorithm. In addition to that, it explains various Elasticsearch features, such as query rewriting, query templates, changes in query modules, and various queries to choose from in a given scenario.

Chapter 3, *Beyond Full Text Search*, describes queries about rescoring, multimatching control, and function score queries. In addition to that, this chapter covers the scripting module of Elasticsearch.

Chapter 4, *Data Modeling and Analytics*, discusses different approaches of data modeling in Elasticsearch and also covers how to handle relationships among documents using parent-child and nested data types, along with focusing on practical considerations. It further discusses the aggregation module of Elasticsearch for the purpose of data analytics.

Chapter 5, *Improving the User Search Experience*, focuses on topics for improving the user search experience using suggesters, which allows you to correct user-query spelling mistakes and build efficient autocomplete mechanisms. In addition to that, it covers how to improve query relevance and how to use synonyms to search.

Chapter 6, *The Index Distribution Architecture*, covers techniques for choosing the right amount of shards and replicas, how routing works, how shard allocation works, and how to alter its behavior. In addition to that, we discuss what query execution preference is and how it allows us to choose where the queries are going to be executed.

Chapter 7, *Low-Level Index Control*, describes how to alter Apache Lucene scoring and how to choose an alternative scoring algorithm. It also covers NRT searching and indexing and transaction log usage and allows you to understand segment merging and tune it for your use case along with the details about removed merge policies inside Elasticsearch 5.x. At the end of the chapter, you will also find information about IO throttling and Elasticsearch caching.

Chapter 8, *Elasticsearch Administration*, focuses on concepts related to administering Elasticsearch. It describes what the discovery, gateway, and recovery modules are, how to configure them, and why you should bother. We also describe what the cat API is and how to back up and restore your data to different cloud services (such as Amazon AWS and Microsoft Azure).

Chapter 9, *Data Transformation and Federated Search*, covers the latest feature of Elasticsearch 5, that is ingest node, which allows us to preprocess data into the Elasticsearch cluster itself before indexing. It further tells us about how federated search works with different clusters using tribe nodes.

Chapter 10, *Improving Performance*, discusses Elasticsearch performance improvements under different loads and what the right way of scaling production clusters is, along with covering the insights into garbage collections and hot threads issues and how to deal with them. It further covers query profiling and query benchmarking. In the end, it explains the general Elasticsearch cluster tuning advice under high query rate scenarios versus high indexing throughput scenarios.

Chapter 11, *Developing Elasticsearch Plugins*, covers Elasticsearch plugins' development by showing and describing in depth how to write your own REST action and language analysis plugin.

Chapter 12, *Introducing Elastic Stack 5.0*, introduces you to the components of Elastic Stack 5.0, covering Elasticsearch, Logstash, Kibana, and Beats.

What you need for this book

This book was written using Elasticsearch 5.0.x, and all the examples and functions should work with it. In addition to that, you'll need a command-line tool that allows you to send HTTP requests such as curl, which are available for most operating systems. Please note that all examples in this book use the mentioned curl tool. If you want to use another tool, please remember to format the request in an appropriate way that is understood by the tool of your choice.

In addition to that, to run examples in Chapter 11, *Developing Elasticsearch Plugins*, you will need a Java Development Kit (JDK) Version 1.8.0_73 and above installed and an editor that will allow you to develop your code (or a Java IDE such as Eclipse). To build the code and manage dependencies in Chapter 11, *Developing Elasticsearch Plugins*, we are using Apache Maven.

The last chapter of this book has been written using Elastic Stack 5.0.0, so you will need to have Logstash, Kibana, and Metricbeat, all comprising the same version.

Who this book is for

This book was written for Elasticsearch users and enthusiasts who are already familiar with the basic concepts of this great search server and want to extend their knowledge of Elasticsearch. It also covers topics such as how Apache Lucene or Elasticsearch works, along with getting aware of the changes from Elasticsearch 1.x to 5.x. In addition to that, readers who want to see how to improve their query relevancy and learn how to extend Elasticsearch with their own plugin may find this book interesting and useful.

If you are new to Elasticsearch and you are not familiar with basic concepts, such as querying and data indexing, you may find it a little difficult to use this book as most of the chapters assume that you have this knowledge already.

Conventions

In this book, you will find a number of styles of text that distinguish between different kinds of information. Here are some examples of these styles, and an explanation of their meaning.

Code words in text are shown as follows: "but not the Elasticsearch term in the document field"

A block of code is set as follows:

```
public class CustomRestActionPlugin extends Plugin implements ActionPlugin
{
  @Override
    public List<Class<? extends RestHandler>> getRestHandlers() {
          return Collections.singletonList(CustomRestAction.class);
      }
}
```

When we wish to draw your attention to a particular part of a code block, the relevant lines or items are set in bold:

```
curl -XGET 'localhost:9200/clients/_search?pretty' -d '{
  "query" : {
   "prefix" : {
    "name" : {
     "prefix" : "j",
     "rewrite" : "constant_score_boolean"
    }
   }
  }
}'
```

Any command-line input or output is written as follows:

```
curl -XPUT 'localhost:9200/mastering_meta/_settings' -d '{
  "index" : {
   "auto_expand_replicas" : "0-all"
  }
}
```

New terms and **important words** are shown in bold. Words that you see on the screen, for example, in menus or dialog boxes, appear in the text like this: "field and hit the **Create** button"

Warnings or important notes appear in a box like this.

Tips and tricks appear like this.

Reader feedback

Feedback from our readers is always welcome. Let us know what you think about this book-what you liked or disliked. Reader feedback is important for us as it helps us develop titles that you will really get the most out of.

To send us general feedback, simply e-mail feedback@packtpub.com, and mention the book's title in the subject of your message.

If there is a topic that you have expertise in and you are interested in either writing or contributing to a book, see our author guide at `www.packtpub.com/authors`.

Customer support

Now that you are the proud owner of a Packt book, we have a number of things to help you to get the most from your purchase.

Downloading the example code

You can download the example code files for this book from your account at `http://www.packtpub.com`. If you purchased this book elsewhere, you can visit `http://www.packtpub.com/support` and register to have the files e-mailed directly to you.

You can download the code files by following these steps:

1. Log in or register to our website using your e-mail address and password.
2. Hover the mouse pointer on the **SUPPORT** tab at the top.
3. Click on **Code Downloads & Errata**.
4. Enter the name of the book in the **Search** box.
5. Select the book for which you're looking to download the code files.
6. Choose from the drop-down menu where you purchased this book from.
7. Click on **Code Download**.

Once the file is downloaded, please make sure that you unzip or extract the folder using the latest version of:

- WinRAR / 7-Zip for Windows
- Zipeg / iZip / UnRarX for Mac
- 7-Zip / PeaZip for Linux

The code bundle for the book is also hosted on GitHub at `https://github.com/PacktPublishing/Mastering-ElasticSearch-5.x-Third-Edition`. We also have other code bundles from our rich catalog of books and videos available at `https://github.com/PacktPublishing/`. Check them out!

Downloading the color images of this book

We also provide you with a PDF file that has color images of the screenshots/diagrams used in this book. The color images will help you better understand the changes in the output. You can download this file from `https://www.packtpub.com/sites/default/files/down loads/MasteringElasticSearch5dotxThirdEdition_ColorImages.pdf`.

Errata

Although we have taken every care to ensure the accuracy of our content, mistakes do happen. If you find a mistake in one of our books-maybe a mistake in the text or the code- we would be grateful if you could report this to us. By doing so, you can save other readers from frustration and help us improve subsequent versions of this book. If you find any errata, please report them by visiting `http://www.packtpub.com/submit-errata`, selecting your book, clicking on the **Errata Submission Form** link, and entering the details of your errata. Once your errata are verified, your submission will be accepted and the errata will be uploaded to our website or added to any list of existing errata under the Errata section of that title.

To view the previously submitted errata, go to `https://www.packtpub.com/books/conten t/support` and enter the name of the book in the search field. The required information will appear under the **Errata** section.

Piracy

Piracy of copyrighted material on the Internet is an ongoing problem across all media. At Packt, we take the protection of our copyright and licenses very seriously. If you come across any illegal copies of our works in any form on the Internet, please provide us with the location address or website name immediately so that we can pursue a remedy.

Please contact us at `copyright@packtpub.com` with a link to the suspected pirated material.

We appreciate your help in protecting our authors and our ability to bring you valuable content.

Questions

If you have a problem with any aspect of this book, you can contact us at `questions@packtpub.com`, and we will do our best to address the problem.

1
Revisiting Elasticsearch and the Changes

Welcome to *Mastering Elasticsearch 5.x, Third Edition*. **Elasticsearch** has progressed rapidly from version 1.x, released in 2014, to version 5.x, released in 2016. During the two-and-a-half-year period since 1.0.0, adoption has skyrocketed, and both vendors and the community have committed bug-fixes, interoperability enhancements, and rich feature upgrades to ensure Elasticsearch remains the most popular NoSQL storage, indexing, and search utility for both structured and unstructured documents, as well as gaining popularity as a log analysis tool as part of the Elastic Stack.

We treat *Mastering Elasticsearch* as a book that will systematize your knowledge about Elasticsearch, and extend it by showing some examples of how to leverage your knowledge in certain situations. If you are looking for a book that will help you start your journey into the world of Elasticsearch, please take a look at *Elasticsearch Essentials*, also published by Packt.

Before going further into the book, we assume that you already know the basic concepts of Elasticsearch for performing operations such as how to index documents, how to send queries to get the documents you are interested in, how to narrow down the results of your queries by using filters, and how to calculate statistics for your data with the use of the aggregation mechanism. However, before getting to the exciting functionality that Elasticsearch offers, we think we should start with a quick overview of **Apache Lucene**, which is a full text search library that Elasticsearch uses to build and search its indices. We also need to make sure that we understand Lucene correctly, as *Mastering Elasticsearch* requires this understanding. By the end of this chapter, we will have covered the following topics:

- An overview of Lucene and Elasticsearch
- Introducing Elasticsearch 5.x

- Latest features introduced in Elasticsearch
- The changes in Elasticsearch after 1.x

An overview of Lucene

In order to fully understand how Elasticsearch works, especially when it comes to indexing and query processing, it is crucial to understand how the Apache Lucene library works. Under the hood, Elasticsearch uses Lucene to handle document indexing. The same library is also used to perform a search against the indexed documents. In the next few pages, we will try to show you the basics of Apache Lucene, just in case you've never used it.

Lucene is a mature, open source, highly performing, scalable, light and, yet, very powerful library written in Java. Its core comes as a single file of the Java library with no dependencies, and allows you to index documents and search them with its out-of-the-box full text search capabilities. Of course, there are extensions to Apache Lucene that allow different language handling, and enable spellchecking, highlighting, and much more, but if you don't need those features, you can download a single file and use it in your application.

Getting deeper into the Lucene index

In order to fully understand Lucene, the following terminologies need to be understood first:

- **Document**: This is a main data carrier used during indexing and search, containing one or more fields, which contains the data we put and get from Lucene.
- **Field**: This is a section of the document which is built of two parts: the name and the value.
- **Term**: This is a unit of search representing a word from the text.
- **Token**: This is an occurrence of a term from the text of the field. It consists of term text, start and end offset, and a type.

Inverted index

Apache Lucene writes all the information to the structure called the **inverted** index. It is a data structure that maps the terms in the index to the documents, not the other way round, as the relational database does. You can think of an inverted index as a data structure, where data is term oriented rather than document oriented.

Let's see how a simple inverted index can look. For example, let's assume that we have the documents with only the title field to be indexed, and they look like the following:

- Elasticsearch Server (document 1)
- Mastering Elasticsearch (document 2)
- Elasticsearch Essentials (document 3)

So, the index (in a very simple way) could be visualized as shown in the following table:

Term	Count	Document : Position
Elasticsearch	3	1:1, 2:2, 3:1
Essentials	1	3:2
Mastering	1	2:1
Server	1	1:2

As you can see, each term points to the number of documents it is present in, along with its position. This allows for a very efficient and fast search such as term-based queries. In addition to this, each term has a number connected to it: the count, telling Lucene how often it occurs.

Segments

Each index is divided into multiple write once and read many times segments. When indexing, after a single segment is written to disk, it can't be updated. For example, the information about deleted documents is stored in a separate file, but the segment itself is not updated.

However, multiple segments can be merged together in a process called **segments merge**. After forcing, segments are merged, or after Lucene decides it is time for merging to be performed, segments are merged together by Lucene to create larger ones. This can be I/O demanding; however, it is needed to clean up some information because during that time some information that is not needed anymore is deleted; for example, the deleted documents. In addition to this, searching with the use of one larger segment is faster than searching against multiple smaller ones holding the same data.

Of course, the actual index created by Lucene is much more complicated and advanced, and consists of more than the terms, their counts, and documents, in which they are present. We would like to tell you about a few of these additional index pieces because even though they are internal, it is usually good to know about them, as they can be very useful.

Norms

A **norm** is a factor associated with each indexed document and stores normalization factors used to compute the score relative to the query. Norms are computed on the basis of index time boosts and are indexed along with the documents. With the use of norms, Lucene is able to provide an index time-boosting functionality at the cost of a certain amount of additional space needed for norms indexation and some amount of additional memory.

Term vectors

Term vectors are small inverted indices per document. They consist of pairs–a term and its frequency–and can optionally include information about the term position. By default, Lucene and Elasticsearch don't enable term vectors indexing, but some functionalities, such as the fast vector highlighting, require them to be present.

Posting formats

With the release of Lucene 4.0, the library introduced the so-called codec architecture, giving developers control over how the index files are written onto the disk. One of the parts of the index is the posting format, which stores fields, terms, documents, term positions and offsets, and, finally, the payloads (a byte array stored at an arbitrary position in the Lucene index, which can contain any information we want). Lucene contains different posting formats for different purposes; for example; one that is optimized for high cardinality fields such as the unique identifier.

Doc values

As we have already mentioned, the Lucene index is the so-called **inverted index**. However, for certain features, such as aggregations, such an architecture is not the best one. The mentioned functionality operates on the document level and not the term level because Elasticsearch needs to uninvert the index before calculations can be done. Because of that, doc values were introduced and an additional structure was used for sorting and aggregations. The doc values store uninverted data for a field that they are turned on for. Both Lucene and Elasticsearch allow us to configure the implementation used to store them, giving us the possibility of memory-based doc values, disk-based doc values, and a combination of the two. Doc values are default in Elasticsearch since the 2.x release.

Document analysis

When we index a document into Elasticsearch, it goes through an analysis phase which is necessary in order to create the inverted indexes. It is a series of steps performed by Lucene which are depicted in following image:

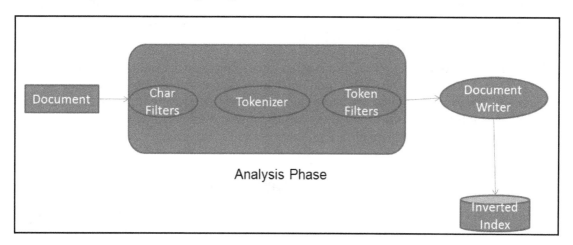

Analysis is done by the analyzer, which is built of a tokenizer and zero or more filters, and can also have zero or more character filters.

A tokenizer in Lucene is used to divide the text into tokens, which are basically terms with additional information, such as its position in the original text and its length. The result of the tokenizer work is a so-called token stream, where the tokens are put one by one and are ready to be processed by filters.

Apart from the tokenizer, the Lucene analyzer is built of zero or more filters that are used to process tokens in the token stream. For example, it can remove tokens from the stream, change them, or even produce new ones. There are numerous filters and you can easily create new ones. Some examples of filters are as follows:

- **Lowercase filter**: This makes all the tokens lowercase
- **ASCII folding filter**: This removes non-ASCII parts from tokens
- **Synonyms filter**: This is responsible for changing one token to another on the basis of synonym rules
- **Multiple language stemming filters**: These are responsible for reducing tokens (actually the text part that they provide) into their root or base forms, the stem

Filters are processed one after another, so we have almost unlimited analysis possibilities with adding multiple filters one after another.

The last thing is the character filtering, which is used before the tokenizer and is responsible for processing text before any analysis is done. One of the examples of the character filter is the HTML tags removal process.

This analysis phase is applied during query time also. However, you can also choose the other path and not analyze your queries. This is crucial to remember because some of the Elasticsearch queries are being analyzed and some are not. For example, the `prefix` query is not analyzed and the match query is analyzed.

What you should remember about indexing and querying analysis is that the index should be matched by the query term. If they don't match, Lucene won't return the desired documents. For example, if you are using stemming and lowercasing during indexing, you need to be sure that the terms in the query are also lowercased and stemmed, or your queries will return no results at all.

Basics of the Lucene query language

Some of the query types provided by Elasticsearch support Apache Lucene query parser syntax. Because of this, it is crucial to understand the Lucene query language.

A query is divided by Apache Lucene into terms and operators. A term, in Lucene, can be a single word or a phrase (a group of words surrounded by double quote characters). If the query is set to be analyzed, the defined analyzer will be used on each of the terms that form the query.

A query can also contain Boolean operators that connect terms to each other forming clauses. The list of Boolean operators is as follows:

- `AND`: This means that the given two terms (left and right operand) need to match in order for the clause to be matched. For example, we would run a query, such as `apache AND lucene`, to match documents with both `apache` and `lucene` terms in a document field.
- `OR`: This means that any of the given terms may match in order for the clause to be matched. For example, we would run a query, such as `apache OR lucene`, to match documents with `apache` or `lucene` (or both) terms in a document field.
- `NOT`: This means that in order for the document to be considered a match, the term appearing after the `NOT` operator must not match. For example, we would run a query `lucene NOT Elasticsearch` to match documents that contain the `lucene` term, but not the `Elasticsearch` term in the document field.

In addition to these, we may use the following operators:

- +: This means that the given term needs to be matched in order for the document to be considered as a match. For example, in order to find documents that match the `lucene` term and may match the `apache` term, we would run a query such as `+lucene apache`.
- −: This means that the given term can't be matched in order for the document to be considered a match. For example, in order to find a document with the `lucene` term, but not the `Elasticsearch` term, we would run a query such as `+lucene -Elasticsearch`.

When not specifying any of the previous operators, the default `OR` operator will be used.

In addition to all these, there is one more thing: you can use parentheses to group clauses together; for example, with something like the following query:

```
Elasticsearch AND (mastering OR book)
```

Querying fields

Of course, just like in Elasticsearch, in Lucene all your data is stored in fields that build the document. In order to run a query against a field, you need to provide the field name, add the colon character, and provide the clause that should be run against that field. For example, if you would like to match documents with the term `Elasticsearch` in the `title` field, you would run the following query:

```
title:Elasticsearch
```

You can also group multiple clauses. For example, if you would like your query to match all the documents having the `Elasticsearch` term and the `mastering book` phrase in the `title` field, you could run a query like the following code:

```
title:(+Elasticsearch +"mastering book")
```

The previous query can also be expressed in the following way:

```
+title:Elasticsearch +title:"mastering book"
```

Term modifiers

In addition to the standard field query with a simple term or clause, Lucene allows us to modify the terms we pass in the query with modifiers. The most common modifiers, which you will be familiar with, are wildcards. There are two wildcards supported by Lucene, the ? and * terms. The first one will match any character and the second one will match multiple characters.

In addition to this, Lucene supports fuzzy and proximity searches with the use of the ~ character and an integer following it. When used with a single word term, it means that we want to search for terms that are similar to the one we've modified (the so-called fuzzy search). The integer after the ~ character specifies the maximum number of edits that can be done to consider the term similar. For example, if we would run a query, such as `writer~2`, both the terms `writer` and `writers` would be considered a match.

When the ~ character is used on a phrase, the integer number we provide is telling Lucene how much distance between the words is acceptable. For example, let's take the following query:

```
title:"mastering Elasticsearch"
```

It would match the document with the `title` field containing `mastering Elasticsearch`, but not `mastering book Elasticsearch`. However, if we ran a query, such as `title:"mastering Elasticsearch"~2`, it would result in both example documents being matched.

We can also use boosting to increase our term importance by using the ^ character and providing a float number. Boosts lower than 1 would result in decreasing the document importance. Boosts higher than 1 would result in increasing the importance. The default boost value is 1. Please refer to the *The changed default text scoring in Lucene – BM25* section in `Chapter 2`, *The Improved Query DSL*, for further information on what boosting is and how it is taken into consideration during document scoring.

In addition to all these, we can use square and curly brackets to allow range searching. For example, if we would like to run a range search on a numeric field, we could run the following query:

```
price:[10.00 TO 15.00]
```

The preceding query would result in all documents with the `price` field between `10.00` and `15.00` inclusive.

In case of string-based fields, we also can run a range query; for example name:`[Adam TO Adria]`.

The preceding query would result in all documents containing all the terms between `Adam` and `Adria` in the `name` field including them.

If you would like your range bound or bounds to be exclusive, use curly brackets instead of the square ones. For example, in order to find documents with the `price` field between `10.00` inclusive and `15.00` exclusive, we would run the following query:

```
price:[10.00 TO 15.00}
```

If you would like your range bound from one side and not bound by the other, for example querying for documents with a price higher than `10.00`, we would run the following query:

```
price:[10.00 TO *]
```

Handling special characters

In case you want to search for one of the special characters (which are +, −, & &, | |, !, (,), { }, [ ], ^, ", ~, *, ?, :, \, /), you need to escape it with the use of the backslash (\) character. For example, to search for the `abc"efg` term you need to do something like `abc"efg`.

An overview of Elasticsearch

Although we've said that we expect the reader to be familiar with Elasticsearch, we would really like to give you a short introduction to the concepts of this great search engine.

As you probably know, Elasticsearch is a distributed full text search and analytic engine that is built on top of Lucene to build search and analysis-oriented applications. It was originally started by *Shay Banon* and published in February 2010. Since then, it has rapidly gained popularity within just a few years and has become an important alternative to other open source and commercial solutions. It is one of the most downloaded open source projects.

The key concepts

There are a few concepts that come with Elasticsearch, and their understanding is crucial to fully understand how Elasticsearch works and operates:

- **Index**: A logical namespace under which Elasticsearch stores data and may be built with more than one Lucene index using shards and replicas.
- **Document**: A document is a JSON object that contains the actual data in key value pairs. It is very important to understand that when a field is indexed for the first time into the index, Elasticsearch creates a data type for that field. Starting from version 2.x, a very strict type checking gets done.
- **Type**: A doc type in Elasticsearch represents a class of similar documents. A type consists of a name such as a user or a blog post, and a mapping including data types and the Lucene configurations for each field.
- **Mapping:** As already mentioned in the *An overview of Lucene* section, all documents are analyzed before being indexed. We can configure how the input text is divided into tokens, which tokens should be filtered out, or what additional processing, such as removing HTML tags, is needed. This is where mapping comes into play–it holds all the information about the analysis chain. Besides the fact that Elasticsearch can automatically discover a field type by looking at its value, in most cases we will want to configure the mappings ourselves to avoid unpleasant surprises.
- **Node**: A single instance of Elasticsearch running on a machine. Elasticsearch nodes can serve different purposes. Of course, Elasticsearch is designed to index and search our data, so the first type of node is the `data` node. Such nodes hold the data and search on them. The second type of node is the `master` node–a node that works as a supervisor of the cluster controlling other nodes' work. The third node type is the `client` node, which is used as a query router. The fourth type of node is the `tribe` node, which was introduced in Elasticsearch 1.0. The `tribe` node can join multiple clusters and thus act as a bridge between them, allowing us to execute almost all Elasticsearch functionalities on multiple clusters just like we would by using a single cluster. Elasticsearch 5.0 has also introduced a new type of node called the `ingest` node, which can be used for data transformation before the data gets indexed.
- **Cluster**: A cluster is a single name under which one or more nodes/instances of Elasticsearch are connected to each other.
- **Shard**: Shards are containers that can be stored on a single node or multiple nodes and are composed of Lucene segments. An index is divided into one or more shards to make the data distributable. For the index, shards once created cannot be increased or decreased.

A shard can be either primary or secondary. A primary shard is the one where all the operations that change the index are directed. A secondary shard is the one that contains duplicate data of the primary shard and helps in quickly searching data as well as in high availability; in case the machine that holds the primary shard goes down, then the secondary shard becomes the primary shard automatically.

- **Replica**: A duplicate copy of the data living in a shard for high availability. Having a replica also provides a faster search experience.

Working of Elasticsearch

Elasticsearch uses the **zen discovery** module for cluster formation. In 1.x, multicast was the default discovery used in Elasticsearch, but in 2.x unicast became the default discovery type. Although, multicast was available in Elasticsearch 2.x as a plugin. Multicast support has completely been removed from Elasticsearch 5.0

When an Elasticsearch node starts, it performs discovery and searches for the list of unicast hosts (master eligible nodes), which are configured in the `elasticsearch.yml` configuration file using the `discovery.zen.ping.unicast.hosts` parameter. By default, the default list of unicast hosts is `["127.0.0.1", "[::1]"]` so that each node, when starting, does not form a cluster only with itself. We will have a detailed section on zen discovery and node configurations in `Chapter 8`, *Elasticsearch Administration*.

Introducing Elasticsearch 5.x

In 2015, Elasticsearch, after acquiring Kibana, Logstash, Beats, and Found, re-branded the company name as Elastic. According to *Shay Banon*, the name change is part of an initiative to better align the company with the broad solutions it provides: future products, and new innovations created by Elastic's massive community of developers and enterprises that utilize the ELK stack for everything from real-time search, to sophisticated analytics, to building modern data applications.

But having several products under one hood resulted in discord among them during the release process and started creating confusion for the users. This resulted in the ELK stack being renamed to Elastic Stack and the company decided to keep releasing all components of the Elastic Stack together. This is so that they will all share the same version number for all the products to keep speed with your deployments, simplify compatibility testing, and make it even easier for developers to add new functionality across the stack.

The very first GA release under Elastic stack is 5.0.0, which will be covered throughout this book. Further, Elasticsearch keeps pace with Lucene version releases to incorporate bug fixes and the latest features into Elasticsearch. Elasticsearch 5.0 is based on Lucene 6, which is a major release from Lucene with some awesome new features and a focus on improving the search speed. We will discuss Lucene 6 in upcoming chapters to let you know how Elasticsearch is going to have some awesome improvements, both from search and storage points of view.

Introducing new features in Elasticsearch

Elasticsearch 5.x has many improvements and has gone through a great refactoring, which caused removal/deprecation of some features. We will keep discussing the removed/improved/new features in upcoming chapters, but for now let's take an overview of the new and improved things in Elasticsearch.

New features in Elasticsearch 5.x

Following are some of the most important features introduced in Elasticsearch version 5.0:

- **Ingest node**: This node is a new type of node in Elasticsearch, which can be used for simple data transformation and enrichment before actual data indexing takes place. The best thing is that any node can be configured to act as an `ingest` node and it is very lighter across the board. You can avoid Logstash for these tasks because the `ingest` node is a Java based implementation of the Logstash filter and comes as a default in Elasticsearch itself.

- **Index shrinking**: By design, once an index is created, there is no provision of reducing the number of shards for that index and this brings a lot of challenges since each shard consumes some resources. Although this design still remains same, to make life easier for users, Elasticsearch has introduced a new `_shrink` API to overcome this problem. This API allows you to shrink an existing index into a newer index with a fewer number of shards.

We will cover the `ingest` node and `shrink` API in detail under `Chapter` `9`, *Data Transformation and Federated Search*.

- **Painless scripting language**: In Elasticsearch, scripting has always been a matter of concern because of its slowness and for security reasons. Elasticsearch 5.0 includes a new scripting language called **Painless**, which has been designed to be fast and secure. Painless is still going through lots of improvements to make it more awesome and easily adaptable. We will cover it under `Chapter` `3`, *Beyond Full Text Search*.

- **Instant aggregations**: Queries have been completely refactored in 5.0; they are now parsed on the coordinating node and serialized to different nodes in a binary format. This allows Elasticsearch to be much more efficient, with more cache-able queries, especially on data separated into time-based indices. This will cause a significant speed up for aggregations.

- **A new completion suggester**: The `completion` suggester has undergone a complete rewrite. This means that the syntax and data structure for fields of type completion have changed, as have the syntax and response of the `completion` suggester requests. The `completion` suggester is now built on top of the first iteration of Lucene's new `suggest` API.

- **Multi-dimensional points**: This is one of the most exciting features of Lucene 6, which empowers Elasticsearch 5.0. It is built using the k-d tree geospatial data structure to offer a fast single- and multi-dimensional numeric range and a geospatial point-in-shape filtering. A multi-dimensional point helps in reducing disk storage, memory utilization, and faster searches.

- **Delete by Query API**: After much demand from the community, Elasticsearch has finally provided the ability to delete documents based on a matching query using the `_delete_by_query` REST endpoint.

New features in Elasticsearch 2.x

Apart from the features discussed just now, you can also benefit from all of the new features that came in Elasticsearch version 2.x. For those who have not had a look at the 2.x series, let's have a quick revamp of the new features which came with Elasticsearch under this series:

- **Reindex API**: In Elasticsearch, re-indexing of documents is almost needed by every user, under several scenarios. The `_reindex` API makes this task very easy and you do not need to worry about writing your own code to do the same. This API, at the simplest level, provides the ability to move data from one index to another but also provides a great control while re-indexing the documents, such as using scripts for data transformation and many other parameters. You can take a look at the reindex API at following URL `https://www.elastic.co/guide/en/elasticsearch/reference/master/docs-reindex.html`.

- **Update by query**: Similar to re-indexing requirements, a user also demands to easily update the documents in place, based on certain conditions, without re-indexing the data. Elasticsearch provided this feature using the `update_by_query` REST endpoint in version 2.x.

- **Tasks API**: The task management API, which is exposed by the `_task` REST endpoint, is used for retrieving information about the currently executing tasks on one or more nodes in the cluster. The following examples show the usage of the `tasks` API:

```
GET /_tasks
GET /_tasks?nodes=nodeId1,nodeId2
GET /_tasks?nodes=nodeId1&actions=cluster;*
```

- Since each task has an ID, you can either wait for the completion of the task or cancel the task in the following way:

```
POST /_tasks/taskId1/_cancel
```

- **Query profiler**: The `Profile` API is an awesome tool to debug the queries and get the insights to know why a certain query is slow and take steps to improve it. This API was released in the 2.2.0 version and provides detailed timing information about the execution of individual components in a search request. You just need to send `profile` as `true` with your query object to get this working for you. For example:

```
curl -XGET 'localhost:9200/_search' -d '{
  "profile": true,
```

```
    "query" : {
      "match" : { "message" : "query profiling test" }
    }
  }'
```

The changes in Elasticsearch

The change list is very long and covering all the change details is out of the scope of this book, since most of the changes are internal level changes which a user should not be worried about. However, we will cover the most important changes an existing Elasticsearch user must know.

Although this book is based on Elasticsearch version 5.0, it is very important for the reader to get to know the changes being made between versions 1.x to 2.x. If you are new to Elasticsearch and are not aware about older versions, you can skip this section.

Changes between 1.x to 2.x

Elasticsearch version 2.x was focused on **resiliency**, **reliability**, **simplification**, and **features**. This release was based on Apache Lucene 5.x and specifically improves query execution and spatial search.

Version 2.x also delivers considerable improvements in index recovery. Historically, Elasticsearch index recovery was extremely painful, whether as part of node maintenance or an upgrade. The bigger the cluster, the bigger the headache. Node failures or a reboot can trigger a shard reallocation storm, and entire shards are sometimes copied over the network, despite having whole data. Users have also reported more than a day of recovery time to restart a single node.

With 2.x, recovery of existing replica shards became almost instant, and there is more lenient reallocation, which avoids reshuffling and makes rolling upgrades much easier and faster. Auto-regulating feedback loops in recent updates also eliminates past worries about merge throttling and related settings.

Elasticsearch 2.x also solved many of the known issues that plagued previous versions, including:

- Mapping conflicts (often yielding wrong results)
- Memory pressures and frequent garbage collections
- Low reliability of data
- Security breaches and split brains
- Slow recovery during node maintenance or rolling cluster upgrades

Mapping changes

Elasticsearch developers earlier assumed an index as a database and a type as a table. This allowed users to create multiple types inside the same index, but eventually became a major source of issues because of restrictions imposed by Lucene.

Fields that have the same name inside multiple types in a single index are mapped to a single field inside Lucene. Incorrect query outcomes and index corruption can result from a field in one document type being of an integer type while a field in another document type being of a string type. Several other issues can lead to mapping refactoring and major restrictions on handling mapping conflicts.

The following are the most significant changes imposed by Elasticsearch version 2.x:

- Field names must be referenced by full name.
- Field names cannot be referenced using a type name prefix.
- Field names can't contain dots.
- Type names can't start with a dot (`.percolator` is an exception)
- Type names may not be longer than 255 characters.
- Types may no longer be deleted. So, if an index contains multiple types, you cannot delete any of the types from the index. The only solution is to create a new index and reindex the data.
- `index_analyzer` and `_analyzer` parameters were removed from mapping definitions.
- Doc values became default.
- A parent type can't pre-exist and must be included when creating child type.
- The `ignore_conflicts` option of the put mappings API got removed and conflicts cannot be ignored anymore.

- Documents and mappings can't contain metadata fields that start with an underscore. So, if you have an existing document that contains a field with _id or _type, it will not work in version 2.x. You need to reindex your documents after dropping those fields.

- The default date format has changed from date_optional_time to strict_date_optional_time, which expects a four-digit year, and a two-digit month and day, (and optionally, a two-digit hour, minute, and second). So a dynamic index set as "2016-01-01" will be stored inside Elasticsearch in "strict_date_optional_time||epoch_millis" format. Please note that if you have been using Elasticsearch older than 1.x then your date range queries might get impacted because of this. For example, if in Elasticsearch 1.x, you have two documents indexed with one having the date as 2017-02-28T12:00:00.000Z and the second having the date as 2017-03-01T11:59:59.000Z, and if you are searching for documents between February 28, 2017 and March 1, 2017, the following query could return both the documents:

```
{
    "range": {
        "created_at": {
            "gte": "2017-02-28",
            "lte": "2017-03-01"
        }
    }
}
```

But in version 2.0 onwards, the same query must use the complete date time to get the same results. For example.

```
{
    "range": {
        "created_at": {
            "gte": "2017-02-28T00:00:00.000Z",
            "lte": "2017-03-01T11:59:59.000Z"
        }
    }
}
```

In addition, you can also use the date match operation in combination with date rounding to get the same results as following query:

```
{
    "range": {
        "doc.created_at": {
            "lte": "2017-02-28||+1d/d",
```

```
        "gte": "2017-02-28",
        "format": "strict_date_optional_time"
    }
  }
}
```

Query and filter changes

Prior to version 2.0.0, Elasticsearch had two different objects for querying data: queries and filters. Each was different in functionality and performance.

Queries were used to find out how relevant a document was to a particular query by calculating a score for each document. Filters were used to match certain criteria and were cacheable to enable faster execution. This means that if a filter matched 1,000 documents, Elasticsearch, with the help of bloom filters, would cache those documents in memory to retrieve them quickly in case the same filter was executed again.

However, with the release of Lucene 5.0, which is used by Elasticsearch version 2.0.0, both queries and filters became the same internal object, taking care of both document relevance and matching.

So, an Elasticsearch query that used to look like the following:

```
{
"filtered" : {
"query": { query definition },
"filter": { filter definition }
 }
}
```

It should now be written like this in version 2.x:

```
{
"bool" : {
"must": { query definition },
"filter": { filter definition }
}
}
```

Additionally, the confusion caused by choosing between a `bool` filter and an `and`/`or` filter has been addressed with the elimination of `and`/`or` filters, and replaced by the `bool` query syntax in the preceding example. Rather than the unnecessary caching and memory requirements that often resulted from a wrong filter, Elasticsearch now tracks and optimizes frequently used filters and doesn't cache for segments with less than 10,000 documents or 3% of the index.

Security, reliability, and networking changes

Starting from 2.x, Elasticsearch now runs under the **Java Security Manager** enabled by default, which streamlines permissions after startup.

Elasticsearch has applied a **durable-by-default** approach to reliability and data duplication across multiple nodes. Documents are now synced to disk before indexing requests are acknowledged, and all file renames are now atomic to prevent partially written files.

On the networking side, based on extensive feedback from system administrators, Elasticsearch removed multicasting, and the default zen discovery has been changed to unicast. Elasticsearch also now binds to the localhost by default, preventing unconfigured nodes from joining public networks.

Monitoring parameter changes

Before version 2.0.0, Elasticsearch used the **SIGAR** library for operating system-dependent statistics. But SIGAR is no longer maintained, and it has been replaced in Elasticsearch by a reliance on stats provided by JVM. Accordingly, we see various changes in the monitoring parameters of the `node info` and `node stats` APIs:

- `network.*` has been removed from `nodes info` and `nodes stats`.
- `fs.*.dev` and `fs.*.disk*` have been removed from `nodes stats`.
- `os.*` has been removed from `nodes stats`, except for `os.timestamp`, `os.load_average`, `os.mem.*`, and `os.swap.*`.
- `os.mem.total` and `os.swap.total` have been removed from `nodes info`.
- From the `_stats` API, `id_cache` parameter, which tells about parent-child data structure memory, usage has also been removed. The `id_cache` can now be fetched from `fielddata`.

Changes between 2.x to 5.x

Elasticsearch 2.x did not see too many releases in comparison to the 1.x series. The last release under 2.x was 2.3.4 and since then Elasticsearch 5.0 was released. The following are the most important changes an existing Elasticsearch user must know before adapting to the latest releases.

 Elasticsearch 5.x requires Java 8 so make sure to upgrade your Java versions before getting started with Elasticsearch.

Mapping changes

From a user's perspective, changes under mappings are the most important changes to know because a wrong mapping will disallow index creation or can lead to unwanted search. Here are the most important changes under this category that you need to know.

No more string fields

The string type is removed in favor of the text and keyword data type. In earlier versions of Elasticsearch, the default mapping for string based fields looked like the following:

```
{
    "content" : {
        "type" : "string"
    }
}
```

Starting from version 5.0, the same will be created using the following syntax:

```
{
    "content" : {
        "type" : "text",
        "fields" : {
            "keyword" : {
                "type" : "keyword",
                "ignore_above" : 256
            }
        }
    }
}
```

This allows you to perform a full-text search on the original field name and to sort and run aggregations on the sub-keyword field.

 Multi-fields are enabled by default for string-based fields and can cause extra overhead if a user is relying on dynamic mapping generation.

However, if you want to create specific mapping for string fields for full-text searches, it will be created as shown in the following example:

```
{
    "content" : {
      "type" : "string"
    }
}
```

Similarly, a `not_analyzed` string field needs to be created using the following mapping:

```
{
    "content" : {
      "type" : "keyword"
    }
}
```

 On all field data types (except for the deprecated string field), the index property now only accepts `true`/`false` instead of `not_analyzed`/no.

Floats are default

Earlier, the default data type for decimal fields used to be double but now it has been changed to float.

Changes in numeric fields

Numeric fields are now indexed with a completely different data structure, called the BKD tree. This is expected to require less disk space and be faster for range queries. You can read the details at the following link:

```
https://www.elastic.co/blog/lucene-points-6.0
```

Changes in geo_point fields

Similar to numeric fields, the geo_point field now also uses the new BKD tree structure and field parameters for geo_point fields are no longer supported: geohash, geohash_prefix, geohash_precision, and lat_lon. Geohashes are still supported from an API perspective, and can still be accessed using the .geohash field extension, but they are no longer used to index geo point data.

For example, in previous versions of Elasticsearch, the mapping of a geo_point field could look like the following:

```
"location":{
      "type": "geo_point",
      "lat_lon": true,
      "geohash": true,
      "geohash_prefix": true,
      "geohash_precision": "1m"
}
```

But, starting from Elasticsearch version 5.0, you can only create mapping of a geo_point field as shown in the following:

```
"location":{
      "type": "geo_point"
    }
```

Some more changes

The following are some very important additional changes you should be aware about:

- Removal of site plugins. The support of site plugins has been completely removed from Elasticsearch 5.0.
- Node clients are completely removed from Elasticsearch as they are considered really bad from a security perspective.

- Every Elasticsearch node, by default, binds to the localhost and if you change the bind address to some non-localhost IP address, Elasticsearch considers the node as production-ready and applies various Bootstrap checks when the Elasticsearch node starts. This is done to prevent your cluster from being blown away in future if you forget to allocate enough resources to Elasticsearch. The following are some of the Bootstrap checks Elasticsearch applies: maximum number of file descriptors check, maximum map count check, and heap size check. Please go to this URL to ensure that you have set all the parameters for Bootstrap checks to be passed
`https://www.elastic.co/guide/en/elasticsearch/reference/master/bootstrap-checks.html`.

> Please note that if you are using OpenVZ virtualization on your servers, then you may find it difficult in setting the maximum map count for running Elasticsearch in the production mode, as this virtualization does not easily allow you to edit the kernel parameters. So you should either speak to your sysadmin to configure `vm.max_map_count` correctly, or move to a platform where you can set it, for example kvm VPS.

- `_optimize` endpoint which was deprecated in 2.x is finally removed and has been replaced by the Force Merge API. For example, an optimize request in version 1.x…

```
curl -XPOST 'http://localhost:9200/test/_optimize?max_num_segments=5'
```

…should be converted to:

```
curl -XPOST
'http://localhost:9200/test/_forcemerge?max_num_segments=5'
```

In addition to these changes, some major changes have been done in search, settings, allocation, merge, and scripting modules, along with cat and Java APIs, which we will cover in subsequent chapters.

Summary

In this chapter, we gave an overview of Lucene, discussing how it works, how the analysis process is done, and how to use the Apache Lucene query language. In addition to that, we discussed the basic concepts of Elasticsearch.

We also introduced Elasticsearch 5.x and covered the latest features introduced in version 2.x as well as 5.x. Finally, we talked about the most important changes and removal of features that Elasticsearch has implemented during the transition from 1.x to 5.x.

In the next chapter, you will learn about the new default scoring algorithm, BM25, and how it is better than the previous TF-IDF algorithm. In addition to that, we will discuss various Elasticsearch features, such as query rewriting, query templates, changes in query modules, and various queries to choose from, in a given scenario.

2
The Improved Query DSL

In the previous chapter, we looked at the overview of Lucene, how it works, how analysis processing is done, and how to use the Apache Lucene query language. In addition to that, we discussed the basic concepts of Elasticsearch. We also introduced Elasticsearch 5.x and covered the latest features introduced in version 2.x as well as 5.x. We also talked about the most important changes/removals of features Elasticsearch has gone through during the transition from 1.x to 5.x. In this chapter, we will dive deep into Elasticsearch, focusing on the Query DSL. We will first go through Lucene similarity algorithm formulas before turning to advanced queries. By the end of this chapter, we will have covered the following topics:

- The changed default text scoring in Lucene: BM25
- Understanding precision and recall
- How BM25 differs from TF-IDF
- Elasticsearch Query DSL
- Understanding bool query syntax
- Which query you should use for your particular use case
- Important changes in Elasticsearch Query DSL
- What query rewrite is and how to use it
- What query templates are and how to use them

The changed default text scoring in Lucene – BM25

Scoring is the most important part of Apache Lucene. It is the process of calculating the score property of a document in a scope of a given query. A score is a factor that describes how well the document matches the query. For score calculation, Lucene supports many algorithms, but since the beginning of Lucene, **TF-IDF** (**term frequency-inverse document frequency**) has been the default scoring algorithm. With the release of Apache Lucene 6.0, one of the major changes in Lucene is the changed default scoring algorithm. The default algorithm is now **BM25** (**Best Matching**). In this section, we will also cover two fundamental concepts of search relevancy: **precision** and **recall**, and after that, we'll look at the new default Apache Lucene scoring mechanism and how it differs from TF-IDF.

Precision versus recall

After executing a search query, an obvious question comes to mind: Have I found the most relevant documents or am I missing important documents in the result set? In addition to that, we also hope that we haven't retrieved lots of junk which are irrelevant to the given query context. It is very difficult to avoid the irrelevant documents while getting back every possible result, but it is possible to perform a measurement of how well a search is performed with the help of two parameters, that is, precision and recall.

Precision and recall are the two fundamental concepts of search relevance that every search engineer should be well aware of. Based on a given search query and the result set (documents returned by the search engine), precision and recall are defined as follows:

- **Precision**: The ratio of the number of relevant documents retrieved to the total number of documents retrieved (both relevant as well as irrelevant). It is expressed as a percentage.
- **Recall**: The ratio of the number of relevant records retrieved to the total number of relevant records in the database. It is also expressed as a percentage.

In Elasticsearch, there are various ways of controlling search relevance and improve recall. During the analysis phase, a search engineer has the power to control Lucene scoring as well as improving the recall. In addition to that, there are various other functionalities such as custom boosting and function score queries available in Elasticsearch, to give more control to the user.

Recalling TF-IDF

TF-IDF, which was the core of the Lucene ranking function, was built on a combination of the **vector space model** (**VSM**) and the **Boolean model** of information retrieval. The main idea behind the Lucene approach is, the more times a query term appears in a document relative to the number of times the term appears in the whole collection, the more relevant that document will be to the query. Lucene also uses the Boolean model to first narrow down the documents that need to be scored based on the use of Boolean logic in the query specification. In order to calculate the score of a document using TF-IDF, multiple factors are taken into account, including:

- **Term frequency**: A term-based factor describing how many times a given term occurs in a document. It is calculated as: the number of times a term appears in a document, divided by the total number of terms in the document. The higher the term frequency, the higher the score of the document will be.
- **Inverse document frequency**: A term-based factor telling the scoring formula how rare the given term is. The higher the inverse document frequency, the rarer the term is. The scoring formula uses this factor to boost documents that contain rare terms. It is calculated as log_e (total number of documents divided by the number of documents with the term t in it).

 While calculating IDF, the `log` is taken because terms such as `the`, `that`, and `is` may appear too many times, and we need to weigh down these frequently appearing terms while increasing the importance of rare terms.

- **Coord**: The coordination factor is based on the number of terms the document has. It is responsible for giving more value to the documents that contain more search terms compared to other documents.
- **Field boost**: The boost value given for a field during querying.
- **Document boost**: The boost value given for a document during indexing.
- **Length norm**: A field-based factor for normalization based on the number of terms a given field contains (calculated during indexing and stored in the index). The longer the field, the lesser boost this factor will give, which means that the Apache Lucene scoring formula will favor documents with fields containing lower terms.
- **Query norm**: A query-based normalization factor that is calculated as a sum of a squared weight of each of the query terms. Query norm is used to allow score comparisons between queries, which, as we said, is not always easy or possible.

In information retrieval, one of the simplest relevancy ranking functions is implemented by summing the TF-IDF weight for each query term, where the weight of each term = *TF(term)*IDF(term)*. Based on the combined weights for all the terms appearing in a single query, a score is calculated that is used to return the results in a sorted order.

At a more complex level, the Lucene practical scoring formula using TF-IDF looks like the following:

$$score(q,d) = coord(q,d) * queryNorm(q) * \sum_{t\ in\ q} (tf(t\ in\ d) * idf(t)^2 * boost(t) * norm(t,d))$$

Where *score(q, d)* reads as the score of the document given a query.

Now, let's take a look at the BM25 scoring technique and its example to understand the use of BM25 and how it differs from TF-IDF.

Introducing BM25 scoring

As we said earlier, BM25 has become the default scoring method since the release of Lucene 6.0. Similar to TF-IDF, BM25 is also a ranking function to score and rank matching documents based on their relevance. BM25 has been widely used by IR researchers and engineers to improve search engine relevance and it is considered as a **state of the art ranking algorithm**. It is based on the probabilistic relevance framework developed in the 1970s and 1980s by Stephen E. Robertson, Karen Spärck Jones, and others.

The complete coverage of BM25 is beyond the scope of this book, but if you are interested in understanding more about it you can refer to the research paper *The Probabilistic Relevance Framework: BM25 and Beyond* by *Stephen Robertson* and *Hugo Zaragoza* which you can find at: http://www.staff.city.ac.uk/~sb317/papers/foundations_bm25_revie w.pdf

In spite of originating from the probabilistic relevance model, BM25 has a lot in common with TF-IDF. Both of the algorithms use the **term frequency**, **inverse document frequency** and field length normalization, but definition of each of these factors is a little different. Both models define a weight for each term as a product of some IDF-function and some TF-function and then summarize that term weight as the score for the whole document towards the given query. Next, we are going to discuss more about these parameters.

BM25 scoring formula

The following is the mathematical representation of the formula used by BM25:

$$\text{bm25}(d) = \sum_{t \in q, f_{t,d} > 0} \log \left(1 + \frac{N - df_t + 0.5}{df_t + 0.5}\right) \cdot \frac{f_{t,d}}{f_{t,d} + k \cdot (1 - b + b\frac{l(d)}{avgdl})}$$

- N is the total number of documents available in the dataset.
- df_t is the number of documents that contain that term.
- k which is also denoted at as $k1$, is the saturation parameter and controls how quickly an increase in term frequency results in term-frequency saturation. The default value of $k1$ is 1.2. Lower values result in quicker saturation, and higher values in slower saturation.
- b is the length parameter which controls how much effect field-length normalization should have. A value of 0.0 disables normalization completely, and a value of 1.0 normalizes fully. The default is 0.75.
- $l(d)$ is the number of tokens in the document.
- $avgdl$ is the average document length in the corpus (complete dataset).
- $f_{t,d}$ is the frequency of a term in the document.

In this formula, k and b are the most important parameters you need to understand and you can tweak the default scoring using these two parameters if you are not satisfied with the default relevancy.

Saturation is described as a parameter to limit the influence of term frequency in a given document. Saturation allows us to tune the influence of term frequency by tweaking the parameter k. While the saturation limit in TF-IDF has no boundary-despite multiplying the square root of the term frequency with some logarithm value-and more frequent terms appearing in a document get a higher weight, BM25 completely removes the problem by introducing $k1$ as a saturation parameter.

Example – tuning BM25 with custom similarity

Let's look at the example of how we can tweak BM25 parameters to create a custom similarity setting for an index and how it affects scoring:

```
curl -XPUT "http://localhost:9200/my_index" -d'
```

```
{
  "settings": {
    "similarity": {
      "my_custom_similarity": {
        "type": "BM25",
        "b": 0,
        "k1": 2
      }
    }
  },
  "mappings": {
    "doc": {
      "properties": {
        "text1": {
          "type":        "text",
          "similarity": "my_custom_similarity"
        },
        "text2": {
          "type":        "text"
        }
      }
    }
  }
}'
```

In the preceding curl request, we have created an index, my_index, with a custom defined similarity with a name, my_custom_similarity, based on existing BM25 provided by Lucene. Please note that we have changed the values of both k1 and b in this custom similarity. Next, we have created a mapping with doc_type called doc, with two fields, text1 and text2. For text1 we have used custom similarity where text2 uses default similarity. Next we will index one document with both the fields having the same text:

```
curl -XPUT "http://localhost:9200/my_index/doc/1" -d'
{
    "text1": "He feels happy. Others feel happy He is being forced into
happiness (is he actually happy?). But The truth is He is actually not
happy at all.",
    "text2": "He feels happy. Others feel happy He is being forced into
happiness (is he actually happy?). But The truth is He is actually not
happy at all."
}'
```

Now, perform a simple match query with the term `happy`, that is, the most frequent term in our data:

```
curl -XGET "http://localhost:9200/my_index/doc/_search" -d'
{"query":{"match":{"text1":"happy"}}}'
```

This will give you a score of 0.5753642 for this document.

Searching on the `text2` field with the following command will give the score of 0.48238015 to this document:

```
curl -XGET "http://localhost:9200/my_index/doc/_search" -d'
{"query":{"match":{"text2":"happy"}}}'
```

How BM25 differs from TF-IDF

In previous sections, we talked about both TF-IDF and BM25. Now let's get a clear picture on what basis they both differ from each other, and how BM25 is better than TF-IDF.

Saturation point

We briefly talked about saturation point in the BM25 scoring formula. Now, to understand the saturation-based scoring problem in TF-IDF: if a single term out of the N terms in your Boolean query occurs many times in a document, it drastically increases the score because its term saturation is weak; `sqrt(termFreq)`. If the query is x or y and a document has 1,000 x's and 0 y's, TF-IDF gives it a great score, even though y never occurred. And so `coord` tries to counteract that behavior.

BM25 performs much better in these scenarios, since it has a much stronger term **saturation**, controlled by its `k1` parameter, such that a single term in your query occurring many times does not increase the score nearly as much as another term going from freq 0 to freq 1. BM25 naturally favors documents that have at least one occurrence among more of the requested query terms. So a document with only five x's and one y, or something similar, will naturally get a better score than the first document with 1,000 x's and 0 y's.

Average document length

The second major difference between TF-IDF and BM25 is the use of the document length in BM25. As an example, if the term "travel" occurs once or twice in an article containing 1,000 terms, it says almost nothing about how much that article is about travel, but *travel* occurring twice in a short tweet, however, means that tweet is very much about travel. TF-IDF performs a very biased measurement of score calculation based on document length, but BM25 uses document length to compensate for the fact that a longer document in general has more words and thus is more likely to have a higher term frequency without necessarily being more pertinent to the term and thus no more relevant to the query. But since some documents actually have a wider scope which makes the longer text justified, BM25 adjusts the term factor using a tuning parameter b, the document length dl, and the average document length $avdl$, as we have seen in its mathematical formula.

Re-factored Query DSL

The release of Elasticsearch 2.0.0 saw a major refactoring in Elasticsearch **Query DSL,** the interface provided by Elasticsearch to write queries in the JSON format. Covering complete Query DSL is out of the scope of this book. But for a person who doesn't have much prior experience with a full text search engine, the number of queries exposed by Elasticsearch can be overwhelming and very confusing. So, we have decided to cover the most frequently used queries, along with making readers aware about how to use queries and filters with revised Query DSL syntax. Thus, this book can serve the purposes of both types of readers: those who are aware of old versions as well as those who are starting with version 5.0.

Choosing the right query for the job

In this section, we will start with different categories of queries available in Elasticsearch, looking at which query to use in which situation.

Query categorization

Of course, categorizing queries is a hard task and the following list of categories is not the only correct one. If you were to ask other Elasticsearch users, they would provide their own categories, or say that each query can be assigned to more than a single category, and they would be right. We also think that there is no single way of categorizing the queries; however, in our opinion, each Elasticsearch query can be assigned to one (or more) of the following categories:

- **Basic queries**: A category that groups queries allowing searching for a part of the index, either in an analyzed or a non-analyzed manner. The key point in this category is that you can nest queries inside a basic query. An example of a basic query is the `term` query.

- **Compound queries**: A category grouping queries that allows us to combine multiple queries or filters inside them, for example a `bool` or `dismax` query.

- **Not analyzed queries**: A category for queries that don't analyze the input and send it as it is to the Lucene index. An example of such a query is the `term` query.

- **Full text search queries**: Quite a large group of queries supporting full text searching, analyzing their content, and possibly providing Lucene query syntax. An example of such a query is the `match` query.

- **Pattern queries**: A group of queries providing support for various wildcards in queries. For example, a `prefix` query can be assigned to this particular group.

- **Similarity supporting queries**: A group of queries sharing a common feature–support for a match of similar words or documents. An example of such a query is the `more_like_this` query.

- **Score altering queries**: A very important group of queries, especially when combined with full text searching. This group includes queries that allow us to modify the score calculation during query execution. An example of such a query that we can assign to this group is the `function_score` query, which we will talk about in detail in `Chapter 3`, *Beyond Full Text Search*.

- **Position aware queries**: Queries that allow us to use term position information stored in the index. A very good example of such a query is the `span_term` query.

- **Structure aware queries**: A group of queries that can work on structured data such as parent-child documents. An example of such a query from this group is the `nested` query, which we will talk about in detail in `Chapter 4`, *Data Modeling and Analytics*.

Now let's talk briefly about the purpose of each of the query categories and then we can cover the scenarios in which they can be applied.

Basic queries

These are queries that are not able to group any other queries. Queries in this group are usually used as parts of more complex queries or as single queries sent against Elasticsearch. You can think about these queries as bricks for building structures–more complex queries. For example, when you need to match a certain phrase without worrying about the ordering of terms in a document and without any additional requirements, you should look at the basic queries. In such a case, the `match` query will be a good opportunity for this requirement and it doesn't need to be added by any other query.

Some examples of the queries from the basic category are as follows:

- `Match`: A query (actually multiple types of queries) used when you need a full text search query that will analyze the provided input. Usually, it is used when you need analysis of the provided text, but you don't need full Lucene syntax support. Because this query doesn't go through the query parsing process, it has a low chance of resulting in a parsing error, and because of this it is a good candidate for handling text entered by the user.
- `match_all`: A simple query matching all documents, useful for situations when we need all the whole index contents returned for aggregations.
- `term`: A simple, not analyzed query that allows us to search for an exact word. An example use case for the `term` query is searching against non-analyzed fields, such as those storing `tags` in our example data. The `term` query is also commonly combined with filtering; for example, filtering on category fields from our example data.

The queries from the basic category are: `match`, `multi_match`, `common`, `fuzzy_like_this`, `geoshape`, `ids`, `match_all`, `query_string`, `simple_query_string`, `range`, `prefix`, `regexp`, `span_term`, `term`, `terms`, `wildcard`.

Compound queries

Compound queries are those that we can use for grouping other queries together and this is their only purpose. If simple queries are bricks for building houses, complex queries are joints for those bricks. Because we can create a virtually indefinite level of nesting of compound queries, we are able to produce very complex queries, and the only thing that limits us is performance.

Some examples of compound queries and their usage are as follows:

- `bool`: One of the most common compound queries that is able to group multiple queries with a Boolean logical operator that allows us to control which part of the query must match, which can, and which should not match. For example, if we would like to find and group together queries matching different criteria, then the `bool` query is a good candidate. The `bool` query should also be used when we want the score of the documents to be a sum of all the scores calculated by the partial queries.
- `dis_max`: A very useful query when we want the score of the document to be mostly associated with the highest boosting partial query, not the sum of all the partial queries (like in the `bool` query). The `dis_max` query generates the union of the documents returned by all the subqueries and scores the documents by the simple equation max (score of the matching clauses) + tie_breaker * (sum of scores of all the other clauses that are not max scoring ones). If you want the max scoring subquery to dominate the score of your documents, then the `dis_max` query is the way to go.

The queries from this category are: `bool`, `boosting`, `constant_score`, `dis_max`, `filtered`, `function_score`, `has_child`, `has_parent`, `indices`, `nested`, `span_first`, `span_multi`, `span_first`, `span_multi`, `span_near`, `span_not`, `span_or`, `span_term`, `top_children`.

Understanding bool queries

Since `bool` queries are the most widely used queries and allow us to wrap up many query clauses together including `bool` clauses, we need to discuss them in detail. The documents are matched based on the combinations of these Boolean clauses that are listed as follows:

- `must`: The queries that are written inside this clause must match in order to return the documents.
- `should`: The queries written inside the `should` clause may or may not have a match, but if the bool query has no `must` clause inside it, then at least one `should` condition needs to be matched in order to return the documents.
- `must_not`: The queries wrapped inside this clause must not appear in the matching documents.
- `filter`: A query wrapped inside this clause must appear in the matching documents. However, this does not contribute to scoring.

The structure of `bool` queries is as follows:

```
{
  "query":{
  "bool":{
  "must":[{}],
  "should":[{}],
  "must_not":[{}]
  "filter":[{}]
  }
  }
  }
```

There are some additional parameters supported by `bool` queries that are listed here:

- `boost`: This parameter controls the score of each query, which is wrapped inside the `must` or `should` clause.
- `minimum_should_match`: This is only used for the `should` clauses. Using this, we can specify how many `should` clauses must match in order to return a document.
- `disable_coord`: The `bool` queries by default use query coordination for all the `should` clauses; it is a good thing to have, since the more clauses get matched, the higher the score a document will get. However, look at the following example where we may need to disable this:

```
{
  "query":{
  "bool":{
  "disable_coord":true,
  "should":[
    {"term":{"text":{"value":"turmoil"}}},
    {"term":{"text":{"value":"riot"}}}
  ]
  }
  }
  }
```

- In the preceding example, inside the text field, we are looking for the terms `turmoil` and `riot`, which are synonyms of each other. In these cases, we do not care how many synonyms are present in the document, since all have the same meaning. In these kinds of scenarios, we can disable the query coordination by setting `disable_coord` to `true`, so that similar clauses do not impact the score factor computation.

Non-analyzed queries

These are queries that are not analyzed and instead the text we provide to them is sent directly to the Lucene index. This means that we either need to be aware exactly how the analysis process is done and provide a proper term, or we need to run the searches against the non-analyzed fields. If you plan to use Elasticsearch as the NoSQL store, this is probably the group of queries you'll be using. They search for the exact terms without analyzing them, that is, with language analyzers.

The following examples should help you understand the purpose of not analyzed queries:

- `term`: When talking about the not analyzed queries, the term query will be the one most commonly used. It provides us with the ability to match documents having a certain value in a field. For example, if we would like to match documents with a certain tag (the tags field in our example data), we would use the term query.
- `Prefix`: Another type of query that is not analyzed. The prefix query is commonly used for autocomplete functionality, where the user provides a text and we need to find all the documents having terms that start with the given text. It is good to remember that even though the prefix query is not analyzed, it is rewritten by Elasticsearch so that its execution is fast.

The queries from this category are: `common`, `ids`, `prefix`, `span_term`, `term`, `terms`, `wildcard`.

Full text search queries

This is a group that can be used when you are building your Google-like search interface. These queries analyze the provided input using the information from the mappings, support Lucene query syntax, support scoring capabilities, and so on. In general, if some part of the query you are sending comes from a user entering some text, you'll want to use one of the full text search queries such as the `query_string`, `match` or `simple_query_string` queries.

A simple example of the full text search queries use case can be seen as follows:

- `simple_query_string`: A query built on top of the Lucene `SimpleQueryParser` (`http://lucene.apache.org/core/6_0_0/queryparser/org/apache/lucene/queryparser/simple/SimpleQueryParser.html`) that was designed to parse human readable queries. In general, if you want your queries not to fail when a query parsing error occurs, and instead figure out what the user wanted to achieve, this is a good query to consider.

The queries from this category are: `match`, `multi_match`, `query_string`, `simple_query_string`.

Pattern queries

Elasticsearch provides us with a few queries that can handle wildcards directly or indirectly: for example, the `wildcard` query and the `prefix` query. In addition to that, we are allowed to use the `regexp` query that can find documents that have terms matching given patterns.

We've already discussed an example using the `prefix` query, so let's focus a bit on the `regexp` query. If you want a query that will find documents having terms matching a certain pattern, then the `regexp` query is probably the only solution for you. For example, if you store logs in your Elasticsearch indices and you would like to find all the logs that have terms starting with the `err` prefix, then having any number of characters and ending with `memory`, the `regexp` query will be the one to look for. However, remember that all the wildcard queries that have expressions matching a large number of terms will be expensive when it comes to performance.

The queries from this category are: `prefix`, `regexp`, `wildcard`.

Similarity supporting queries

We can think of similarity supporting queries as a family of queries that allow us to search for similar terms or documents to the one we passed to the query. For example, if we would like to find documents that have terms similar to the `crimea` term, we could run a `fuzzy` query. Another use case for this group of queries is providing us with a *Did you mean:* like functionality. If we would like to find documents that have titles similar to the input we've provided, we would use the `more_like_this` query. In general, you would use a query from this group whenever you need to find documents having terms or fields similar to the provided input.

The queries from this category are: `fuzzy_like_this`, `fuzzy`, `more_like_this`, `more_like_this_field`.

Score altering queries

This is a group of queries used for improving search precision and relevance. They allow us to modify the score of the returned documents by providing not only a custom boost factor, but also some additional logic. A very good example of a query from this group is the `function_score` query that provides us with a possibility of using functions, which results in a document score modification based on mathematical equations. For example, if you would like documents that are closer to a given geographical point to be scored higher, then using the `function_score` query provides you with such a possibility.

The queries from this category are: `boosting`, `constant_score`, `function_score`, `indices`.

Position aware queries

This is a family of queries that allow us to match not only certain terms but also the information about the terms' positions. The most significant queries from this group are all the span queries in Elasticsearch. We can also say that the `match_phrase` query can be assigned to this group as it also looks at the position of the indexed terms, at least to some extent. If you want to find groups of words that are a certain distance in the index from other words, such as, `find me the documents that have mastering and Elasticsearch terms near each other and are followed by second and edition terms no further than three positions away`, then span queries is the way to go. However, you should remember that span queries will be removed in future versions of the Lucene library and thus from Elasticsearch as well. This is because these queries are resource-intensive and require a vast amount of CPU to be properly handled.

The queries from this category are: `match_phrase`, `span_first`, `span_multi`, `span_near`, `span_not`, `span_or`, `span_term`.

Structure aware queries

The last group of queries is the structure aware queries. The queries that can be assigned to this group are as follows:

- `nested`
- `has_child`
- `has_parent`
- `top_children`

Basically, all the queries that allow us to search inside structured documents and don't require us to flatten the data can be classified as structure aware queries. If you are looking for a query that will allow you to search inside the children document, nested documents, or for children having certain parents, then you need to use one of the queries that are mentioned in the preceding terms. If you want to handle relationships in the data, this is the group of queries you should look for; however, remember that although Elasticsearch can handle relations, it is still not a relational database.

The use cases

As we already know which groups of queries can be responsible for which tasks and what we can achieve using queries from each group, let's have a look at some example use cases for each of the groups, so that we can have a better view of what the queries are useful for. Please note that this is not a full and comprehensive guide to all the queries available in Elasticsearch, but instead a simple example of what can be achieved.

Example data

Let's create an index with the name `library` and index some sample data into it. The mapping for our library index would look like the following and it can be found in the `library.json` file provided with this book:

```
{
  "book": {
    "properties": {
      "author": {
        "type": "text"
```

```
        },
        "characters": {
          "type": "text"
        },
        "copies": {
          "type": "long"
        },
        "otitle": {
          "type": "text"
        },
        "tags": {
          "type": "keyword"
        },
        "title": {
          "type": "text"
        },
        "year": {
          "type": "long"
        },
        "available": {
          "type": "boolean"
        },
        "review": {
          "type": "nested",
          "properties": {
            "nickname": {
              "type": "text"
            },
            "text": {
              "type": "text"
            },
            "stars": {
              "type": "integer"
            }
          }
        }
      }
    }
  }
}
```

The data that we will use is provided with this book in the books.json file. The example documents from that file look like the following:

```
{ "index" : { "_index" : "library", "_type" : "books", "_id" : "1" } }
{"title":"All Quiet on the Western Front","otitle":"Im Westen nichts
Neues","author":"Erich Maria Remarque","year":1929,"characters":["Paul
Bäumer","Albert Kropp","Haie Westhus","Fredrich Müller","Stanislaus
Katczinsky","Tjaden"],"tags":["novel"],"copies":1,"available":true,"section
```

```
":3}
{"index":{"_index":"library","_type":"book","_id":"2"}}
{"title":"Catch-22","author":"Joseph
Heller","year":1961,"characters":["John Yossarian","Captain
Aardvark","Chaplain Tappman","Colonel Cathcart","Doctor
Daneeka"],"tags":["novel"],"copies":6,"available":false,"section":1}
{"index":{"_index":"library","_type":"book","_id":"3"}}
{"title":"The Complete Sherlock Holmes","author":"Arthur Conan
Doyle","year":1936,"characters":["Sherlock Holmes","Dr. Watson","G.
Lestrade"],"tags":[],"copies": 0, "available":false, "section":12}
```

 Please note that doing a copy-paste from the e-book to run the examples can result in errors because of formatting and character encoding issue.

To create the index using the provided mappings and to index the data, we would run the following commands:

```
curl -XPUT 'localhost:9200/library'
curl -XPUT 'localhost:9200/library/book/_mapping' -d @library.json
curl -s -XPOST 'localhost:9200/_bulk' --data-binary @books.json
```

We used the bulk method of indexing documents in the previous example; now let us add two additional documents to our `library` index using individual documents in separate `curl` requests.

The commands used for indexing two additional documents are as follows:

```
curl -XPOST "http://localhost:9200/library/book/4" -d'
{
  "title": "The Sorrows of Young Werther",
  "author": "Johann Wolfgang von Goethe",
  "available": true,
  "characters": ["Werther", "Lotte", "Albert", " Fräulein von B"],
  "copies": 1,
  "otitle": "Die Leiden des jungen Werthers",
  "section": 4,
  "tags": ["novel", "classics"],
  "year": 1774,
  "review": [{ "nickname": "Anna", "text": "Could be good, but not my
style", "stars": 3} ]
}'
curl -XPOST "http://localhost:9200/library/book/5" -d'
{
  "title": "The Peasants",
  "author": "Władysław Reymont",
```

```
      "available": true,
      "characters": [ "Maciej Boryna", "Jankiel", "Jagna Paczesiówna",
"Antek Boryna" ],
      "copies": 4,
      "otitle": "Chłopi",
      "section": 4,
      "tags": [ "novel", "polish", "classics" ],
      "year": 1904,
      "review": [ { "nickname": "anonymous",  "text": "awsome  book",
"stars": 5    },  { "nickname": "Jane","text": "Great book, but    too
long", "stars": 4 },
         { "nickname": "Rick", "text": "Why bothe,  when you can find it on
the internet", "stars": 3 } ]
    }'
```

Basic queries use cases

Let's look at simple use cases for the basic queries group.

Searching for values in range

One of the simplest queries that can be run is a query matching documents in a given range of values. Usually, such queries are a part of a larger query or a filter. For example, a query that would return books with the number of copies from 1 to 3 inclusive would look as follows:

```
curl -XGET 'localhost:9200/library/_search?pretty' -d '{
  "query" : {
   "range" : {
    "copies" : {
     "gte" : 1,
     "lte" : 3
    }
   }
  }
}'
```

Compound queries use cases

Let's now see how we can use compound queries to group other queries together.

A Boolean query for multiple terms

Imagine a situation where your users can show a number of tags the books returned by what the query should contain. The thing is that we require only 75 percent of the provided tags to be matched if the number of tags provided by the user is higher than three, and all the provided tags to be matched if the number of tags is three or less:

```
curl -XGET "http://localhost:9200/library/_search?pretty" -d'
{
  "query": {
    "bool": {
      "should": [
        {"term": {"tags": {"value": "novel"}}},
        {"term": {"tags": {"value": "polish" }}},
        {"term": {"tags": {"value": "classics"}}},
        {"term": {"tags": {"value": "criminal"}}}
      ],
      "minimum_should_match": "3<75%"
    }
  }
}'
```

Boosting some of the matched documents

One of the simplest examples is using the `bool` query to boost some documents by including a non-mandatory query part that is used for boosting. For example, if we would like to find all the books that have at least a single copy and boost the ones that are published after 1950, we could use the following query:

```
curl -XGET 'localhost:9200/library/_search?pretty' -d '{
  "query" : {
  "bool" : {
    "must" : [ { "range" : { "copies" : { "gte" : 1 } } } ],
    "should" : [ { "range" : {  "year" : { "gt" : 1950 } } } ]
  }
  }
}'
```

Ignoring lower scoring partial queries

The `dis_max` query, as we have already covered, allows us to control how influential the lower scoring partial queries are. For example, if we only want to assign the score of the highest scoring partial query for the documents matching Young Werther in the title field or Werther in the characters field, we would run the following query:

Source filtering – Using _source and fields parameters

In the following command, we have marked _source as false to avoid returning any field in the response, so only meta fields will be returned. The main point to note here is that earlier versions of Elasticsearch used to provide two ways of retrieving selected fields in the response; the first using the source parameter and the second using the fields parameter. The usage of _source has remained the same across versions but the fields parameter can be used for only those fields which are marked as stored in the mapping. Fetching a non-stored field using the fields parameter will give query parsing exception.

```
curl -XGET "http://localhost:9200/library/_search?pretty" -d'
{
  "query" : {
   "dis_max" : {
    "tie_breaker" : 0.0,
    "queries" : [
     { "match" : { "title" : "Young Werther" } },
     { "match" : { "characters" : "Werther" } }
    ]
   }
  },
  "_source": false
}'
```

The result for the preceding query should look as follows:

```
{
    "took": 11,
    "timed_out": false,
    "_shards": {
        "total": 5,
        "successful": 5,
        "failed": 0
    },
    "hits": {
        "total": 1,
        "max_score": 1.1537418,
        "hits": [
            {
                "_index": "library",
                "_type": "book",
                "_id": "4",
                "_score": 1.1537418
            }
```

```
        ]
    }
}
```

Now let's see the score of the partial queries alone. To do that, we will run the partial queries using the following commands:

```
curl -XGET "http://localhost:9200/library/_search?pretty" -d'
{
 "query" : {
  "match" : {
     "title" : "Young Werther"
     }
 },"_source": false
}'
```

And the response is as follows:

```
{
    "took": 4,
    "timed_out": false,
    "_shards": {
       "total": 5,
       "successful": 5,
       "failed": 0
    },
    "hits": {
       "total": 1,
       "max_score": 1.1537418,
       "hits": [
          {
             "_index": "library",
             "_type": "book",
             "_id": "4",
             "_score": 1.1537418
          }
       ]
    }
}
```

And the next command is as follows:

```
curl -XGET "http://localhost:9200/library/_search?pretty" -d'
{
  "query": {
    "match": {
      "characters": "Werther"
      }
```

```
    },
    "_source": false
  }'
```

As you can see, the score of the document returned by our `dis_max` query is equal to the score of the highest scoring partial query (the first partial query). That is because we've set the `tie_breaker` property to 0.0.

Not analyzed queries use cases

Let's look at two example use cases for queries that are not processed by any of the defined analyzers.

Limiting results to given tags

One of the simplest examples of the not analyzed query is the `term` query provided by Elasticsearch. You'll probably very rarely use the `term` query alone; however, it may be commonly used in compound queries. For example, let's assume that we would like to search for all the books with the `novel` value in the `tags` field. To do that, we would run the following command:

```
curl -XGET 'localhost:9200/library/_search?pretty' -d '{
  "query" : {
    "term" : {
      "tags" : "novel"
    }
  }
}'
```

Full text search queries use cases

Full text search is a broad topic and so are the use cases for the full text queries. However, let's look at two simple examples of queries from that group.

Using Lucene query syntax in queries

Sometimes, it is good to be able to use Lucene query syntax as it is. We talked about this syntax in the *Lucene query language* section in Chapter 1, *Revisiting Elasticsearch and the Changes*. For example, if we would like to find books having sorrows and young terms in their title, with the von goethe phrase in the author field, and not having more than five copies, we could run the following query:

```
curl -XGET "http://localhost:9200/library/_search?pretty" -d'
{
  "query": {
    "query_string": {
      "query": "+title:sorrows +title:young +author:"von goethe"-
copies:{5 TO *]"
    }
  }
}'
```

As you can see, we've used the Lucene query syntax to pass all the matching requirements and we've let the query parser construct the appropriate query.

Handling user queries without errors

Sometimes, queries coming from users can contain errors. For example, let's look at the following query:

```
curl -XGET 'localhost:9200/library/_search?pretty' -d '{
  "query" : {
   "query_string" : {
    "query" : "+sorrows +young "",
    "default_field" : "title"
   }
  }
}'
```

The response would contain the following reason, along with the detailed cause of the query failure:

```
"reason": "Failed to parse query [+sorrows +young "]",
```

This means that the query was not properly constructed and a parse error happened. That's why the simple_query_string query was introduced. It uses a query parser that tries to handle user mistakes and tries to guess how the query should look. Our query using that parser would look as follows:

```
curl -XGET 'localhost:9200/library/_search?pretty' -d '{
```

```
    "query" : {
     "simple_query_string" : {
      "query" : "+sorrows +young "",
      "fields" : [ "title" ]
     }
    }
   }'
```

If you run the preceding query, you would see that the proper document has been returned by Elasticsearch, even though the query is not properly constructed.

Pattern queries use cases

There are multiple use cases for the wildcard queries; however, we wanted to show you the following two.

Autocomplete using prefixes

A very common use case provides autocomplete functionality on the indexed data. As we know, the prefix query is not analyzed and works on the basis of terms indexed in the field. So the actual functionality depends on what tokens are produced during indexing. For example, let's assume that we would like to provide autocomplete functionality on any token in the title field and the user provided the wes prefix. A query that would match such a requirement looks as follows:

```
curl -XGET 'localhost:9200/library/_search?pretty' -d '{
  "query" : {
   "prefix" : {
    "title" : "wes"
   }
  }
 }'
```

Pattern matching

If we need to match a certain pattern and our analysis chain is not producing tokens that allow us to do so, we can turn to the regexp query. One should remember, though, that this kind of query can be expensive during execution and thus should be avoided. Of course, this is not always possible. One thing to remember is that the performance of the regexp query depends on the chosen regular expression. If you choose a regular expression that will be rewritten into a high number of terms, then performance will suffer.

Let's now see the example usage of the regexp query. Let's assume that we would like to find documents that have a term starting with wat, then followed by two characters and ending with the n character, and those terms should be in the characters field. To match this requirement, we could use a regexp query like the one used in the following command:

```
curl -XGET 'localhost:9200/library/_search?pretty' -d '{
  "query" : {
   "regexp" : {
    "characters" : "wat..n"
   }
  }
}'
```

Similarity supporting queries use cases

Let's look at a couple of simple use cases about how we can find similar documents and terms.

Finding terms similar to a given one

A very simple example is using the fuzzy query to find documents having a term similar to a given one. For example, if we would like to find all the documents having a value similar to younger, we could run the following query:

```
curl -XGET 'localhost:9200/library/_search?pretty' -d '{
  "query" : {
   "fuzzy" : {
    "title" : {
     "value" : "younger",
     "fuzziness" : 3,
     "max_expansions" : 50
    }
   }
  }
}'
```

Score altering query use cases

Elasticsearch provides function_score queries as a great tool to alter the score of matching documents; we will cover them in Chapter 3, *Beyond Full Text Search*.

Decreasing importance of books with a certain value

Sometimes, it is good to be able to decrease the importance of certain documents, while still showing them in the results list. For example, we may want to show all books, but put the ones that are not available on the bottom of the results list by lowering their score. We don't want sorting on availability because sometimes a user may know what he or she is looking for and the score of a full text search query should also be important. However, if our use case is that we want the books that are not available on the bottom of the results list, we could use the following command to get them:

```
curl -XGET 'localhost:9200/library/_search?pretty' -d '{
  "query" : {
   "boosting" : {
    "positive" : {
     "match_all" : {}
    },
    "negative" : {
     "term" : {
      "available" : false
     }
    },
    "negative_boost" : 0.2
   }
  }
}'
```

Pattern query use cases

These are not very commonly used because of how resource hungry they are. Pattern aware queries allow us to match documents having phrases and terms in the right order. Let's look at some examples.

Matching phrases

This is the simplest position aware query possible and the most performing one from the queries assigned in this group. For example, a query that would only match the document `leiden des jungen` phrase in the `otitle` field would look as follows:

```
curl -XGET 'localhost:9200/library/_search?pretty' -d '{
  "query" : {
   "match_phrase" : {
    "otitle" : "leiden des jungen"
   }
  }
}'
```

Spans, spans everywhere

Of course, the phrase query is very simple when it comes to position handling. What if we would like to run a query to find documents that have the des jungen phrase not more than two positions after the die term and just before the werthers term? This can be done with span queries, and the following command shows how such a query could look:

```
curl -XGET "http://localhost:9200/library/_search?pretty" -d'
{"query":{"span_near":{"clauses":[{"span_near":{"clauses":[{"span_term":{"o
title":"die"}},{"span_near":{"clauses":[{"span_term":{"otitle":"des"}},{"sp
an_term":{"otitle":"jungen"}}],"slop":0,"in_order":true}}],"slop":2,"in_ord
er":false}},{"span_term":{"otitle":"werthers"}}],"slop":0,"in_order":true}}
}'
```

Please note that span queries are not analyzed.

Some more important changes in Query DSL

The following are some of the most important changes in Elasticsearch Query DSL, which an existing user must be aware of:

- The missing query (earlier know as the missing filter) has been completely removed and you need to use must_not in place of the missing query.
- AND/OR filters which were known as AND/OR queries in Elasticsearch 2.x have been removed completely in favor of the bool query. For AND, you need to use a must Boolean clause whereas for OR, you need to use a should clause.
- The search type count has been removed from Query DSL, and to get the only count of documents or while using aggregation you need to use the size parameter as 0 instead.
- The search type scan has also been removed, and all the benefits of the scan type can now be achieved by doing a scroll request that sorts documents in _doc order, for example:

```
GET /index_name/doc_ype/_search?scroll=10m
{
  {"sort":["_doc"]}
}
```

- The filtered query has been completely removed in Elasticsearch 5.x

Query rewrite explained

We have already talked about scoring, which is valuable knowledge, especially when trying to improve the relevance of our queries. We also think that when debugging your queries, it is valuable to know how all the queries are executed; therefore, it is because of this that we decided to include this section on how query rewrite works in Elasticsearch, why it is used, and how to control it.

If you have ever used queries, such as the `prefix` query and the `wildcard` query, basically any query that is said to be **multiterm**, you've probably heard about query rewriting. Elasticsearch does that because of performance reasons. The rewrite process is about changing the original, expensive query to a set of queries that are far less expensive from Lucene's point of view, and thus speed up the query execution. The rewrite process is not visible to the client, but it is good to know that we can alter the rewrite process behavior. For example, let's look at what Elasticsearch does with a prefix query.

Prefix query as an example

The best way to illustrate how the rewrite process is done internally is to look at an example and see what terms are used instead of the original query term. Let's say we have the following data in our index:

```
curl -XPUT 'localhost:9200/clients/client/1' -d '{
  "id":"1", "name":"Joe"
}'
curl -XPUT 'localhost:9200/clients/client/2' -d '{
  "id":"2", "name":"Jane"
}'
curl -XPUT 'localhost:9200/clients/client/3' -d '{
  "id":"3", "name":"Jack"
}'
curl -XPUT 'localhost:9200/clients/client/4' -d '{
  "id":"4", "name":"Rob"
}'
```

We would like to find all the documents that start with the `j` letter. As simple as that, we run the following query against our `clients` index:

```
curl -XGET 'localhost:9200/clients/_search?pretty' -d '{
  "query" : {
   "prefix" : {
    "name" : {
     "prefix" : "j",
     "rewrite" : "constant_score_boolean"
    }
   }
  }
 }'
```

We've used a simple `prefix` query; we've said that we would like to find all the documents with the `j` letter in the `name` field. We've also used the rewrite property to specify the query rewrite method, but let's skip it for now, as we will discuss the possible values of this parameter in the later part of this section.

As the response to the previous query, we've got the following:

```
{
  "took" : 2,
  "timed_out" : false,
  "_shards" : {
    "total" : 5,
    "successful" : 5,
    "failed" : 0
  },
  "hits" : {
    "total" : 3,
    "max_score" : 1.0,
    "hits" : [ {
      "_index" : "clients",
      "_type" : "client",
      "_id" : "3",
      "_score" : 1.0,
      "_source":{
  "id":"3", "name":"Jack"
}
    }, {
      "_index" : "clients",
      "_type" : "client",
      "_id" : "2",
      "_score" : 1.0,
      "_source":{
  "id":"2", "name":"Jane"
```

```
        }
    }, {
        "_index" : "clients",
        "_type" : "client",
        "_id" : "1",
        "_score" : 1.0,
        "_source":{
    "id":"1", "name":"Joe"
    }
        } ]
    }
}
```

As you can see, in response we've got the three documents that have the contents of the name field starting with the desired character. We didn't specify the mappings explicitly, so Elasticsearch has guessed the name field mapping and has set it to string-based and analyzed it. You can check this by running the following command:

curl -XGET 'localhost:9200/clients/client/_mapping?pretty'

Elasticsearch's response will be similar to the following code:

```
{
  "clients" : {
    "mappings" : {
      "client" : {
        "properties" : {
          "id" : {
            "type" : "text",
            "fields" : {
              "keyword" : {
                "type" : "keyword",
                "ignore_above" : 256
              }
            }
          },
          "name" : {
            "type" : "text",
            "fields" : {
              "keyword" : {
                "type" : "keyword",
                "ignore_above" : 256
              }
            }
          }
        }
      }
    }
  }
}
```

```
      }
    }
```

 If you are a user of an Elasticsearch version below 5.0 and surprised by the preceding mapping, then please see the *Mapping changes under changes between 2.x to 5.x* section in `Chapter 1`, *Revisiting Elasticsearch and the Changes.*

Getting back to Apache Lucene

Now let's take a step back and look at Apache Lucene again. If you recall what the Lucene inverted index is built of, you can tell that it contains a term, a count, a document pointer, and the terms position in the document (if you can't recall, please refer to the *An overview of Lucene* section in `Chapter 1`, *Revisiting Elasticsearch and the Changes*. So, let's see how the simplified view of the index may look for the previous data we've put to the `clients` index, as shown in the following table:

Term	Count	Document : Position
Jack	1	3:1
Jane	1	2:1
Joe	1	1:1
Rob	1	4:1

What you see in the column with the term text is quite important. If we look at Elasticsearch and Apache Lucene internals, you can see that our prefix query was rewritten to the following Lucene query:

```
ConstantScore(name:jack name:jane name:joe)
```

We can check the portions of the rewrite using the Elasticsearch API. First of all, we can use the Explain API by running the following command:

```
curl -XGET 'localhost:9200/clients/client/1/_explain?pretty' -d '{
  "query" : {
   "prefix" : {
    "name" : {
     "prefix" : "j",
     "rewrite" : "constant_score_boolean"
    }
   }
  }
}'
```

The result would be as follows:

```
{
  "_index" : "clients",
  "_type" : "client",
  "_id" : "1",
  "matched" : true,
  "explanation" : {
    "value" : 1.0,
    "description" : "sum of:",
    "details" : [
      {
        "value" : 1.0,
        "description" : "ConstantScore(name:joe), product of:",
        "details" : [
          {
            "value" : 1.0,
            "description" : "boost",
            "details" : [ ]
          },
          {
            "value" : 1.0,
            "description" : "queryNorm",
            "details" : [ ]
          }
        ]
      },
      .
      .
      .
    ]
}
```

We can see that Elasticsearch used a constant score query with the `joe` term against the `name` field.

Query rewrite properties

Of course, the `rewrite` property of multiterm queries can take more than a single `constant_score_boolean` value. We can control how the queries are rewritten internally. To do that, we place the `rewrite` parameter inside the JSON object responsible for the actual query, for example, like the following code:

```
{
  "query" : {
    "prefix" : {
      "name" : "j",
      "rewrite" : "constant_score_boolean"
```

```
        }
    }
}
```

 Elasticsearch has a **Boolean query limit** of 1,024. This means you can use a maximum of 1,024 terms inside a `bool` query. This limit can be increased by setting the `indices.query.bool.max_clause_count` property in the `elasticsearch.yml` file. However, please remember that the more Boolean queries are produced, the lower the query performance may be.

The `rewrite` property can take the following values:

- `scoring_boolean`: This rewrite method translates each generated term into a Boolean `should` clause in a Boolean query. This rewrite method causes the score to be calculated for each document. Because of that, this method may be CPU demanding for queries where many terms may exceed the Boolean query limit.
- `constant_score_boolean`: This rewrite method is similar to the `scoring_boolean` rewrite method described previously, but is less CPU demanding because scoring is not computed, and instead of that, each term receives a score equal to the query boost (1 by default and can be set using the boost property). Because this rewrite method also results in Boolean `should` clauses being created, similar to the `scoring_boolean` rewrite method, this method can also hit the maximum Boolean clauses limit.
- `constant_score (default)`: This is the default rewrite method available in Elasticsearch and performs similar to `constant_score_boolean` when there are few matching terms and–otherwise it visits all matching terms in sequence and marks documents for that term. Matching documents are assigned a constant score equal to the query's boost.
- `top_terms_N`: This rewrite method translates each generated term into a Boolean `should` clause in a Boolean query and keeps the scores as computed by the query. However, unlike the `scoring_boolean` rewrite method, it only keeps the `N` number of top scoring terms to avoid hitting the maximum Boolean clauses limit and increases the final query performance.

- `top_terms_boost_N`: This is a rewrite method similar to the `top_terms_N` one, but the scores are not computed; instead the documents are given the score equal to the value of the `boost` property (one by default).

- `top_terms_blended_freqs_N`: This rewrite method first translates each term into the `should` clause in a Boolean query, but all term queries compute scores as if they had the same frequency. The frequency used is the maximum frequency of all matching terms. It only uses the top scoring terms so it will not overflow the Boolean query limit. Here also, the `N` controls the size of the top scoring terms to use.

An example

If we would like our example query to use the `top_terms_N` with *N* equal to 2, our query would look like the following:

```
curl -XGET 'localhost:9200/clients/client/_search?pretty' -d '{
  "query" : {
    "prefix" : {
      "name" : {
       "prefix" :"j",
       "rewrite" : "top_terms_2"
      }
    }
  }
}'
```

If you look at the results returned by Elasticsearch, you'll notice that, unlike our initial query, the documents were given a score different to the default 1.0:

```
{
  "took" : 4,
  "timed_out" : false,
  "_shards" : {
    "total" : 5,
    "successful" : 5,
    "failed" : 0
  },
  "hits" : {
    "total" : 3,
    "max_score" : 0.6931472,
    "hits" : [
      {
        "_index" : "clients",
        "_type" : "client",
```

```
        "_id" : "2",
        "_score" : 0.6931472,
        "_source" : {
          "id" : "2",
          "name" : "Jane"
        }
      },
      {
        "_index" : "clients",
        "_type" : "client",
        "_id" : "1",
        "_score" : 0.2876821,
        "_source" : {
          "id" : "1",
          "name" : "Joe"
        }
      },
      {
        "_index" : "clients",
        "_type" : "client",
        "_id" : "3",
        "_score" : 0.2876821,
        "_source" : {
          "id" : "3",
          "name" : "Jack"
        }
      }
    ]
  }
}
```

This is because the `top_terms_N` keeps the score for N top scoring terms.

Which rewrite type should you use?

The answer to this question greatly depends on your use case, but to summarize, if you can live with lower precision and relevancy (but higher performance), you can go for the top N rewrite method. If you need high precision and thus more relevant queries (but lower performance), choose the Boolean approach.

Query templates

When the application grows, it is very probable that the environment will start to be more and more complicated. In your organization, you probably have developers who specialize in particular layers of the application. For example, you have at least one frontend designer and an engineer responsible for the database layer. It is very convenient to have the development divided into several modules because you can work on different parts of the application in parallel, without the need for constant synchronization between individuals and the whole team. Of course, the book you are currently reading is not a book about project management, but search, so let's stick to that topic. In general, it would be useful, at least sometimes, to be able to extract all queries generated by the application, give them to a search engine, and let him/her optimize them, in terms of both performance and relevance. In such a case, the application developers would only have to pass the query itself to Elasticsearch and not care about the structure, query DSL, filtering, and so on.

Introducing search templates

Search templates were introduced in the release of Elasticsearch 1.1.0 and they have a dedicated search template API endpoint: _search/template. Search templates are very helpful in cases when we already know what type of queries should be sent to Elasticsearch, but the query structure is not final. By using the query templates, we can quickly supply the basic version of the query, let the application specify the parameters, and modify the query on the Elasticsearch side until the query parameters change. We will be using the same library index we have created while learning about queries use cases in *The use cases* section in this chapter.

 Apart from _search/template API, Elasticsearch had a template query also which used to accept a query template and a map of key/value pairs to fill in template parameters. But in Elasticsearch 5.0, the template query is deprecated and will be removed in future releases. So you are advised to switch to the search template API.

Let's assume that one of our queries needs to return the most relevant books from our `library` index. We also allow users to choose whether they are interested in books that are available or the ones that are not available. In such a case, we will need to provide two parameters: the phrase itself and the Boolean that specifies the availability. The first, simplified example of our query could look as follows:

```
{
    "query": {
        "bool": {
            "must": {
                "match": {
                    "_all": QUERY
                }
            },
            "filter": {
                "term": {
                    "available": BOOLEAN
                }
            }
        }
    }
}
```

In some of the examples in this chapter, we have used the `_all` field for query purposes. If you are not aware about the `_all` field, it is a special field maintained by Elasticsearch in which data of all the fields are copied by Elasticsearch itself, and this is enabled by default. However, there is an issue opened on GitHub for disabling this field in upcoming versions. You can follow its progress at `https://github.com/elastic/elasticsearch/issues/19784`

`QUERY` and `BOOLEAN` are placeholders for variables that will be passed to the query by the application. Of course, this query is too simple for our use case, but as we already said, this is only its first version–we will improve it in just a second.

Having our first query, we can now create our first template. Let's change our query a bit so that it looks as follows:

```
{
    "inline": {
        "query": {
            "bool": {
                "must": {
                    "match": {
                        "_all": "{{phrase}}"
                    }
```

```
      },
      "filter": {
        "term": {
          "available": "{{avail}}"
        }
      }
    }
  }
},
"params": {
  "phrase": "front",
  "avail": true
}
}
```

 In the preceding example, you can see inline parameter, which is used while creating templates. In earlier versions, the template keyword was used but it was removed in favor of inline.

You can see that our placeholders were replaced by {{phrase}} and {{avail}}, and a new section, params, was introduced. When encountering a section such as {{phrase}}, Elasticsearch will go to the params section and look for a parameter called phrase and use it. In general, we've moved the parameter values to the params section, and in the query itself we use references using the {{var}} notation, where var is the name of the parameter from the params section. In addition, the query itself is nested in the inline element. This way we can parameterize our queries.

Let's now send the preceding query to the /library/_search/template REST endpoint (not /library/_search as we usually do) using the GET HTTP method. To do this, we will use the following command:

```
curl -XGET "http://localhost:9200/library/_search/template?pretty" -d'
{
  "inline": {
    "query": {
      "bool": {
        "must": {
          "match": {
            "_all": "{{phrase}}"
          }
        },
        "filter": {
          "term": {
            "available": "{{avail}}"
          }
        }
```

```
            }
          }
        }
      },
      "params": {
        "phrase": "front",
        "avail": true
      }
    }'
```

The preceding query will return one document with the title, *All Quiet on the Western Front*.

The Mustache template engine

Elasticsearch uses Mustache templates (see: `http://mustache.github.io/`) to generate resulting queries from templates. As you have already seen, every variable is surrounded by double curly brackets; this is specific to Mustache and is a method of dereferencing variables in this template engine. The full syntax of the Mustache template engine is beyond the scope of this book, but we would like to briefly introduce you to the most interesting parts of it: conditional expression, loops, and default values.

 The complete documentation of Mustache is available at `http://mustache.github.io/mustache.5.html`

Conditional expressions

The `{{val}}` expression results in inserting the value of the `val` variable. The `{{#val}}` and `{{/val}}` expressions insert the values placed between them if the variable called `val` computes to `true`.

Let's take a look at the following example:

```
curl -XGET 'localhost:9200/library/_search/template?pretty' -d '{
  "inline": "{ {{#limit}}"size": 2 {{/limit}}}",
  "params": {
    "limit": false
  }
}'
```

The preceding command returns all documents indexed in the `library` index. However, if we change the `limit` parameter to `true` and send the query once again, we would only get two documents. That's because the conditional would be `true` and the template would be activated. In the preceding command, the `{{#val}}` and `{{/val}}` expressions are equal to `{{#limit}}"size": 2 {{/limit}}`. It is also important to see that the size parameter is used with the escaped character to make the request a valid JSON string. Otherwise, the request would have failed and Elasticsearch would return the following error:

```
{
    "error": {
        "root_cause": [
            {
                "type": "json_parse_exception",
                "reason": "Unexpected character ('s' (code 115)):
was expecting comma to separate OBJECT entries\n at [Source:
org.elasticsearch.transport.netty4.ByteBufStreamInput@6ce7498d;
line: 2, column: 29]"
            }
        ],
        "type": "json_parse_exception",
        "reason": "Unexpected character ('s' (code 115)): was
expecting comma to separate OBJECT entries\n at [Source: org
.elasticsearch.transport.netty4.ByteBufStreamInput@6ce7498d;
line: 2, column: 29]"
    },
    "status": 500
}
```

Loops

Loops are defined exactly the same as conditionals–between expression `{{#val}}` and `{{/val}}`. If the variable from the expression is an array, you can insert current values using the `{{.}}` expression.

For example, if we would like the template engine to iterate through an array of terms and create a terms query using them, we could run a query using the following command:

```
curl -XGET 'localhost:9200/library/_search/template?pretty' -d '{
    "inline": {
        "query": {
            "terms": {
                "title": [
                    "{{#title}}",
```

```
        "{{.}}",
        "{{/title}}"
      ]
    }
  }
},
"params": {
  "title": [ "front", "complete" ]
}
}'
```

With the preceding query, you will get two hits in the response.

Default values

The default value tag allows us to define what value (or whole part of the template) should be used if the given parameter is not defined. The syntax for defining the default value for a variable called var is as follows:

```
{{var}}{{^var}}default value{{/var}}
```

For example, if we would like to have the default value of complete for the phrase parameter in our template query, we could send a query using the following command:

```
curl -XGET 'localhost:9200/library/_search/template?pretty' -d '{
  "inline": {
    "query": {
      "term": {
        "title": "{{phrase}}{{^phrase}}complete{{/phrase}}"
      }
    }
  },
  "params": {
    "phrase": "front"
  }
}'
```

The preceding command will result in Elasticsearch finding all documents with the term front in the title field. However, if the phrase parameter was not defined in the params section, the term crime will be used instead. You can try it by removing the params object from the preceding command.

Storing templates in files

Regardless of the way we defined our templates previously, we were still a long way from decoupling them from the application. We still needed to store the whole query in the application; we were only able to parameterize the query. Fortunately, there is a simple way to change the query definition so it can be read dynamically by Elasticsearch from the `config/scripts` directory.

For example, let's create a file called `bookList.mustache` (in the `/etc/elasticsearch/scripts/` directory) with the following contents:

```
{
  "query": {
    "bool": {
      "must": {
        "match": {
          "_all": "{{phrase}}"
        }
      },
      "filter": {
        "term": {
          "available": "{{avail}}"
        }
      }
    }
  }
}
```

We can now use the contents of that file in a query by specifying the template name (the name of the template is the name of the file without the `.mustache` extension). For example, if we would like to use our `bookList` template, we would send the following command:

```
curl -XGET 'localhost:9200/library/_search/template?pretty' -d '{
  "file": "bookList",
  "params": {
    "phrase": "front",
    "avail": true
  }
}'
```

In the preceding command, notice the file parameter for loading the template from the Elasticsearch `config/scripts` directory.

The very convenient fact is that Elasticsearch can see the changes in the file without the need for a node restart. Of course, we still need to have the template file stored on all Elasticsearch nodes that are capable of handling the query execution.

Storing templates in a cluster

Templates can be also be stored in the Elasticsearch cluster state, and they can be used using `_id` of the template. Usually template names are used as `_id`.

For example, you can use the following `curl` request to store your template in Elasticsearch:

```
curl -XPOST "http://localhost:9200/_search/template/template1" -d'
{
"template": {
    "query": {
      "bool": {
        "must": {
          "match": {
            "_all": "{{phrase}}"
          }
        },
        "filter": {
          "term": {
            "available": "{{avail}}"
          }
        }
      }
    }
  }
}'
```

Please pay special attention to the use of `template` elements instead of `inline`, which we have been using throughout this section.

To use the preceding template at query time, the following request needs to be made:

```
curl -XGET "http://localhost:9200/library/_search/template?pretty" -d'
{
 "id": "template1",
 "params": {
   "phrase": "front",
   "avail": true
 }
}'
```

The template we have indexed with id `template1`, can be retrieved using the following commands.

```
curl -XGET "http://localhost:9200/_search/template/template1"
```

You can see the output of the command, in which it is shown that Elasticsearch uses the Mustache and stores the template body as a JSON string:

```
{
  "lang": "mustache",
  "_id": "template1",
  "found": true,
  "template":
"{"query":{"bool":{"must":{"match":{"_all":"{{phrase}}"}},"filter":{"term":
{"available":"{{avail}}"}}}}}"
}
```

This template can be deleted with the following curl request:

```
curl -XDELETE "http://localhost:9200/_search/template/template1"
```

Summary

In this chapter, we explained scoring and its new default similarity ranking algorithm, BM25, along with explaining the difference between BM25 and TF-IDF, the previous ranking algorithm used in Apache Lucene. In addition to that, we discussed precision and recall, the fundamentals of search relevancy.

After that, we discussed Elasticsearch Query DSL in detail and covered the important queries with their use cases. We also saw the new `bool` query syntax and how one can use filters within the query context of the `bool` query. The chapter also covered a detailed discussion about using query rewrites and using search templates along with the Mustache template engine.

In the next chapter, you will learn about query rescoring and how search works in multimatch scenarios, such as cross-field matching and phrase matching. We will also cover various ways to use scripting in Elasticsearch.

3
Beyond Full Text Search

In the previous chapter, we saw how scoring and relevancy work in a full text search. We also discussed the Elasticsearch Query DSL in detail and covered the important queries with their use cases. Finally, we talked about using query rewrites and using search templates along with the Mustache template engine. In this chapter, we will focus on topics which are more than just a full text search and we'll learn how to alter the default scoring of Apache Lucene using custom methods. We will also learn about scripting modules of Elasticsearch in detail. By the end of this chapter, we will have covered the following topics:

- Controlling multimatching
- Controlling the score using the function score query
- Optimizing queries and score recalculation using the query rescore
- Extended information regarding Elasticsearch scripting
- The new scripting language: Painless
- Understanding Lucene expressions

Controlling multimatching

It is often required to search the terms in more than one field in a single query. This can be easily done using the `multi_match` query available in Elasticsearch. But, what's more important is to know and control the score calculation while using the `multi_match` queries. The `multi_match` query is built over a simple `match` query to allow for searching inside multiple fields.

Multimatch types

In this section, we will cover the different flavors of `multi-match` queries, which are mainly controlled using the `type` property. The following are the available types:

- The `best_fields` type
- The `most_fields` type
- The `cross_fields` type
- The `phrase` type
- The `phrase_prefix` type

Best fields matching

To use the `best_fields` type matching, one needs to set the `type` property of the `multi_match` query to the `best_fields` query. This type of multimatching will generate a `match` query for each field specified in the `fields` property and it is best used for searching for multiple words in the same best matching field. For example, let's look at the following query:

```
curl -XGET 'localhost:9200/library/_search?pretty' -d '{
  "query" : {
    "multi_match" : {
      "query" : "complete conan doyle",
      "fields" : [ "title", "author", "characters" ],
      "type" : "best_fields",
      "tie_breaker" : 0.8
    }
  }
}'
```

The preceding query would be translated into a query similar to the following one:

```
curl -XGET 'localhost:9200/library/_search?pretty' -d '{
  "query" : {
    "dis_max" : {
      "queries" : [
        {
          "match" : {
            "title" : "complete conan doyle"
          }
        },
        {
          "match" : {
```

```
            "author" : "complete conan doyle"
          }
        },
        {
          "match" : {
            "characters" : "complete conan doyle"
          }
        }
      ],
      "tie_breaker" : 0.8
    }
  }
}'
```

If you look at the results for both of the preceding queries, you will notice the following:

```
{
  "took": 3,
  "timed_out": false,
  "_shards": {
    "total": 5,
    "successful": 5,
    "failed": 0
  },
  "hits": {
    "total": 1,
    "max_score": 0.7364661,
    "hits": [
      {
        "_index": "library",
        "_type": "book",
        "_id": "3",
        "_score": 0.7364661,
        "_source": {
          "title": "The Complete Sherlock Holmes",
          "author": "Arthur Conan Doyle",
          "year": 1936,
          "characters": [
            "Sherlock Holmes",
            "Dr. Watson",
            "G. Lestrade"
          ],
          "tags": [],
          "copies": 0,
          "available": false,
          "section": 12
        }
      }
```

```
        ]
    }
}
```

Both queries resulted in exactly the same results and the same scores calculated for the document. One thing to remember is how the score is calculated. If the `tie_breaker` value is present, the score for each document is the sum of the score for the best matching field and the score of the other matching fields multiplied by the `tie_breaker` value. If the `tie_breaker` value is not present, the document is assigned a score equal to the score of the best matching field.

There is one more question when it comes to `best_fields` matching: what happens when we would like to use the AND operator or the `minimum_should_match` property? The answer is simple: `best_fields` matching is translated into many `match` queries and both the `operator` property and the `minimum_should_match` property are applied to each of the generated `match` queries. Because of that, a query such as the following wouldn't return any documents in our case:

```
curl -XGET 'localhost:9200/library/_search?pretty' -d '{
  "query" : {
    "multi_match" : {
      "query" : "complete conan doyle",
      "fields" : [ "title", "author", "characters" ],
      "type" : "best_fields",
      "operator" : "and"
    }
  }
}'
```

This is because the preceding query would be translated into:

```
curl -XGET 'localhost:9200/library/_search?pretty' -d '{
  "query" : {
    "dis_max" : {
      "queries" : [
        {
          "match" : {
            "title" : {
              "query" : "complete conan doyle",
              "operator" : "and"
            }
          }
        },
        {
          "match" : {
            "author" : {
```

```
              "query" : "complete conan doyle",
              "operator" : "and"
          }
        }
      },
      {
        "match" : {
          "characters" : {
            "query" : "complete conan doyle",
            "operator" : "and"
          }
        }
      }
    ]
  }
 }
}'
```

And the preceding query looks as follows on the Lucene level:

```
(+title:complete +title:conan +title:doyle) | (+author:complete
+author:conan +author:doyle) | (+characters:complete    +characters:conan
+characters:doyle)
```

We don't have any document in the index that has the `complete`, `conan`, and `doyle` terms in a single field. However, if we would like to match the terms in a different field, we can use the `cross_fields` matching.

Cross fields matching

The `cross_fields` type matching is perfect when we want all the terms from the query to be found in the mentioned fields inside the same document. Let's recall our previous query, but this time instead of `best_fields` matching, let's use the `cross_fields` matching type:

```
curl -XGET 'localhost:9200/library/_search?pretty' -d '{
  "query" : {
    "multi_match" : {
      "query" : "complete conan doyle",
      "fields" : [ "title", "author", "characters" ],
      "type" : "cross_fields",
      "operator" : "and"
    }
  }
}'
```

This time, the results returned by Elasticsearch were as follows:

```
{
  "took": 3,
  "timed_out": false,
  "_shards": {
    "total": 5,
    "successful": 5,
    "failed": 0
  },
  "hits": {
    "total": 1,
    "max_score": 0.79400253,
    "hits": [
      {
        "_index": "library",
        "_type": "book",
        "_id": "3",
        "_score": 0.79400253,
        "_source": {
          "title": "The Complete Sherlock Holmes",
          "author": "Arthur Conan Doyle",
          "year": 1936,
          "characters": [
            "Sherlock Holmes",
            "Dr. Watson",
            "G. Lestrade"
          ],
          "tags": [],
          "copies": 0,
          "available": false,
          "section": 12
        }
      }
    ]
  }
}
```

This is because our query was translated into the following Lucene query:

```
+(title:complete author:complete characters:complete)    +(title:conan
author:conan characters:conan) +(title:doyle    author:doyle
characters:doyle)
```

The results will only contain documents having all the terms in any of the mentioned fields. Of course, this is only the case when we use the AND Boolean operator. With the OR operator, we will get documents having at least a single match in any of the fields. One more thing that is taken care of when using the `cross_fields` type is the problem of different term frequencies for each field. Elasticsearch handles that by blending the term frequencies for all the fields that are mentioned in a query. To put it simply, Elasticsearch gives almost the same weight to all the terms in the fields that are used in a query.

Most fields matching

Another type of `multi_field` configuration is the `most_fields` type. As the official documentation states, it was designed to help run queries against documents that contain the same text analyzed in different ways. One of the examples is having multiple languages in different fields. For example, if we would like to search for books that have `Die leiden` terms in their title or original title, we could run the following query:

```
curl -XGET 'localhost:9200/library/_search?pretty' -d '{
  "query" : {
    "multi_match" : {
      "query" : "Die Leiden",
      "fields" : [ "title", "otitle" ],
      "type" : "most_fields"
    }
  }
}'
```

Internally, the preceding request would be translated to the following query:

```
curl -XGET 'localhost:9200/library/_search?pretty' -d '{
  "query" : {
    "bool" : {
      "should" : [
        {
          "match" : {
            "title" : "die leiden"
          }
        },
        {
          "match" : {
            "otitle" : "die leiden"
          }
        }
      ]
    }
  }
}
```

```
}'
```

The resulting documents are given a score equal to the sum of scores from each `match` query divided by the number of matching `match` clauses.

Phrase matching

The phrase matching is very similar to the `best_fields` matching that we have already discussed. However, instead of translating the query using `match` queries, it uses `match_phrase` queries. Let's take a look at the following query:

```
curl -XGET 'localhost:9200/library/_search?pretty' -d '{
  "query" : {
    "multi_match" : {
      "query" : "sherlock holmes",
      "fields" : [ "title", "author" ],
      "type" : "phrase"
    }
  }
}'
```

Because we use the phrase matching, it would be translated into the following:

```
curl -XGET 'localhost:9200/library/_search?pretty' -d '{
  "query" : {
    "dis_max" : {
      "queries" : [
        {
          "match_phrase" : {
            "title" : "sherlock holmes"
          }
        },
        {
          "match_phrase" : {
            "author" : "sherlock holmes"
          }
        }
      ]
    }
  }
}'
```

Phrase with prefixes matching

This is exactly the same as the phrase matching, but instead of using the match_phrase query, the match_phrase_prefix query is used. Let's assume we run the following query:

```
curl -XGET 'localhost:9200/library/_search?pretty' -d '{
  "query" : {
    "multi_match" : {
      "query" : "sherlock hol",
      "fields" : [ "title", "author" ],
      "type" : "phrase_prefix"
    }
  }
}'
```

What Elasticsearch would do internally is run a query similar to the following one:

```
curl -XGET 'localhost:9200/library/_search?pretty' -d '{
  "query" : {
    "dis_max" : {
      "queries" : [
        {
          "match_phrase_prefix" : {
            "title" : "sherlock hol"
          }
        },
        {
          "match_phrase_prefix" : {
            "author" : "sherlock hol"
          }
        }
      ]
    }
  }
}'
```

As you can see, by using the type property of the multi_match query, you can achieve different results without the need for writing complicated queries. What's more, Elasticsearch will also take care of the scoring and problems related to it.

Controlling scores using the function score query

In most cases, you are good to go with the default scoring algorithms of Elasticsearch to return the most relevant results. However, some cases require you to have more control over the calculation of a score. This is especially required while implementing domain-specific logics where you need to implement a very specific scoring formula and alter the final score. Elasticsearch provides you with the `function_score` query to take control of all these things.

The `function_score` query allows you to take complete control of how a score needs to be calculated for a particular query. The syntax of the `function_score` query is given as follows:

```
{
  "query": {"function_score": {
    "query": {},
    "boost": "boost for the whole query",
    "functions": [
      {}
    ],
    "max_boost": number,
    "score_mode": "(multiply|max|...)",
    "boost_mode": "(multiply|replace|...)",
    "min_score" : number
  }}
}
```

The `function_score` query has two parts: The first is a base query that finds the overall pool of results you want. The second part is a list of functions which are used to adjust the scoring. These functions can be applied on each document that matches the main query in order to alter or completely replace the original query `_score`.

> In a `function_score` query, each function is composed of an optional filter that tells Elasticsearch which records should have their scores adjusted (defaults to all records), and a description of how to adjust the score.

The other parameters that can be used with the `function_score` query are as follows:

- The `boost` parameter is an optional parameter which defines the `boost for the whole query`.
- The `max_boost` parameter is the maximum boost that will be applied by the `function_score`.
- The `boost_mode` parameter is an optional parameter, which defaults to `multiply`. It defines how the combined result of score functions will influence the final score together with the sub-query score. The other possible values can be `replace` (only the function score is used, and the query score is ignored), `max` (max of the query score and function score), `min` (min of the query score and function score), `sum` (the query score and function score are added), `avg`, or `multiply` (the query score and function score are multiplied).
- The `score_mode` parameter specifies how the results of individual score functions will be aggregated. Possible values can be `first` (the first function that has a matching filter is applied), `avg`, `max`, `sum`, `min`, and `multiply`.
- The `min_score` parameter is the minimum score to be used. It is used for excluding non-relevant documents that do not meet a certain score threshold specified using this parameter.

Built-in functions under the function score query

The following are the built-in functions available to be used with the `function_score` query:

- The `weight` function
- The `field_value_factor` function
- The `script_score` function
- Decay functions – `linear`, `exp`, `gauss`

Let's look at them one by one.

The weight function

The `weight` function allows you to apply a simple boost to each document without the boost being normalized: a `weight` of 2 results in 2 * _score. For example:

```
curl -XGET "http://localhost:9200/library/_search" -d'
{
  "query": {
    "function_score": {
      "query": {
        "match": {
          "tags": "novel"
        }
      },
      "functions": [
        {
          "filter": {
            "term": {
              "tags": "classics"
            }
          },
          "weight": 2
        }
      ],
      "boost_mode": "replace"
    }
  }
}'
```

The preceding query will match all the books which belong to the `novel` category, but will give a higher score to books that also belongs to the `classics` category. Please note that `boost_mode` is set to `replace` which will cause the _score calculated by `query` to be overridden by the `weight` function for our particular `filter` clause. The query output will contain the books on top with a _score of 2, which belongs to both the `novel` and `classics` categories.

The field value factor function

This uses the value of a field in the document to alter the _score:

```
curl -XGET "http://localhost:9200/library/_search" -d'
{
  "query": {
    "function_score": {
      "query": {
```

```
      "term": {
        "tags": {
          "value": "novel"
        }
      }
    },
    "functions": [
      {
        "field_value_factor": {
          "field": "year"
        }
      }
    ],
    "boost_mode": "multiply"
  }
 }
}'
```

The preceding query finds all the books with `novel` in their `tags` but influences the total score depending on the `year` in which that book is published. So the greater the value of the `year`, the higher ranking the book will get. Please note that `boost_mode` is set to `multiply` which will yield the following formula for final scoring:

```
_score = _score * doc['total_experience'].value
```

But there are two issues with this approach. First, if the field which is used for influencing the score using `field_value_factor` has a value of zero, it will reset the final score to zero. Second, the Lucene _score usually falls within the range zero to 10, so if the value of the field is greater than 10, it will completely swamp the effect of the full text search score.

To get rid of this problem, apart from using the `field` parameter, the `field_value_factor` function provides you with the following extra parameters to be used:

- The `factor` parameter: An optional factor to multiply the field value with. It defaults to 1.
- The `modifier` parameter: A mathematical modifier to apply to the field value, which can be one of `none`, `log`, `log1p`, `log2p`, `ln`, `ln1p`, `ln2p`, `square`, `sqrt`, or `reciprocal`. It defaults to `none`.

The script score function

This is the most powerful function available in Elasticsearch. It uses a custom script to take complete control of the scoring logic. You can write a custom script to implement the logic you need. Scripting allows you to write from simple to very complex logics. Scripts are cached too, to allow faster executions for repetitive queries. Let's look at the following example:

```
{
  "script_score": {
    "script": "doc['year'].value"
  }
}
```

Look at the special syntax for accessing the field values inside the `script` parameter. This is how the value of fields is accessed using the Painless scripting language which we will look at in upcoming sections of this chapter. You will also see lots of examples of using `script_score` throughout this chapter.

Decay functions – linear, exp, and gauss

Decay functions come in three types: `linear`, `exp` (that is, exponential), and `gauss` (that is, Gaussian). All these three decay functions work only on numeric, date, and geo-point fields. They are used when we want to work with this sliding scale based on some numbers or distance. All three functions take the same parameter as the following and are required for controlling the shape of the curve created for decay: `origin`, `scale`, `decay`, and `offset`.

The point of origin is used for calculating distance. For date fields, the default is `now` (the current timestamp). The `scale` parameter defines the distance from the origin at which the computed score will the equal `decay` parameter. The `origin` and `scale` parameters can be thought of as your min and max, defining a bounding box within which the curve will be defined. If we want to give more boosts to the documents which have been published in the last 10 days, it would be best to define the `origin` as the current timestamp, and the `scale` as 10d. The `offset` defines that the decay function will only compute the decay function for documents with a distance greater than the defined `offset`. The default is `0`.

Finally, the decay option alters how severely the document is demoted based on its position. The default decay value is 0.5. Let's assume we run the following query:

```
curl -XGET "http://localhost:9200/library/_search" -d'
{
   "query": {
     "function_score": {
       "query": {
         "match_all": {}
       },
       "functions": [
         {
           "exp": {
             "year": {
               "origin": "2016",
               "scale": "100"
             }
           }
         }
       ],
       "boost_mode": "multiply"
     }
   }
}'
```

In the preceding query, we have used the exponential decay function which tells Elasticsearch to start decaying the score calculation after a value of 100 from the given origin. So, books which are published more than 100 years ago from the given origin will be ranked low but not discarded. These books can still be ranked higher if we combine other function's score queries such as weight or field_value_factor with the decay function, and combine the results of all the functions together.

Query rescoring

One of the great features provided by Elasticsearch is the ability to change the ordering of documents after they are returned by a query. Actually, Elasticsearch does a simple trick–it recalculates the score of top matching documents, so only part of the document in the response is reordered. The reasons why we want to do this can vary. One of the reasons may be performance. For example, calculating target ordering is very costly because scripts are used and we would like to do this on the subset of documents returned by the original query. You can imagine that rescore gives us many great opportunities for business use cases. Now, let's look at this functionality and how we can benefit from using it.

What is query rescoring?

Rescoring in Elasticsearch is the process of recalculating the score for a defined number of documents returned by the `query`. This means that Elasticsearch first takes N documents for a given `query` (or the `post_filter` phase) and calculates their score using a provided `rescore` definition. For example, if we would take a term query and ask for all the documents that are available, we can use `rescore` to recalculate the score for 100 documents only, not for all documents returned by the `query`. Rescoring is commonly used if a scoring algorithm is too costly to be executed across the entire document set but efficient enough to be executed on the top-N documents scored by a faster retrieval method.

If you are not aware about `post_filter` you can read about it more at `https://www.elastic.co/guide/en/elasticsearch/reference/master/search-request-post-filter.html`

Let's start with a simple query that looks as follows:

```
{
  "query" : {
    "match_all" : {}
  }
}
```

It matches all the documents from the index the query is run against. Every document returned by the `query` will have the score equal to `1` because of the `match_all` query. This is enough to show how rescoring affects our result set.

Structure of the rescore query

Let's now modify our query so that it uses the rescore functionality. Basically, let's assume that we want the score of the document to be equal to the value of the `year` field. The query that does that would look as follows:

```
{
  "query": {
    "match_all": {}
  },
  "rescore": {
    "query": {
      "rescore_query": {
        "function_score": {
          "query": {
```

```
        "match_all": {}
      },
      "script_score": {
        "script": {
          "inline": "doc['year'].value",
          "lang": "painless"
        }
      }
    }
  }
 }
}
"_source": ["title", "available"]
}
```

Let's now look at the preceding query in more detail. The first thing you may have noticed is the `rescore` object. The mentioned object holds the `query` that will affect the scoring of the documents returned by the `query`. In our case, the logic is very simple, we just assign the value of the `year` field as the score of the document.

 When using `curl`, you need to escape the script value, so the `doc['year'].value` would look like `doc[\"year\"].value`.

We can save this query in the `query.json` file and send it using the following command:

```
curl -XGET localhost:9200/library/book/_search?pretty -d @query.json
```

The document that Elasticsearch should return should be as follows (please note that we've omitted the structure of the response so that it is as simple as it can be):

```
{
  "took": 6,
  "timed_out": false,
  "_shards": {
    "total": 5,
    "successful": 5,
    "failed": 0
  },
  "hits": {
    "total": 5,
    "max_score": 1,
    "hits": [
      {
        "_index": "library",
        "_type": "book",
```

```
          "_id": "2",
          "_score": 1962,
          "_source": {
            "available": false,
            "title": "Catch-22"
          }
        },
        {
          "_index": "library",
          "_type": "book",
          "_id": "3",
          "_score": 1937,
          "_source": {
            "available": false,
            "title": "The Complete Sherlock Holmes"
          }
        },
        {
          "_index": "library",
          "_type": "books",
          "_id": "1",
          "_score": 1930,
          "_source": {
            "available": true,
            "title": "All Quiet on the Western Front"
          }
        },
        {
          "_index": "library",
          "_type": "book",
          "_id": "5",
          "_score": 1905,
          "_source": {
            "available": true,
            "title": "The Peasants"
          }
        },
        {
          "_index": "library",
          "_type": "book",
          "_id": "4",
          "_score": 1775,
          "_source": {
            "available": true,
            "title": "The Sorrows of Young Werther"
          }
        }
      }
    ]
```

```
            }
        }
```

As we can see, Elasticsearch found all the documents from the original query. Now look at the score of the documents. Elasticsearch took the first *N* documents and applied the second query to them. In the result, the score of those documents is the sum of the score from the first and second queries. As you know, scripts execution can be demanding when it comes to performance. That's why we've used it in the rescore phase of the query. If our initial `match_all` query returns thousands of results, calculating script-based scoring for all those can affect query performance. Rescore gives us the possibility to only calculate such scoring on the top *N* documents and thus reduce the performance impact.

Let's look at another example of query rescoring–to understand it better–and how to tune the rescore functionality behavior using the available parameters as follows:

```
curl -XPOST "http://localhost:9200/library/_search" -d'
{
  "query" : {
    "match" : {
      "title" : {
        "operator" : "or",
        "query" : "The Complete",
        "type" : "boolean"
      }
    }
  },
  "rescore" : {
    "window_size" : 50,
    "query" : {
      "score_mode":"max",
      "rescore_query" : {
        "match" : {
          "title" : {
            "query" : "The Sorrows",
            "type" : "boolean",
            "operator" : "and"
          }
        }
      },
      "query_weight" : 0.7,
      "rescore_query_weight" : 1.2
    }
  },
  "_source": ["title", "available"]
}'
```

In the preceding query, first the main query is executed on the index, which matches the documents which have `The` or `Complete` in the title, and then on all the matching documents the `rescore_query` is executed. The final score is altered using the `rescore_query` which has `The` and `Sorrows` both available in the `title` field. You can see that there are some additional parameters used in this query which are: `window_size`, `score_mode`, `query_weight`, and `rescore_query_weight`. Let us see what they mean in the next section.

Rescore parameters

In the `query` under the `rescore` object, we are allowed to use the following parameters:

- The `window_size` parameter (defaults to the sum of the `from` and `size` parameters) is the number of documents used for rescoring on every shard. Please note that the sum of the `from` and `size` parameter cannot be more than the `index.max_result_window` index setting which defaults to `10,000`.
- The `score_mode` parameter (defaults to `total`) is the way to combine the final score for each document. It supports the following parameters:
  - The `total` parameter: Adds the original score and the `rescore_query` score. It is the default parameter of `score_mode`.
  - The `multiply` parameter: Multiplies the original score by the `rescore_query` score. It is useful for `function_query` rescores.
  - The `avg` parameter: Averages the original score and the `rescore_query` score.
  - The `max` parameter: Takes the maximum of the original score and the `rescore_query` score.
  - The `min` parameter: Takes the minimum of the original score and the `rescore_query` score.
- The `query_weight` parameter (defaults to `1`): The resulting score of the original query will be multiplied by this value before adding the score generated by `rescore`.
- The `rescore_query_weight` parameter (defaults to `1`): The resulting score of the `rescore` will be multiplied by this value before adding the score generated by the original query

To sum up, the target score for the document is equal to the following:

```
original_query_score * query_weight + rescore_query_score *
rescore_query_weight
```

To sum up

Sometimes, we want to show results where the ordering of the first documents on the page is affected by additional rules. Unfortunately, this cannot be achieved by the rescore functionality. The first idea points to the `window_size` parameter, but this parameter, in fact, is not connected with the first documents on the result list, but with the number of results returned on every shard. In addition, the `window_size` value cannot be less than page size (Elasticsearch will set the `window_size` value to the value of the `size` property, when `window_size` is lower than `size`). Also, one very important thing: rescoring cannot be combined with sorting because sorting is done before the changes to the documents, scores are done by rescoring, and thus sorting won't take the newly calculated score into consideration.

Elasticsearch scripting

One of the great things in Elasticsearch is its scripting capabilities. In those scenarios where the API is just not enough, Elasticsearch allows you to write your own custom logic in a script. You can use this script for calculating the score, text-based scoring, data filtering, data analysis, and doing partial updates to the documents. Although scripting can be slow in some cases, such as calculating the score for each document, we think that this part of Elasticsearch is important. Scripting is supported in many APIs including search, sorting, aggregations, and document updates.

The syntax

The script follows the following pattern whenever it is used in any Elasticsearch API:

```
"script": {
  "lang":    "...",
  "inline" | "id" | "file": "...",
  "params": { ... }
}
```

Let us understand the script parameters:

- The `lang` parameter is the language the script is written in, which defaults to `painless`.
- The `inline | id | file` parameter is the script itself, which may be specified as `inline`, `id`, or `file`. This is a way to specify the source of the script. An inline script is specified `inline`, a stored script with the specified `id` is retrieved from the cluster state, and a file script is retrieved from a `file` in the `config/scripts` directory.
- The `params` parameter is any named parameter that should be passed into the script.

Scripting changes across different versions

Elasticsearch scripting has seen lots of refactoring starting from version 1.0 and in the versions that came after that. Because of those changes, some users are always lost as to why their scripts stopped working when upgrading to some other versions of Elasticsearch and what is happening in general. Here are some highlights of scripting changes in Elasticsearch:

- **Deprecation and removal of MVEL**: The first default scripting language introduced in Elasticsearch was MVEL which was replaced by Groovy in the release of Elasticsearch Version 1.4. MVEL was finally removed in the later release.
- **Deprecation of Groovy**: Starting from Elasticsearch Version 5.0, the Groovy scripting language is deprecated and might be removed from future versions of Elasticsearch. Groovy is replaced by the new language, Painless. You can still use Groovy but you need to enable dynamic scripting in the `elasticsearch.yml` file. For using Painless, there are no additional settings required.
- **Deprecation of additional language plugins**: Elasticsearch used to have language plugin supports for JavaScript as well as Python, but along with Groovy, both of these languages are marked as deprecated in Elasticsearch 5.0.0 in favor of Painless.

 Please visit the following URL if you want to enable dynamic scripting in Elasticsearch. It explains very well about the fine grained control for enabling dynamic scripts in different search contexts:
`https://www.elastic.co/guide/en/elasticsearch/reference/5.x/modu les-scripting-security.html`

In addition to Painless, the following scripting languages are still supported in Elasticsearch out of the box:

- Lucene expressions, which are primarily used for fast custom ranking and sorting
- Mustache is used for search templates and has already been discussed in `Chapter 2`, *The Improved Query DSL*
- Java, also known as native scripts, is the best way to implement them by writing custom plugins

> In this chapter, we will cover the Painless and Lucene expressions in detail. We will not be covering Groovy, JavaScript, or Python language scripting, since they have already been marked as deprecated and are going to be removed soon.

Painless – the new default scripting language

With the release of Elasticsearch 5.0, we can use a new scripting language that has become the default: Painless. It is a simple and secure scripting language available in Elasticsearch by default and does not require any plugin to be installed. Painless is designed specifically for use with Elasticsearch and can safely be used with inline and stored scripting, without worrying about any security issues or configuration changes.

Using Painless as your scripting language

There is not much documentation available on the Painless scripting language yet but according to the Elasticsearch official documentation, Painless syntax is similar to Groovy. Although we will cover how to use Painless with some examples in the next sections, lets first learn about the basics of Painless syntax and semantics.

Variable definition in scripts

Painless allows us to define variables in scripts used in Elasticsearch. To define a new variable, we use the `def` keyword followed by the variable name and its value. For example, to define a variable named `sum` and assign an initial value of `0` to it, we would use the following snippet of code:

```
def sum = 0
```

Of course, we are not only bound to simple variables definition. We can define lists, for example, a list of four values as follows:

```
def listOfValues = [0, 1, 2, 3]
```

Conditionals

We are also allowed to use conditional statements in scripts. For example, we can use standard if...elseif...else structures:

```
def total = 0;
for (def i = 0; i < doc['tags'].length; i++)
  {
    if (doc['tags'][i] == 'novel')
      { total += 1; }
    else if (doc['tags'][i] == 'classics')
      {total+=10; }
    else
      {total+=20}
  }
return total
```

Please note that while passing the scripts in the query, the scripts need to be properly formatted as a string and special care needs to be taken to avoid the newline characters. For instance, the preceding logic when used in the query will look like the following:

```
{
  "query": {
    "function_score": {
      "query": {
        "match_all": {}
      },
      "min_score": 1,
      "script_score": {
        "script": {
          "inline": "def total = 0; for (int i = 0; i < doc['tags'].length;
i++)  { if (doc['tags'][i] == 'novel'){ total += 1;} else if
(doc['tags'][i] == 'classics') {total+=10;} else {total+=20}} return
total;",
          "lang": "painless"
        }
      }
    }
  }
}
```

The score of the preceding query will be equal to the total value calculated and returned based on the `tags` matched inside each document. Also, we have used a special parameter, `min_score`, which is used for discarding any document in the response which has a value below the threshold value specified for `min_score`.

Loops

Of course, we can also use loops when using Elasticsearch scripts and Painless as the language in which scripts are written. Let's start with the `while` loop that is going to be executed until the statement in the parenthesis is true as follows:

```
def i = 2;
def sum = 0;
while (i > 0)
    {
        sum = sum + i;
        i--;
    }
```

The preceding loop will be executed twice and ended. In the first iteration, the `i` variable will have the value of 2, which means that the `i > 0` statement is true. In the second iteration, the value of the `i` variable will be 1, which again makes the `i > 0` statement true. In the third iteration, the `i` variable will be 0, which will cause the `while` loop not to execute its body and exit.

We can also use the `for` loop, which you are probably familiar with if you've used programming languages before. For example, to iterate 10 times over the `for` loop body, we could use the following code:

```
def sum = 0;
for (def i = 0; i < 10; i++)
    {
        sum += i;
    }
```

Or we could iterate over a list of values as follows:

```
def sum = 0;
for ( i in [0, 1, 2, 3, 4, 5, 6, 7, 8, 9] )
    {
        sum += i;
    }
```

An example

Now, after seeing some of the basics of Painless, let's try to run an example script that will modify the score of our documents. We will implement the following algorithm for the score calculation:

- If the `year` field holds the value lower than `1800`, we will give the book a score of `1.0`.
- If the `year` field is between `1800` and `1900`, we will give the book a score of `2.0`.
- The rest of the books should have the score equal to the value of the `year` field minus `1000`.

The query that does the preceding example looks as follows:

```
curl -XGET "http://localhost:9200/library/_search?pretty" -d'
{
  "_source": [
    "_id",
    "_score",
    "title",
    "year"
  ],
  "query": {
    "function_score": {
      "query": {
        "match_all": {}
      },
      "script_score": {
        "script": {
          "inline": "def year = doc["year"].value; if (year < 1800) {return
1.0 } else if (year < 1900) { return 2.0 } else { return year - 1000 }",
          "lang": "painless"
        }
      }
    }
  }
}'
```

The result returned by Elasticsearch for the preceding query is as follows:

```
{
  "took": 10,
  "timed_out": false,
  "_shards": {
    "total": 5,
    "successful": 5,
```

```
            "failed": 0
        },
        "hits": {
            "total": 5,
            "max_score": 961,
            "hits": [
                {
                    "_index": "library",
                    "_type": "book",
                    "_id": "2",
                    "_score": 961,
                    "_source": {
                        "year": 1961,
                        "title": "Catch-22"
                    }
                },
                {
                    "_index": "library",
                    "_type": "book",
                    "_id": "3",
                    "_score": 936,
                    "_source": {
                        "year": 1936,
                        "title": "The Complete Sherlock Holmes"
                    }
                },
                {
                    "_index": "library",
                    "_type": "books",
                    "_id": "1",
                    "_score": 929,
                    "_source": {
                        "year": 1929,
                        "title": "All Quiet on the Western Front"
                    }
                },
                {
                    "_index": "library",
                    "_type": "book",
                    "_id": "5",
                    "_score": 904,
                    "_source": {
                        "year": 1904,
                        "title": "The Peasants"
                    }
                },
                {
                    "_index": "library",
```

```
            "_type": "book",
            "_id": "4",
            "_score": 1,
            "_source": {
               "year": 1774,
               "title": "The Sorrows of Young Werther"
            }
         }
      ]
   }
}
```

As you can see, our script worked as we wanted it to.

Sorting results based on scripts

Let's see an example to sort the documents based on the value of a string (keyword) field:

```
curl -XGET "http://localhost:9200/library/_search" -d'
{
  "query": {
    "match_all": {}
  },
  "sort": {
    "_script": {
      "type": "string",
      "order": "desc",
      "script": {
        "lang": "painless",
        "inline": "doc[\"tags\"].value"
      }
    }
  },"_source": "tags"
}'
```

 To perform sorting on numeric fields, you need to specify the type parameter of the script object as a number.

The preceding query sorts the results based on the `tags` in descending order. The response of the query looks as follows:

```
{
    "took": 2,
    "timed_out": false,
    "_shards": {
        "total": 5, "successful": 4, "failed": 1,
        "failures": [
            {
                "shard": 4,
                "index": "library",
                "node": "PONCbrNJR6uu_0dghowrVA",
                "reason": {
                    "type": "null_pointer_exception",
                    "reason": null
                }
            }
        ]
    },
    "hits": {
        "total": 4,
        "max_score": null,
        "hits": [
            {
                "_index": "library", "_type": "book","_id": "2","_score": null,
                "_source": {
                    "tags": ["novel"]
                },
                "sort": ["novel"]
            },
            {
                "_index": "library","_type": "books","_id": "1","_score": null,
                "_source": {
                    "tags": ["novel"]
                },
                "sort": ["novel"]
            },
            {
                "_index": "library", "_type": "book", "_id": "5","_score":
null,
                "_source": {
                    "tags": ["novel", "polish", "classics"]
                },
                "sort": ["classics"]
            },
            {
                "_index": "library", "_type": "book", "_id": "4", "_score":
```

```
null,
            "_source": {
                "tags": ["novel","classics"]
            },
            "sort": ["classics"]
        }
    ]
  }
}
```

In the response, you will find that there is a failure which says the reason for the failure is `null_pointer_exception`. The reason for this failure is because one of our documents contains an empty array of `tags`.

Sorting based on multiple fields

There are some cases where it is necessary to sort the documents based on the combined value of the two fields. For example, sorting based on the values of first name and last name. We can do this in the following way:

```
{
    "query": {
        "match_all": {}
    },
    "sort": {
        "_script": {
            "type": "string",
            "order": "asc",
            "script": {
                "lang": "painless",
                "inline": "doc[\"first.keyword\"].value + \" \" +
doc[\"last.keyword\"].value"
            }
        }
    }
}
```

 If you want to explore more about Painless, you can do so at, https://www.elastic.co/guide/en/elasticsearch/reference/master/m odules-scripting-painless.html.

Lucene expressions

Lucene expressions are a very powerful tool for easy scoring adjustments, without writing custom Java code. The thing that makes Lucene expressions very handy is that using them is very fast–their execution is as fast as native scripts since each expression is compiled to Java bytecode, to achieve native code-like performance, yet they are like dynamic scripts with some limitations. This section will show you what you can do with Lucene expressions.

The basics

Lucene provides functionality to compile a JavaScript expression to a Java bytecode. This is how Lucene expressions work and why they are as fast as native Elasticsearch scripts. Lucene expressions can be used in the following Elasticsearch functionalities:

- Scripts responsible for sorting
- Aggregations that work on numeric fields
- In the `function_score` query under the `script_score` query
- In queries using `script_fields`

In addition to this, you have to remember that:

- Lucene expressions can be only used on numeric fields
- Stored fields can't be accessed using Lucene expressions
- Missing values for a field will be given a value of zero
- You can use `_score` to access the document score and `doc['field_name'].value` to access the value of a single valued numeric field in the document
- No loops are possible, only single statements

An example

Knowing the preceding information, we can try using Lucene expressions to modify the score of our documents. Let's go back to our `library` index and try to increase the score of the given document by 10% of the year it was originally released. To do this, we could run the following query:

```
curl -XGET "http://localhost:9200/library/_search?pretty" -d'
{
```

```
      "_source": [
        "_id",
        "_score",
        "title"
      ],
      "query": {
        "function_score": {
          "query": {
            "match_all": {}
          },
          "script_score": {
            "script": {
              "inline": "_score + doc[\"year\"].value * percentage",
              "lang": "expression",
              "params": {
                "percentage": 0.1
              }
            }
          }
        }
      }
    }'
```

The query is very simple, but let's discuss its structure. First, we are using the `match_all`
query wrapped in the `function_score` query, because we want all documents to match
and we want to use the script for scoring. We are also setting the script language to
`expression` (by setting the `lang` property to `expression`) to tell Elasticsearch that our
script is a Lucene expressions script. Of course, we provide the script and we parameterize
it, just like we would with any other script. The results of the preceding query look as
follows:

```
{
  "took": 3,
  "timed_out": false,
  "_shards": {
    "total": 5,
    "successful": 5,
    "failed": 0
  },
  "hits": {
    "total": 5,
    "max_score": 197.1,
    "hits": [
      {
        "_index": "library",
        "_type": "book",
        "_id": "2",
```

```
        "_score": 197.1,
        "_source": {
            "title": "Catch-22"
        }
    },
    {
        "_index": "library",
        "_type": "book",
        "_id": "3",
        "_score": 194.6,
        "_source": {
            "title": "The Complete Sherlock Holmes"
        }
    },
    {
        "_index": "library",
        "_type": "books",
        "_id": "1",
        "_score": 193.9,
        "_source": {
            "title": "All Quiet on the Western Front"
        }
    },
    {
        "_index": "library",
        "_type": "book",
        "_id": "5",
        "_score": 191.4,
        "_source": {
            "title": "The Peasants"
        }
    },
    {
        "_index": "library",
        "_type": "book",
        "_id": "4",
        "_score": 178.4,
        "_source": {
            "title": "The Sorrows of Young Werther"
        }
    }
    ]
  }
}
```

As we can see, Elasticsearch did what it was asked to do.

Summary

We have covered lots of important topics in this chapter. We first started with how to work with different type of multimatch queries under different scenarios, then we started to learn about custom scoring in Elasticsearch using the function score, and also learned about query rescoring for recalculating the score on a defined number of documents returned by the query. We finally discussed one of the most important modules of Elasticsearch, that is scripting, and learned how to work with the new default scripting language: Painless.

In the next chapter, we will see different approaches to the data modeling in Elasticsearch and will learn how to handle relationships among documents using parent-child and nested data types, along with focusing on practical considerations.

4
Data Modeling and Analytics

In the previous chapter, we discussed searching across different fields with the help of different variants of multimatch queries, then we went through one of the most powerful features of **Elasticsearch**: function score queries, which give more power to the user for controlling document relevancy by using custom scores. Finally, we covered the scripting module of Elasticsearch in detail. In this chapter, we will see how we can deal with the general problems of structuring data in Elasticsearch and the different data modeling techniques. We will also discuss the aggregation module of Elasticsearch for data analytics purposes. By the end of this chapter, we will have covered the following topics:

- Data modeling techniques in Elasticsearch
- Managing relational data in Elasticsearch using parent-child and nested types
- Data analytics using aggregations
- The new aggregation category: Matrix aggregation

Data modeling techniques in Elasticsearch

Defining the structure of data is one of the key things to getting the search speed right, as well as making updates easier and non-expensive. If we compare it to the SQL world, most of the NoSQL solutions fail to provide relational mappings and queries. Elasticsearch, in spite of being a NoSQL document store, provides some ways to manage this relational data. However, there are always some trade-offs which we must be aware of before choosing a solution for defining the schema of the index. There are primarily four ways to define document structure in Elasticsearch:

- Flat structure (application side joins)
- Data denormalization

- Nested objects
- Parent-child relationships

Flat structures, In flat structures, we index the documents in simple key-value pairs or sometimes in the form of plain objects; these are the simplest and fastest ones. Storing data in this format allows for faster indexing as well as faster query execution. But it is hard to maintain the relation among different entities while indexing the documents in this way because Elasticsearch is not aware of how one entity relates to another. When following this approach, we often need to perform application side joins in the code to find the relation among documents. However, this is not appropriate for large scale data.

Data denormalization, This is the other technique, in which we duplicate the fields inside documents just for the sake of maintaining the relation of one entity to the other. This approach helps us in maintaining the flat structure and at the same time we can maintain the relation by keeping one or more fields in each document. This approach has the advantage of speed but can take up too much space because in some scenarios we have to deal with too many duplicates. We will see an example of this approach in an upcoming section.

Nested and parent-child, Relationships are out-of-the box solutions provided by Elasticsearch for managing relational data. In the upcoming section, we will see both of them in detail.

Managing relational data in Elasticsearch

While Elasticsearch is gaining more and more attention, it is no longer used only as a search engine. It is seen as a data analysis solution and sometimes as a primary data store. Having a single data store that enables fast and efficient full text searching often seems like a good idea. We can not only store documents, but also search them and analyze their contents, bringing meaning to the data. This is usually more than we could expect from traditional SQL databases. However, if you have any experience with SQL databases, when dealing with Elasticsearch, you soon realize the necessity of modeling relationships between documents. Unfortunately, it is not easy and many of the habits and good practices from relation databases won't work in the world of the inverted index that Elasticsearch uses. Let's have a look at all the available possibilities in Elasticsearch on how the relational data can be managed.

The object type

Elasticsearch tries to interfere as little as possible when modeling your data and turning it into an inverted index. Unlike the relational databases, Elasticsearch can index structured objects naturally. It means that if you have a JSON document, you can index it without problems and Elasticsearch adapts to it. Let's look at the following code:

```
{
    "title": "Title",
    "quantity": 100,
    "edition": {
        "isbn": "1234567890",
        "circulation": 50000
    }
}
```

As you can see, the preceding code has two simple properties in flattened format and a nested object inside it (the `edition` one) with additional properties. The mapping for our example is simple and looks as follows (it is also stored in the `relations.json` file provided with the book):

```
{
    "properties": {
        "title": {
            "type": "text"
        },
        "quantity": {
            "type": "integer"
        },
        "edition": {
            "type": "object",
            "properties": {
                "isbn": {
                    "type": "keyword"
                },
                "circulation": {
                    "type": "integer"
                }
            }
        }
    }
}
```

Unfortunately, everything will work only when the inner object is connected to its parent with a one-to-one relation. If you add the second object, for example, like the following, Elasticsearch will flatten it:

```
{
    "title": "Title",
    "quantity": 100,
    "edition": [
        {
            "isbn": "1234567890",
            "circulation": 50000
        },
        {
            "isbn": "9876543210",
            "circulation": 2000
        }
    ]
}
```

To Elasticsearch, the preceding code would look more or less like the following one (of course, the _source field will still look like the preceding document):

```
{
    "title": "Title",
    "quantity": 100,
    "edition": {
        "isbn": [ "1234567890", "9876543210" ],
        "circulation": [50000, 2000 ]
    }
}
```

This is not exactly what we want, and such representation will cause problems when you search for books containing editions with the given ISBN numbers and circulation. Simply, cross-matches will happen—Elasticsearch will return books containing editions with given ISBNs and any circulation.

We can test this by indexing our document by using the following command:

```
curl -XPOST 'localhost:9200/rel_natural/book/1' -d '{
"title": "Title",
"quantity": 100,
"edition": [
  {
    "isbn": "1234567890",
    "circulation": 50000
  },
  {
```

```
      "isbn": "9876543210",
      "circulation": 2000
    }
  ]
}'
```

Now, if we run a simple query to return documents with the `isbn` field equal to `1234567890` and the `circulation` field equal to `2000`, we shouldn't get any documents. Let's test that by running the following query:

```
curl -XGET "http://localhost:9200/rel_natural/_search?pretty" -d'
{
 "_source" : [ "_id", "title" ],
 "query" : {
  "bool" : {
   "must" : [
     {
      "term" : {
       "edition.isbn" : "1234567890"
      }
     },
     {
      "term" : {
       "edition.circulation" : 2000
      }
     }
    ]
   }
  }
}'
```

What we got as a result from Elasticsearch is as follows:

```
{
    "took": 3,
    "timed_out": false,
    "_shards": {
       "total": 5,
       "successful": 5,
       "failed": 0
    },
    "hits": {
       "total": 1,
       "max_score": 1.287682,
       "hits": [
           {
               "_index": "rel_natural",
               "_type": "book",
```

```
            "_id": "1",
            "_score": 1.287682,
            "_source": {
                "title": "Title"
            }
        }
    ]
}
}
```

This cross-finding can be avoided by rearranging the mapping and document so that the source document looks like the following:

```
{
    "title": "Title",
    "quantity": 100,
    "edition": {
        "isbn": ["1234567890", "9876543210"],
        "circulation_1234567890": 50000,
        "circulation_9876543210": 2000
    }
}
```

Now, you can use the preceding query, which uses the relationships between fields at the cost of greater complexity of query building. The important problem is that the mappings would have to contain information about all the possible values of the fields—this is not something that we would like to go for when having more than a couple of possible values. From the other side, this still does not allow us to create more complicated queries, such as all books with a circulation of more than 10,000 and ISBN numbers starting with 23. In such cases, a better solution would be to use nested objects.

To summarize, the object type is handy only for the simplest cases when problems with cross-field searching do not exist—for example, when you don't want to search inside nested objects, or you only need to search on one of the fields without matching on the others.

The nested documents

From a mapping point of view, the definition of a nested document differs only in the use of the nested type instead of object (which Elasticsearch will use by default when guessing types). For example, let's modify our previous example so that it uses nested documents:

```
{
    "properties": {
```

```
      "title": {
        "type": "text"
      },
      "quantity": {
        "type": "integer"
      },
      "edition": {
        "type": "nested",
        "properties": {
          "isbn": {
            "type": "keyword"
          },
          "circulation": {
            "type": "integer"
          }
        }
      }
    }
  }
}
```

When we are using the nested documents, Elasticsearch creates one document for the main object (we can call it a parent one, but that can bring confusion when talking about the parent-child functionality) and additional documents for inner objects. During normal queries, these additional documents are automatically filtered out and not searched or displayed. This is called a **block join** in Apache Lucene (you can read more about Apache Lucene block join queries in a blog post written by Lucene committer Mike McCandless, available at

`http://blog.mikemccandless.com/2012/01/searching-relational-content-with.html`).
For performance reasons, Lucene keeps these documents together with the main document, in the same segment block.

This is why the nested documents have to be indexed at the same time as the main document; because both sides of the relation are prepared before storing them in the index and both sides are indexed at the same time. Some people refer to nested objects as an index-time join. This strong connection between documents is not a big problem when the documents are small and the data is easily available from the main data store. But what if documents are quite big, one of the relationship parts changes a lot, and reindexing the second part is not an option? The next problem is what if a nested document belongs to more than one main document? These problems do not exist in the parent-child functionality.

If we get back to our example, and we create another index with our nested mapping and we index the same documents again, we need to change our query to use the nested query too, and you will see that no documents will be returned because there is no match for such a query in a single nested document. Our nested query will look as follows:

```
curl -XGET "http://localhost:9200/rel_nested/_search?pretty" -d'
{
  "_source": ["_id", "title"],
  "query": {
    "nested": {
      "path": "edition",
      "query": {
        "bool": {
          "must": [
            {
              "term": {
                "edition.isbn": "1234567890"
              }
            },
            {
              "term": {
                "edition.circulation": 2000
              }
            }
          ]
        }
      }
    }
  }
}'
```

Note that in the preceding query we are using a nested query with a path parameter as the name of the field which is nested.

A nested query always follows the following syntax:

```
{
  "query": {
    "nested": {
      "path": "path_to_nested_doc",
      "query": {}
    }
  }
}
```

Parent – child relationship

When talking about the parent-child functionality, we have to start with its main advantage—the true separation between documents—and each part of the relation can be indexed independently. The first cost of this advantage is more complicated queries and thus slower queries. Elasticsearch provides special query and filter types, which allow us to use this relation. This is why it is sometimes called a query-time join. The second disadvantage, which is more significant, is present in the bigger applications and multi-node Elasticsearch setups. Let's see how the parent-child relationship works in the Elasticsearch cluster that contains multiple nodes.

 Please note that unlike nested documents, the children documents can be queried without the context of the parent document, which is not possible with nested documents.

Parent-child relationship in the cluster

To better show the problem, let's create an index which holds the documents in a parent-child relationship. In our index, `rel_pch`, there are going to be two document types. The first is the `book` which hold the parents, and the second is `editions` which holds the child documents:

```
curl -XPUT "http://localhost:9200/rel_pch?pretty" -d'
{
  "settings": {
    "number_of_replicas": 0,
    "number_of_shards": 5
  },
  "mappings": {
    "book": {
      "properties": {
        "title": {
          "type": "text"
        }
      }
    },
    "edition": {
      "_parent": {
        "type": "book"
      },
      "properties": {
        "isbn": {
          "type": "keyword"
```

```
          },
          "circulation": {
            "type": "integer"
          }
        }
      }
    }
  }
}'
```

 From Elasticsearch version 2.0 onwards, the mapping for the parent type can be added at the same time as the mapping for the child type, but cannot be added before the child type.

In the preceding mapping, you can see mapping for the edition document type contains the `_parent` parameter, which specifies the name of the parent document type.

The last step is to import data to these indices. The script which we have provided with this book generates about 10,000 child type records; an example document looks as follows:

```
{"index": {"_index": "rel_pch", "_type": "edition", "_id": "1",
  "_parent": "1"}}
{"isbn" : "no1", "circulation" : 501}
```

The assumption is simple: we have 10,000 documents of child type (`edition`) but the key is the `_parent` field. In our example, it will always be set to 1, so all 10,000 editions belong to that one particular book. This example is rather extreme, but it lets us point out an important thing.

First let's look at the following screenshot which shows how documents are stored across different shards for our parent-child index:

index	shard	prirep	state	docs	store	ip	node
rel_pch	3	p	STARTED	10000	644.9kb	127.0.0.1	J2h6MUi
rel_pch	4	p	STARTED	0	130b	127.0.0.1	J2h6MUi
rel_pch	2	p	STARTED	0	130b	127.0.0.1	J2h6MUi
rel_pch	1	p	STARTED	0	130b	127.0.0.1	J2h6MUi
rel_pch	0	p	STARTED	0	130b	127.0.0.1	J2h6MUi

The output shown in the preceding screenshot is taken by running the following command using the `_cat` API of Elasticsearch:

```
curl -XGET localhost:9200/_cat/shards?v
```

The index, `rel_pch`, which contains only our children documents for now (we haven't indexed any parent document yet), has five shards, but four of them are empty and one contains all 10,000 documents! So something is not right—all the documents we indexed are located in one particular shard. This is because Elasticsearch will always put documents with the same parent in the same shard (in other words, the `routing` parameter value for children documents is always equal to the `parent` parameter value). Our example shows that in situations when some parent documents have substantially more children, we can end up with uneven shards, which may cause performance and storage issues—for example, some shards may be idling, while others will be constantly overloaded.

To prove this, let's index the parent of all these children with `_id` as 1:

```
curl -XPUT "http://localhost:9200/rel_pch/book/1" -d'
{
   "title": "Mastering Elasticsearch"
}'
```

And, when you run the command `curl -XGET localhost:9200/_cat/shards?v` again, you will find that the shard which contained 10,000 documents now has 10,001 documents, which is because both parent and child documents exist in the same shard.

Finding child documents with a parent ID query

Elasticsearch has two dedicated queries for parent-child relationship documents. The `has_parent` and `has_child`. But starting from version 5.0, there is a new `parent_id` query which helps to find all the child documents of a given parent. For example:

```
curl -XGET "http://localhost:9200/rel_pch/edition/_search" -d'
{
   "query": {
     "parent_id": {
       "type": "edition",
       "id": "1"
     }
   }
}'
```

This will find all child documents which have `parent_id` as 1. This `query` has two required parameters. The first is `type`, which is the document `type` of the child document and the second is `id`, which is the `_id` of the parent document.

A few words about alternatives

As we have seen, the handling of relations between documents can cause different problems for Elasticsearch. Of course, this is not only the case with Elasticsearch because full text search solutions are extremely valuable for searching and data analysis, and not for modeling relationships between data. If it is a big problem for your application, and the full text capability is not a core part of it, you may consider using an SQL database that allows full text searching to some extent. Of course, these solutions won't be as flexible and fast as Elasticsearch, but we have to pay the price if we need full relationship support. However, in most other cases, the change of data architecture and the elimination of relations by denormalization will be sufficient.

An example of data denormalization

Taking the same example of our dataset, books and the editions, we can keep them in a denormalized way as follows:

```
{ "isbn": "no1",  "circulation": 501,  "book_id": 1,  "book_title":
"Mastering Elasticsearch"}
{ "isbn": "no2",  "circulation": 502,  "book_id": 1,  "book_title":
"Mastering Elasticsearch"}
```

...and so on.

This approach allows for very fast indexing as well as faster searches but it has two disadvantages:

- More storage overhead, because of data duplication, (we are duplicating `book_id` and `book_title` in each document).
- If you want to search in the `book_title` field, you will get the number equal to the documents in which that title appears. So, if there are 10,000 editions of a single book and we search for the number of books with `Elasticsearch` in the `title`, we will get 10,000 hits instead of just 1 hit.

Data analytics using aggregations

Elasticsearch is a search engine at its core but what makes it more usable is its ability to perform complex data analytics in an easy and simple way. The volume of data is growing rapidly and companies want to perform analysis on data in real-time. Whether it is log, real-time streaming of data, or static data, Elasticsearch works wonderfully in creating a summarization of data through its aggregation capabilities.

In the previous editions of *Mastering Elasticsearch* we have covered a lot of ground on aggregations but we will revisit the important aggregations in this chapter again, and then cover the new aggregation type which is introduced in Elasticsearch version 5.x.

Instant aggregations in Elasticsearch 5.0

Aggregations were too costly at the beginning of Elasticsearch and used to be the biggest consumer of memory. In Elasticsearch 1.4, there was a new feature which was known as **shard query cache**, which was further renamed **shard request cache**. The benefit of this cache is that, when a search request is run against an index or against more than one index, each involved shard executes the search locally and returns its local results to the coordinating node, which combines these shard-level results into a global result set. The shard request cache module caches the local results on each shard which allows frequently used (and potentially heavy) search requests to return results almost instantly.

Until version 5.0, this feature was disabled by default because of two obvious problems: ordering in JSON is not deterministic so although two requests may be logically the same, when rendered to JSON strings they may not be equal. The shard cache key is based on the whole JSON string and the same queries could not benefit from the cache.

Most of the time, users' queries are time-based and particularly relative to the current time so subsequent requests will tend to have slightly different time ranges. So, enabling this caching would likely be a waste of memory most of the time since there would rarely be a cache hit.

But during all these years, Elasticsearch developers put a large amount of effort into avoiding these issues and making shard-level cache aggregations instant, providing as a default feature. This was possible because of the major query refactoring in search execution.

Before 5.0, search requests on each node used to receive the original search request in JSON format, and used to parse the query along with information available from the shard (like mappings) to actually create the Lucene query that was then executed as part of the query phase.

In 5.0, this overhead was removed completely. Query parsing now happens on only the coordinating node which receives the request and changes the search request into a serializable intermediate format (an intermediary query object which every node understands) independent of the mappings available. These intermediary query objects are then parsed on every node to convert into actual Lucene queries based on the mappings and information present in the shards. We will cover caching in detail in `Chapter 7`, *Low-Level Index Control*.

The shard request cache is enabled in Elasticsearch 5.0 by default for all requests with `"size":0`. This cache is most useful for analytics use cases where the user is mainly interested in getting a high overview of data using aggregation results without returning the documents in the response.

Revisiting aggregations

In Elasticsearch version 1.x, only two categories of aggregations were available: **metric** and **bucket.** Then, in version 2.0 there was a third category of aggregation included with the name **pipeline aggregation**. Let's see what these categories mean and which aggregations are supported under these three different categories.

Metric aggregations

Metric aggregations allow you to find out the statistical measurement of the data, which includes the following:

- **Computing basic stats**: The `min`, `max`, `sum`, and `value_count` aggregation
- **Computing basic stats in one go**: `stats` aggregation
- **Computing extended statistics**: The `extended_stats` aggregation, which apart from including basic stats, also provides stats such as `sum_of_squares`, variance and `std_deviation` on the values of a field

- **Computing distinct counts**: `cardinality` aggregation, which helps in finding the total unique value of a field.
- The syntax of all the metric aggregations is the same and looks as follows:

```
{
  "aggs": {
    "aggaregation_name": {
      "aggrigation_type": {
        "field": "name_of_the_field"
      }
    }
  },"size": 0
}
```

Where `aggaregation_name` is the name of the aggregation you want to assign, for example, `total_unique_records`, `aggrigation_type` is the type of aggregation to be used, such as `stats`, `min`, `max`, and cardinality and finally, the `field` parameter contains the name of the field on which you want to execute the aggregation.

 Please note that `search_type` count has been removed from Elasticsearch version 5.0 and you should always use the `size` parameter as 0, while executing the aggregation queries and not being concerned about the document to be returned in the response.

Bucket aggregations

- Bucket aggregations provide a simple way of grouping the documents that meet a certain criteria. They are used to categorize documents, for example:

  The category of books can fall into the buckets of horror or romantic.

  The category of an employee can be either male or female.

- Elasticsearch offers a wide variety of buckets to categorize documents in many ways such as by days, age range, popular terms, or location geo-points. However, all of them work on the same principle: document categorization based on some criteria.

- The most interesting part is that bucket aggregations can be nested within each other. This means that a bucket can contain other buckets within it. Since each of the buckets defines a set of documents, one can create another aggregation on that bucket, which will be executed in the context of its parent bucket. For example, a country-wise bucket can include a state-wise bucket, which can further include a city-wise bucket.
- Bucket aggregations are further categorized into two forms: single buckets that contain only a single bucket in the response, and multi-buckets that contain more than one bucket in the response. For example, a `terms aggregation` belongs to a multi-bucket category since it provides the top unique terms and their frequency in a field, whereas a `filter aggregation` just provides a single bucket in response containing the total doc count of the matching filter.
- We are not covering bucket aggregations in detail because they have existed for a very long time and are very easy to understand. If you still want to explore more on this family of aggregations, please visit the official documentation on Elastic at `https://www.elastic.co/guide/en/elasticsearch/reference/master/search-aggregations-bucket.html`.

Pipeline aggregations

Pipeline aggregations were one of the most awesome features introduced in Elasticsearch version 2.0. These aggregations are used to perform computation on the buckets produced as a result of the earlier aggregation. Pipeline aggregations are broadly classified into two types:

- **Parent**: A pipeline aggregation computes its output (bucket/aggregation) and this output gets added to the bucket/aggregation of the parent aggregation.
- **Sibling**: An existing aggregation becomes an input of a pipeline of aggregations and you get new aggregations at the same level as the sibling aggregation instead of it becoming part of existing buckets on the input aggregations.

Pipeline aggregations are further categorized as follows:

- Sibling pipeline aggregations:
    - Avg bucket aggregation
    - Max bucket aggregation
    - Min bucket aggregation
    - Sum bucket aggregation
    - Stats bucket aggregation
    - Extended stats bucket aggregation

- Percentile bucket aggregation
- Moving average aggregation
- Parent pipeline aggregations:
    - Derivative aggregation
    - Cumulative sum aggregation
    - Bucket script aggregation
    - Bucket selector aggregation
    - Serial differencing aggregation

Pipeline aggregations don't support sub-aggregations but they do support aggregation chaining using a `bucket_path` parameter, thus in a chain of pipeline aggregations the final output contains the output of each aggregation in the chain. The syntax of the `bucket_path` is as follows:

```
AGG_SEPARATOR       =   '>'
METRIC_SEPARATOR    =   '.'
AGG_NAME            =   <the name of the aggregation>
METRIC              =   <the name of the metric (in case of multi-value
metrics aggregation)>
PATH                =   <AGG_NAME> [ <AGG_SEPARATOR>, <AGG_NAME> ]* [
<METRIC_SEPARATOR>, <METRIC> ]
```

For example, `"buckets_path": "AGG_NAME>METRIC"` tells us that `bucket_path` refers to an aggregation and the metric in that aggregation.

We will explain some of these aggregations with the help of examples. But for that we need to index some data inside the `books` index to run the example aggregation queries. Our data looks like the following and you can get it with the book in `book_transactions.txt` for testing on your own:

```
{ "index": {}}
{ "price" : 1000, "category" : "databases", "sold" : "2016-10-26" }
{ "index": {}}
{ "price" : 2000, "category" : "databases", "sold" : "2016-11-15" }
{ "index": {}}
{ "price" : 3000, "category" : "networking", "sold" : "2016-05-28" }
{ "index": {}}
{ "price" : 1500, "category" : "programming", "sold" : "2016-07-22" }
{ "index": {}}
{ "price" : 1200, "category" : "networking", "sold" : "2016-08-11" }
{ "index": {}}
{ "price" : 2000, "category" : "databases", "sold" : "2016-11-12" }
{ "index": {}}
{ "price" : 800, "category" : "databases", "sold" : "2016-01-23" }
```

```
{ "index": {}}
{ "price" : 2500, "category" : "programming", "sold" : "2016-02-11" }
{ "index": {}}
{ "price" : 20000, "category" : "databases", "sold" : "2016-12-15" }
{ "index": {}}
{ "price" : 3000, "category" : "networking", "sold" : "2016-03-28" }
{ "index": {}}
{ "price" : 500, "category" : "programming", "sold" : "2016-07-12" }
{ "index": {}}
{ "price" : 700, "category" : "networking", "sold" : "2016-09-14" }
{ "index": {}}
{ "price" : 2000, "category" : "databases", "sold" : "2016-05-27" }
{ "index": {}}
{ "price" : 800, "category" : "databases", "sold" : "2016-01-04" }
{ "index": {}}
{ "price" : 2500, "category" : "programming", "sold" : "2016-01-18" }
```

To index this data, we just have to run the following command:

```
curl -XPOST localhost:9200/books/transactions/_bulk --data-binary
@book_transactions.txt
```

As you can see, this data is about transactions under certain categories which are sold in different months of 2016.

Now, let's see some examples of aggregation pipelining.

Calculating average monthly sales using avg_bucket aggregation

Following is an example of using aggregation pipeline in which we are calculating average monthly sales from overall transactions:

```
curl -XGET "http://localhost:9200/books/transactions/_search?pretty" -d'
{
    "aggs":{
        "sales_per_month":{
            "date_histogram":{
                "field":"sold",
                "interval":"month",
                "format":"yyyy-MM-dd"
            },
            "aggs":{
                "monthly_sum":{
                    "sum":{
                        "field":"price"
                    }
                }
```

```
            }
        },
        "avg_monthly_sales":{
            "avg_bucket":{
                "buckets_path":"sales_per_month>monthly_sum"
            }
        }
    },"size": 0
}'
```

The output of the preceding request looks as follows:

```
{
    "took": 12,
    "timed_out": false,
    "_shards": {"total": 5, "successful": 5, "failed": 0},
    "hits": { "total": 15, "max_score": 0, "hits": [] },
    "aggregations": {
        "sales_per_month": {
            "buckets": [
                {
                    "key_as_string": "2016-01-01",
                    "key": 1451606400000,
                    "doc_count": 3,
                    "monthly_sum": {
                        "value": 185000
                    }
                },
                {
                    "key_as_string": "2016-02-01",
                    "key": 1454284800000,
                    "doc_count": 1,
                    "monthly_sum": {
                        "value": 25000
                    }
                },
                {
                    "key_as_string": "2016-03-01",
                    "key": 1456790400000,
                    "doc_count": 1,
                    "monthly_sum": {
                        "value": 30000
                    }
                },
                {
                    "key_as_string": "2016-04-01",
                    "key": 1459468800000,
                    "doc_count": 0,
```

```
            "monthly_sum": {
                "value": 0
            }
        },
        {
            "key_as_string": "2016-05-01",
            "key": 1462060800000,
            "doc_count": 2,
            "monthly_sum": {
                "value": 50000
            }
        },
        {
            "key_as_string": "2016-06-01",
            "key": 1464739200000,
            "doc_count": 0,
            "monthly_sum": {
                "value": 0
            }
        },
        {
            "key_as_string": "2016-07-01",
            "key": 1467331200000,
            "doc_count": 2,
            "monthly_sum": {
                "value": 20000
            }
        },
        {
            "key_as_string": "2016-08-01",
            "key": 1470009600000,
            "doc_count": 1,
            "monthly_sum": {
                "value": 12000
            }
        },
        {
            "key_as_string": "2016-09-01",
            "key": 1472688000000,
            "doc_count": 1,
            "monthly_sum": {
                "value": 7000
            }
        },
        {
            "key_as_string": "2016-10-01",
            "key": 1475280000000,
            "doc_count": 1,
```

```
                 "monthly_sum": {
                     "value": 10000
                 }
             },
             {
                 "key_as_string": "2016-11-01",
                 "key": 1477958400000,
                 "doc_count": 2,
                 "monthly_sum": {
                     "value": 40000
                 }
             },
             {
                 "key_as_string": "2016-12-01",
                 "key": 1480550400000,
                 "doc_count": 1,
                 "monthly_sum": {
                     "value": 20000
                 }
             }
         ]
     },
     "avg_monthly_sales": {
         "value": 39900
     }
   }
 }
```

In the output, you can see that it contains the bucket `sales_per_month` generated by `date_histogram` bucket aggregation and each nested bucket contains the total amount of sales in each month which has been calculated using the sum metric aggregation.

The sibling pipeline aggregation, `avg_monthly_sale` generates the aggregation value of average total monthly sales. The key point of this calculation is the usage of the `buckets_path` syntax under `avg_bucket` aggregation:

```
"avg_monthly_sales":{
       "avg_bucket":{
           "buckets_path":"sales_per_month>monthly_sum"
       }
   }
```

Similarly, you can calculate `min`, `max`, and `sum` of monthly sales, using the following syntaxes:

```
{
    "min_bucket":{
            "buckets_path":"sales_per_month>monthly_sum"
        }
}
{
    "max_bucket":{
            "buckets_path":"sales_per_month>monthly_sum"
        }
}
{
    "sum_bucket":{
            "buckets_path":"sales_per_month>monthly_sum"
        }
}
{
    "extended_stats_bucket":{
            "buckets_path":"sales_per_month>monthly_sum"
        }
}
```

Calculating the derivative for the sum of the monthly sale

Calculating the derivative for the sum of the monthly sale can be done using the derivative aggregation which belongs to a parent pipeline aggregation category:

```
curl -XGET "http://localhost:9200/books/transactions/_search?pretty" -d'
    {
        "aggs": {
            "sales_per_month": {
                "date_histogram": {
                    "field": "sold",
                    "interval": "month",
                    "format": "yyyy-MM-dd"
                },
                "aggs": {
                    "monthly_sum": {
                        "sum": {
                            "field": "price"
                        }
                    },
                    "sales_deriv": {
                        "derivative": {
                            "buckets_path": "monthly_sum"
```

```
                        }
                    }
                }
            }
        },"size": 0
    }'
```

The output of the preceding request looks as follows:

```
{
    "took": 20,
    "timed_out": false,
    "_shards": {
        "total": 5,
        "successful": 5,
        "failed": 0
    },
    "hits": {
        "total": 15,
        "max_score": 0,
        "hits": []
    },
    "aggregations": {
        "sales_per_month": {
            "buckets": [
                {
                    "key_as_string": "2016-01-01",
                    "key": 1451606400000,
                    "doc_count": 3,
                    "monthly_sum": {
                        "value": 185000
                    }
                },
                {
                    "key_as_string": "2016-02-01",
                    "key": 1454284800000,
                    "doc_count": 1,
                    "monthly_sum": {
                        "value": 25000
                    },
                    "sales_deriv": {
                        "value": -160000
                    }
                },
                {
                    "key_as_string": "2016-03-01",
                    "key": 1456790400000,
                    "doc_count": 1,
```

```
                        "monthly_sum": {
                            "value": 30000
                        },
                        "sales_deriv": {
                            "value": 5000
                        }
                    }
                    .
                    .
                    .
                    12 more results...
                ]
            }
        }
    }
}
```

In the response, you can see that for the bucket there is no derivative calculated since there was nothing available for the comparison, whereas in the second month the derivative is calculated by taking the values of the first and second month together.

The new aggregation category – Matrix aggregation

Matrix aggregation is included in Elasticsearch aggregation categories with the release of Elasticsearch 5.0. It provides a way to operate on multiple fields and produce a matrix of results based on the values extracted from those fields.

At the time of writing this book, there is only one aggregation type supported in this category: Matrix stats.

Understanding matrix stats

This aggregation computes the numeric stats on a set of given fields. To understand it more, lets create an index named person which contains data on the height of 10 people and also contains different self-esteem values (on a scale of 1 to 10) for each person based on their height. (This example is just for illustration purposes and it is not likely that one's self-esteem lowers because of height):

```
curl -XPUT "http://localhost:9200/persons/person/_mapping" -d'
{"properties": {"self_esteem":{"type": "float"}}}'
```

Please note that we are defining the data type for the `self_esteem` field in advance, otherwise you will get an error of type conversion between `float` and `long` while indexing the data.

The following is our sample data to find the relationships between `height` and `self_esteem`:

```
{"index": {"_index": "persons", "_type": "person", "_id": "1"}}
{"height":165,"self_esteem":7.2}
{"index": {"_index": "persons", "_type": "person", "_id": "2"}}
{"height":175,"self_esteem":8}
{"index": {"_index": "persons", "_type": "person", "_id": "3"}}
{"height":154,"self_esteem":5.3}
{"index": {"_index": "persons", "_type": "person", "_id": "4"}}
{"height":165,"self_esteem":7.2}
{"index": {"_index": "persons", "_type": "person", "_id": "5"}}
{"height":160,"self_esteem":6}
{"index": {"_index": "persons", "_type": "person", "_id": "6"}}
{"height":145,"self_esteem":4.5}
{"index": {"_index": "persons", "_type": "person", "_id": "7"}}
{"height":150,"self_esteem":5}
{"index": {"_index": "persons", "_type": "person", "_id": "8"}}
{"height":162,"self_esteem":6.1}
{"index": {"_index": "persons", "_type": "person", "_id": "9"}}
{"height":156,"self_esteem":5.8}
{"index": {"_index": "persons", "_type": "person", "_id": "10"}}
{"height":160,"self_esteem":6}
```

Now let's index this data using the bulk API:

```
curl -XPOST localhost:9200/_bulk --data-binary @persons.txt
```

Now, to calculate the statistical measures which describe the degree of relationships between two variables, `height` and `self_esteem`, we can use the `matrix_stats` aggregation as follows:

```
curl -XGET "http://localhost:9200/persons/_search?pretty" -d'
{
  "aggs": {
    "matrixstats": {
      "matrix_stats": {
        "fields": [
          "height",
          "self_esteem"
        ]
      }
    }
  },"size": 0
}'
```

The output of the preceding aggregation query looks like the following:

```
{
  "took": 3,
  "timed_out": false,
  "_shards": {
    "total": 5,
    "successful": 5,
    "failed": 0
  },
  "hits": {
    "total": 10,
    "max_score": 0,
    "hits": []
  },
  "aggregations": {
    "matrixstats": {
      "fields": [
        {
          "name": "self_esteem",
          "count": 10,
          "mean": 6.1099999904632565,
          "variance": 1.1721109714508229,
          "skewness": 0.2987179705001951,
          "kurtosis": 2.180068994686735,
          "covariance": {
            "self_esteem": 1.1721109714508229,
            "height": 8.953332879808213
          },
          "correlation": {
```

```
            "self_esteem": 1,
            "height": 0.9734162963071297
        }
    },
    {
        "name": "height",
        "count": 10,
        "mean": 159.2,
        "variance": 72.17777777777775,
        "skewness": 0.10355198975247665,
        "kurtosis": 2.6850634873449977,
        "covariance": {
            "self_esteem": 8.953332879808213,
            "height": 72.17777777777775
        },
        "correlation": {
            "self_esteem": 0.9734162963071297,
            "height": 1
        }
    }
    ]
    }
  }
}
```

Where ,these are the parameters:

- count: Number of per field samples included in the calculation.
- mean: The average value for each field.
- variance: Per field measurement for how spread out the samples are from the mean.
- skewness: Per field measurement quantifying the asymmetric distribution around the mean.
- kurtosis: Per field measurement quantifying the shape of the distribution.
- covariance: A matrix that quantitatively describes how changes in one field are associated with another.
- correlation: The covariance matrix scaled to a range of -1 to 1, inclusive. Describes the relationship between field distributions.

Dealing with missing values

If a value is missing in some of the documents for the fields you are calculating matrix stats for, by default they are ignored. But if you want then you can provide a default value for all the missing values using the `missing` parameter. For example:

```
{
   "aggs": {
     "matrixstats": {
       "matrix_stats": {
         "fields": [
            "height",
            "self_esteem"
         ],
     "missing": {"self_esteem" : 6}
        }
      }
   },"size": 0
}
```

Summary

In this chapter, we started with the general problems of structuring data in Elasticsearch and the different approaches to data modeling. We have shown you how relational data can be managed using nested and parent-child data types. We further discussed the aggregation module of Elasticsearch for data analytics purposes, including the concept of instant aggregation introduced in Elasticsearch 5.0, along with all four categories of aggregations, that is, metric, bucket, pipeline, and the latest matrix aggregation available in Elasticsearch.

Our next chapter will focus on topics for improving the user search experience using suggesters, which allows you to correct user query spelling mistakes and build efficient autocomplete mechanisms. In addition to that, you'll see how to improve query relevance by using different queries and the Elasticsearch functionality. Finally, the chapter will cover how to use synonyms with Elasticsearch.

5
Improving the User Search Experience

In the previous chapter, we extended our knowledge with different approaches to data modeling, and discussed how relational data can be managed using nested and parent-child data types. We also talked about the aggregation module of Elasticsearch for data analytics purposes, including the concept of instant aggregations introduced in Elasticsearch 5.0, along with all four categories of aggregations, for instance, metric, bucket, pipeline, and the latest matrix aggregation available in Elasticsearch. In this chapter, we will focus on the topics for improving the user search experience using suggesters, which allow you to correct user query spelling mistakes and build efficient autocomplete mechanisms. In addition to that, we'll also cover how to implement synonym search in the applications. By the end of this chapter, we will have covered the following topics:

- Using the Elasticsearch suggesters to correct user spelling mistakes
- Using the `term` suggester to suggest single words
- Using the `phrase` suggester to suggest whole phrases
- Configuring suggest capabilities to match your needs
- Using the `completion` suggester for the autocomplete functionality
- Implementing custom autocomplete for partial matching
- Working with synonyms

Correcting user spelling mistakes

One of the simplest ways to improve the user search experience is to correct spelling mistakes either automatically, or by just showing the correct query phrase and allowing the user to use it. For example, this is what **Google** shows us when we type in `elasticsaerch` instead of `Elasticsearch`:

Starting from version 0.90.0 Beta1, Elasticsearch allows us to use the suggest API to correct user spelling mistakes. With the newer versions of Elasticsearch, the API was changed, bringing new features and becoming more and more powerful. In this section, we will try to bring you a comprehensive guide on how to use the suggest API provided by Elasticsearch, both in simple use cases and in ones that require more configuration.

Testing data

For the purposes of this section, we need a bit more data than a few documents. In order to get the data, we have decided to index some news documents from *Wikipedia dump*.

Let's follow the given steps for downloading and importing data into the index:

1. Download the dump file:

```
wget
https://github.com/bharvidixit/mastering-elasticsearch-5.0/raw/master/chapt
er-5/enwikinews-20160926-cirrussearch-content.json.gz
```

2. Take the downloaded file path into a variable; in addition, export the index name into a variable as well:

```
export dump=enwikinews-20160926-cirrussearch-content.json.gz
export index=wikinews
```

3. Create a directory with name `chunks` and split the downloaded compressed JSON file into multiple parts inside the directory:

```
mkdir chunks
cd chunks
zcat ../$dump | split -a 10 -l 500 - $index
```

4. Now index the data into Elasticsearch running on `localhost` with the following code:

```
exportes=localhost:9200
for file in *; do
echo -n "${file}:   "
took=$(curl -s -XPOST $es/$index/_bulk?pretty --data-binary @$file
 | grep took | cut -d':' -f 2 | cut -d',' -f 1)
printf '%7s\n' $took
[ "x$took" = "x" ] || rm $file
done
```

Once the data is indexed with the name `wikinews`, the index will have 21067 documents. You can find the script `index_wikinews.sh` provided with this book download and load the data into index.

Getting into technical details

Introduced in version 0.90.3, the suggest API is not the simplest one available in Elasticsearch. In order to get the desired suggest, we need to add a new suggest section to the query. In addition to this, we have multiple suggest implementations that allow us to correct user spelling mistakes, create the autocomplete functionality, and so on. All this gives us a powerful and flexible mechanism that we can use in order to make our search better.

Of course, the suggest functionality works on our data, so if we have a small set of documents in the index, the proper suggestion may not be found. When dealing with a smaller data set, Elasticsearch has fewer words in the index and, because of that, it has fewer candidates for suggestions. On the other hand, the more data, the bigger the possibility that we will have data that has some mistakes; however, we can configure Elasticsearch internals to handle such situations.

Please note that the layout of this chapter is a bit different. We start by showing you a simple example on how to query for suggestions and how to interpret user suggest query responses without getting into all the configuration options too much. We do this because we don't want to overwhelm you with technical details, but we want to show you what you can achieve. The nifty configuration parameters come later.

Suggesters

Before we continue with querying and analyzing the responses, we would like to write a few words about the available suggester types—the functionality responsible for finding suggestions when using the Elasticsearch suggest API. Elasticsearch allows us to use four suggesters currently: the `term` one, the `phrase` one, the `completion` one, and the `context` one. The first two allow us to correct spelling mistakes, while the third and fourth ones allow us to develop a very fast autocomplete functionality. However, for now, let's not focus on any particular suggester type, but let's look at the query possibilities and the responses returned by Elasticsearch. We will try to show you the general principles, and then we will get into more detail about each of the available suggesters.

Using a suggester under the _search endpoint

Before Elasticsearch 5.0, there was a possibility to get suggestions for a given text by using a dedicated _suggest REST endpoint. But in Elasticsearch 5.0, this dedicated _suggest endpoint has been deprecated in favor of using the suggest API. In this release, the suggest-only search requests have been optimized for performance reasons and we can execute the suggestions _search endpoint. Similar to a `query` object, we can use a `suggest` object and what we need to provide inside the `suggest` object is the text to analyze and the type of used suggester (term or phrase). So, if we would like to get suggestions for the words `chrimes in wordl` (note that we've misspelled the word on purpose), we would run the following query:

 The dedicated endpoint _suggest has been deprecated in Elasticsearch version 5.0 and might be removed in future releases, so be advised that you should use the suggestion request under the _search endpoint. All the examples covered in this chapter use the same _search endpoint for the suggest request.

```
curl -XPOST "http://localhost:9200/wikinews/_search?pretty" -d'
{
```

```
"suggest": {
"first_suggestion": {
"text": "chrimes in wordl",
"term": {
"field": "title"
}
}
}
}'
```

As you can see, the suggestion request is wrapped inside the `suggest` object and is sent to Elasticsearch in its own object with the name we chose (in the preceding case, it is `first_suggestion`). Next, we specify the text for which we want the suggestion to be returned using the `text` parameter. Finally, we add the `suggester` object, which is either `term` or `phrase`. The `suggester` object contains its configuration, which for the `term` suggester used in the preceding command, is the field we want to use for suggestions (the `field` property).

We can also send more than one suggestion at a time by adding multiple suggestion names. For example, if in addition to the preceding suggestion, we also include a suggestion for the word `arest`, we would use the following command:

```
curl -XPOST "http://localhost:9200/wikinews/_search?pretty" -d'
{
    "suggest": {
        "first_suggestion": {
            "text": "chrimes in wordl",
            "term": {
                "field": "title"
            }
        },
        "second_suggestion": {
            "text": "arest",
            "term": {
                "field": "text"
            }
        }
    }
}'
```

Understanding the suggester response

Let's now look at the example response for the suggestion query we have executed. Although the response will differ for each suggester type, let's look at the response returned by Elasticsearch for the first command we've sent in the preceding code that used the `term` suggester:

```
{
"took" : 5,
"timed_out" : false,
"_shards" : {
"total" : 5,
"successful" : 5,
"failed" : 0
},
"hits" : {
"total" : 0,
"max_score" : 0.0,
"hits" : [ ]
},
"suggest" : {
"first_suggestion" : [
{
"text" : "chrimes",
"offset" : 0,
"length" : 7,
"options" : [
{
"text" : "crimes",
"score" : 0.8333333,
"freq" : 36
},
{
"text" : "choices",
"score" : 0.71428573,
"freq" : 2
},
{
"text" : "chrome",
"score" : 0.6666666,
"freq" : 2
},
{
"text" : "chimps",
"score" : 0.6666666,
"freq" : 1
},
```

```
{
"text" : "crimea",
"score" : 0.6666666,
"freq" : 1
}
]
},
{
"text" : "in",
"offset" : 8,
"length" : 2,
"options" : [ ]
},
{
"text" : "wordl",
"offset" : 11,
"length" : 5,
"options" : [
{
"text" : "world",
"score" : 0.8,
"freq" : 436
},
{
"text" : "words",
"score" : 0.8,
"freq" : 6
},
{
"text" : "word",
"score" : 0.75,
"freq" : 9
},
{
"text" : "worth",
"score" : 0.6,
"freq" : 21
},
{
"text" : "worst",
"score" : 0.6,
"freq" : 16
}
]
}
]
}
}
```

As you can see in the preceding response, the `term` suggester returns a list of possible suggestions for each term that was present in the `text` parameter of our `first_suggestion` section. For each term, the `term` suggester will return an array of possible suggestions with additional information. Looking at the data returned for the `word1` term, we can see the original word (the `text` parameter), its offset in the original `text` parameter (the `offset` parameter), and its length (the `length` parameter).

The `options` array contains suggestions for the given word and will be empty if Elasticsearch doesn't find any suggestions. Each entry in this array is a suggestion and is characterized by the following properties:

- `text`: This is the text of the suggestion.
- `score`: This is the suggestion score; the higher the score, the better the suggestion will be.
- `freq`: This is the frequency of the suggestion. The frequency represents how many times the word appears in documents in the index we are running the suggestion query against. The higher the frequency, the more documents will have the suggested word in its fields and the higher the chance that the suggestion is the one we are looking for.

 Please remember that the `phrase` suggester response will differ from the one returned by the `terms` suggester, and we will discuss the response of the `phrase` suggester later in this section.

Multiple suggestion types for the same suggestion text

There is one more possibility-if we have the same suggestion text, but we want multiple suggestion types, we can embed our suggestions in the `suggest` object and place the `text` property as the `suggest` object option. For example, if we would like to get suggestions for the `arest` text for the `text` field and for the `title` field, we could run the following command:

```
curl -XGET 'localhost:9200/wikinews/_search?pretty' -d '{
"query" : {
"match_all" : {}
},
"suggest" : {
"text" : "arest",
"first_suggestion" : {
"term" : {
"field" : "text"
```

```
    }
  },
  "second_suggestion" : {
  "term" : {
  "field" : "title"
  }
  }
  }
  }'
```

We now know how to make a query with suggestions returned. Let's now look at each of the available suggester types in more detail.

The term suggester

The `term` suggester works on the basis of the edit distance, which means that the suggestion with the fewest characters that need to be changed or removed to make the suggestion look like the original word is the best one. For example, let's take the words `worl` and `work`. In order to change the `worl` term to `work`, we need to change the `l` letter to `k`, so it means a distance of one. Of course, the text provided to the suggester is analyzed and then terms are chosen to be suggested. Let's now look at how we can configure the Elasticsearch `term` suggester.

Configuring the Elasticsearch term suggester

The Elasticsearch `term` suggester supports multiple configuration properties that allow us to tune its behavior to match our needs and to work with our data. Of course, we've already seen how it works in *Using a suggester under the _search endpoint* section and what it can give us, so we will concentrate on configuration now.

Common term suggester options

The common `term` suggester options can be used for all the suggester implementations that are based on the `term` suggester. Currently, these are the `phrase` suggesters and, of course, the base `term` suggester. The available options are:

- `text`: This is the text we want to get the suggestions for. This parameter is required in order for the suggester to work.
- `field`: This is another required parameter. The `field` parameter allows us to set which field the suggestions should be generated for. For example, if we only want to consider the `title` field `terms` in suggestions, we should set this parameter value to the `title`.
- `analyzer`: This is the name of the analyzer that should be used to analyze the text provided in the `text` parameter. If not set, Elasticsearch will use the analyzer used for the field provided by the `field` parameter.
- `size`: This is the maximum number of suggestions that are allowed to be returned by each term provided in the `text` parameter. It defaults to `5`.
- `sort`: This allows us to specify how suggestions are sorted in the result returned by Elasticsearch. By default, this is set to a score, which tells Elasticsearch that the suggestions should be sorted by the suggestion score first, suggestion document frequency next, and finally, by the term. The second possible value is the frequency, which means that the results are first sorted by the document frequency, then by score, and finally, by the term.
- `suggest_mode`: This is another suggestion parameter that allows us to control which suggestions will be included in the Elasticsearch response. Currently, there are three values that can be passed to this parameter: `missing`, `popular`, and `always`. The default `missing` value will tell Elasticsearch to generate suggestions to only those words that are provided in the `text` parameter that don't exist in the index. If this property is set to `popular`, then the `term` suggester will only suggest terms that are more popular (exist in more documents) than the original term for which the suggestion is generated. The last value, which is `always`, will result in a suggestion generated for each of the words in the `text` parameter.

Additional term suggester options

In addition to the common `term` suggester options, Elasticsearch allows us to use additional ones that will only make sense for the `term` suggester itself. These options are as follows:

- `lowercase_terms`: When set to `true`, this will tell Elasticsearch to make all terms that are produced from the `text` field after analysis lowercase.

- `max_edits`: This defaults to 2 and specifies the maximum edit distance that the suggestion can have for it to be returned as a term suggestion. Elasticsearch allows us to set this value to only 1 or 2. Setting this value to 1 can result in fewer suggestions or no suggestions at all for words with many spelling mistakes. In general, if you see many suggestions that are not correct (because of errors) you can try setting `max_edits` to 1.

- `prefix_length`: Because spelling mistakes usually don't appear at the beginning of the word, Elasticsearch allows us to set how much of the suggestion's initial characters must match with the initial characters of the original term. By default, this property is set to 1. If we are struggling with the suggester performance increasing, this value will improve the overall performance, because less suggestions will be needed to be processed by Elasticsearch.

- `min_word_length`: This defaults to 4 and specifies the minimum number of characters a suggestion must have in order to be returned on the suggestions list.

- `shard_size`: This defaults to the value specified by the `size` parameter and allows us to set the maximum number of suggestions that should be read from each shard. Setting this property to values higher than the `size` parameter can result in more accurate document frequency (this is because of the fact that terms are held in different shards for our indices unless we have a single shard index created) being calculated but will also result in degradation of the spellchecker's performance.

- `max_inspections`: This defaults to 5 and specifies how many candidates Elasticsearch will look at in order to find the words that can be used as suggestions. Elasticsearch will inspect a maximum of `shard_size` multiplied by the `max_inspections` candidates for suggestions. Setting this property to values higher than the default 5 may improve the suggester accuracy but can also decrease the performance.

- `min_doc_freq`: This defaults to `0f`, which means not enabled. It allows us to limit the returned suggestions to only those that appear in the number of documents higher than the value of this parameter (this is a per-shard value and not a globally counted one). For example, setting this parameter to `2` will result in suggestions that appear in at least two documents in a given shard. Setting this property to values higher than `0` can improve the quality of returned suggestions; however, it can also result in some suggestions not being returned because it has a low shard document frequency. This property can help us with removing suggestions that come from a low number of documents and may be erroneous. This parameter can be specified as a percentage; if we want to do this, its value must be less than `1`. For example, `0.01` means 1 percent, which again means that the minimum frequency of the given suggestion needs to be higher than `1` percent of the total term frequency (of course, per shard).

- `max_term_freq`: This defaults to `0.01f` and specifies the maximum threshold in number of documents a `suggest` text token can exist in order to be included. Similar to the `min_doc_freq` parameter, it can be either provided as an absolute number (such as `4` or `100`), or it can be a percentage value if it is beyond `1` (for example, `0.01` means 1 percent). Please remember that this is also a per-shard frequency. The higher the value of this property, the better the overall performance of the spellchecker will be. In general, this property is very useful when we want to exclude terms that appear in many documents from spellchecking, because they are usually correct terms.

- `string_distance`: This specifies which algorithm should be used to compare how similar terms are when comparing them to each other. This is an expert setting. These options are available: `internal`, which is the default comparison algorithm based on an optimized implementation of the Damerau-Levenshtein similarity algorithm; `damerau_levenshtein`, which is the implementation of the Damerau-Levenshtein string distance algorithm (`http://en.wikipedia.org/wiki/Damerau%E2%80%93Levenshtein_distance`); `levenstein`, which is the implementation of the Levenshtein distance (`http://en.wikipedia.org/wiki/Levenshtein_distance`), `jarowinkler`, which is an implementation of the Jaro-Winkler distance algorithm (`http://en.wikipedia.org/wiki/Jaro%E2%80%93Winkler_distance`), and finally, `ngram`, which is an n-gram based distance algorithm.

Because of the fact that we've used the `term` suggester during the initial examples, we decided to skip showing you how to query `term` suggesters and how the response looks. If you want to see how to query this suggester and what the response looks like, please refer to the beginning of the *Suggesters* section in this chapter.

The phrase suggester

The `term` suggester provides a great way to correct user spelling mistakes on a per-term basis. However, if we would like to get back phrases, it is not possible to do that when using this suggester. This is why the `phrase` suggester was introduced. It is built on top of the `term` suggester and adds additional phrase calculation logic to it so that whole phrases can be returned instead of individual terms. It uses N-gram based language models to calculate how good the suggestion is and will probably be a better choice to suggest whole phrases instead of the `term` suggester. The n-gram approach divides terms in the index into grams-word fragments built of one or more letters. For example, if we would like to divide the word `mastering` into bi-grams (a two letter n-gram), it would look like this: `ma as stteerri in ng`.

 If you want to read more about n-gram language models, refer to the Wikipedia article available at the following link:
`http://en.wikipedia.org/wiki/Language_model#N-gram_models`

Usage example

Before we continue with all the possibilities, we have to configure the `phrase` suggester; let's start with showing you an example of how to use it. This time, we will run a simple query to the _search endpoint with only the `suggest` section in it. We do this by running the following command:

```
curl -XGET "localhost:9200/wikinews/_search?pretty" -d'
{
"query": {
"match_all": {}
},
"suggest": {
"text": "Unitd States",
"our_suggestion": {
"phrase": {
"field": "text"
}
}
}
}'
```

As you can see in the preceding command, it is almost the same as we sent when using the `term` suggester, but instead of specifying the `term` suggester type, we've specified the `phrase` type. The response to the preceding command will be as follows:

```
{
"took" : 58,
"timed_out" : false,
"_shards" : {
"total" : 5,
"successful" : 5,
"failed" : 0
},
"hits" : {
"total" : 21067,
"max_score" : 1.0,
"hits" : [
...
]
},
"suggest" : {
"our_suggestion" : [
{
"text" : "Unitd States",
"offset" : 0,
"length" : 12,
"options" : [
{
"text" : "united states",
"score" : 0.002762749
},
{
"text" : "unit states",
"score" : 6.516915E-4
},
{
"text" : "units states",
"score" : 5.88379E-4
},
{
"text" : "unity states",
"score" : 5.200962E-4
},
{
"text" : "unite states",
"score" : 4.2309557E-4
}
]
}
```

```
        ]
    }
}
```

As you can see, the response is very similar to the one returned by the term suggester, but instead of a single word being returned as the suggestion for each term from the text field, it is already combined and Elasticsearch returns whole phrases. Of course, we can configure additional parameters in the phrase section and now we will look at what parameters are available for usage. Of course, the returned suggestions are sorted by their score by default.

Configuring the phrase suggester

The phrase suggester configuration parameter can be divided into three groups: **basic parameters** that define the general behavior, the **smoothing models configuration** to balance N-gram weights, and **candidate generators** that are responsible for producing the list of terms suggestions that will be used to return final suggestions.

 Because the phrase suggester is based on the term suggester, it can also use some of the configuration options provided by it. These options are field, text, size, analyzer, and shard_size. Refer to the term suggester description earlier in this chapter to find out what they mean.

Basic configuration

In addition to the properties mentioned in the preceding phrase, the suggester exposes the following basic options:

- highlight: This allows us to use suggestions highlighting. With the use of the pre_tag and post_tag properties, we can configure what prefix and postfix should be used to highlight suggestions. For example, if we would like to surround suggestions with the <b> and </b> tags, we should set pre_tag to <b> and post_tag to </b>.
- gram_size: This is the maximum size of the n-gram that is stored in the field and is specified by the field property. If the given field doesn't contain N-grams, this property should be set to 1 or not passed with the suggestion request at all. If not set, Elasticsearch will try to detect the proper value of this parameter by itself. For example, for fields using a shingle filter (https://www.elastic.co/guide/en/elasticsearch/reference/current/analysis-shingle-tokenfilter.html), the value of this parameter will be set to the max_shingle_size property (of course, if not set explicitly).

- `confidence`: This is the parameter that allows us to limit the suggestion based on its score. The value of this parameter is applied to the score of the input phrase (the score is multiplied by the value of this parameter), and this score is used as a threshold for generated suggestions. If the suggestion score is higher than the calculated threshold, it will be included in the returned results; if not, then it will be dropped. For example, setting this parameter to `1.0` (which is the default value of it) will result in suggestions that are scored higher than the original phrase. On the other hand, setting it to `0.0` will result in the suggester returning all the suggestions (limited by the `size` parameter) no matter what their score is.

- `max_errors`: This is the property that allows us to specify the maximum number (or the percentage) of terms that can be erroneous (not correctly spelled) in order to create a correction using it. The value of this property can be either an integer number such as `1` or `5`, or it can be a float between 0 and 1, which will be treated as a percentage value. If we set it as a float, it will specify the percentage of terms that can be erroneous. For example, a value of `0.5` will mean `50` percent. If we specify an integer number, such as `1` or `5`, Elasticsearch will treat it as a maximum number of erroneous terms. By default, it is set to `1`, which means that at most, a single term can be misspelled in a given correction.

- `separator`: This defaults to a whitespace character and specifies the separator that will be used to divide terms in the resulting bigram field.

- `collate`: This allows us to check each suggestion against a specified query (using the `query` property inside the `collate` object). The provided query is run as a template query and exposes the `{{suggestion}}` variable that represents the currently processed suggestion. By including an additional parameter called `prune` (in the `collate` object) and setting it to `true`, Elasticsearch will include the information if the suggestion matches the query (this information will be included in the `collate_match` property in the results). In addition to this, the query preference can be included by using the `preference` property (which can take the same values as the ones used during the normal query processing).

- `real_word_error_likehood`: This is a percentage value, which defaults to `0.95` and specifies how likely it is that a term is misspelled even though it exists in the dictionary (built of the index). The default value of `0.95` tells Elasticsearch that `5%` of all terms that exist in its dictionary are misspelled. Lowering the value of this parameter will result in more terms being taken as misspelled ones even though they may be correct.

Let's now look at an example of using some of the previously mentioned parameters, for example, suggestions highlighting. If we modify our initial phrase suggestion query and add highlighting, the command would look as follows:

```
curl -XGET "http://localhost:9200/wikinews/_search?pretty" -d'
{
"suggest": {
"text": "chrimes in wordl",
"our_suggestion": {
"phrase": {
"field": "text",
"highlight": {
"pre_tag": "<b>",
"post_tag": "</b>"
},
"collate": {
"prune": true,
"query": {
"inline": {
"match": {
"title": "{{suggestion}}"
}
}
}
}
}
}
}'
```

The result returned by Elasticsearch for the preceding query would be as follows:

```
{
"took" : 81,
"timed_out" : false,
"_shards" : {
"total" : 5,
"successful" : 5,
"failed" : 0
},
"hits" : {
"total" : 0,
"max_score" : 0.0,
"hits" : [ ]
},
"suggest" : {
"our_suggestion" : [
{
```

```
"text" : "chrimes in wordl",
"offset" : 0,
"length" : 16,
"options" : [
{
"text" : "crimes in would",
"highlighted" : "<b>crimes</b> in <b>would</b>",
"score" : 1.6482786E-4,
"collate_match" : true
},
{
"text" : "crimes in world",
"highlighted" : "<b>crimes</b> in <b>world</b>",
"score" : 1.5368809E-4,
"collate_match" : true
},
{
"text" : "choices in would",
"highlighted" : "<b>choices</b> in <b>would</b>",
"score" : 6.684227E-5,
"collate_match" : true
},
{
"text" : "choices in world",
"highlighted" : "<b>choices</b> in <b>world</b>",
"score" : 6.325384E-5,
"collate_match" : true
},
{
"text" : "crimes in words",
"highlighted" : "<b>crimes</b> in <b>words</b>",
"score" : 4.8852085E-5,
"collate_match" : true
}
]
}
]
}
}
```

As you can see, the suggestions were highlighted.

Configuring smoothing models

A **smoothing model** is a functionality of the phrase suggester whose responsibility is to measure the balance between the weight of infrequent n-grams that don't exist in the index and the frequent ones that exist in the index. It is rather an expert option and if you want to modify these n-grams, you should check suggester responses for your queries in order to see whether your suggestions are proper for your case. Smoothing is used in language models, to avoid situations where the probability of a given term is equal to zero. The Elasticsearch `phrase` suggester supports multiple smoothing models.

 You can find out more about language models at `http://en.wikipedia.org/wiki/Language_model`

In order to set which smoothing model we want to use, we need to add an object called smoothing and include a smoothing model name we want to use inside of it. Of course, we can include the properties we need or want to set for the given smoothing model. For example, we could run the following command:

```
curl -XGET "http://localhost:9200/wikinews/_search?pretty" -d'
{
"suggest": {
"text": "chrimes in world",
"generators_example_suggestion": {
"phrase": {
"analyzer": "standard",
"field": "text",
"smoothing": {
"linear": {
"trigram_lambda": 0.1,
"bigram_lambda": 0.6,
"unigram_lambda": 0.3
}
}
}
}
}
}'
```

The response of the preceding request looks as follows and looks much better than previous suggestions:

```
{
"took" : 6,
"timed_out" : false,
```

```
"_shards" : {
"total" : 5,
"successful" : 5,
"failed" : 0
},
"hits" : {
"total" : 0,
"max_score" : 0.0,
"hits" : [ ]
},
"suggest" : {
"generators_example_suggestion" : [
{
"text" : "chrimes in world",
"offset" : 0,
"length" : 16,
"options" : [
{
"text" : "crimes in world",
"score" : 1.6559726E-4
},
{
"text" : "choices in world",
"score" : 6.815534E-5
},
{
"text" : "chrome in world",
"score" : 4.6913046E-5
},
{
"text" : "crises in world",
"score" : 4.5373123E-5
},
{
"text" : "crimea in world",
"score" : 3.5583496E-5
}
]
}
]
}
}
```

There are three smoothing models available in Elasticsearch. Let's now look at them.

Stupid backoff is the default smoothing model used by the Elasticsearch phrase suggester. In order to alter it or force its usage, we need to use the `stupid_backoff` name. The `stupid backoff` smoothing model is an implementation that will use a lower ordered n-gram (and will give it a discount equal to the value of the `discount` property) if the higher order n-gram count is equal to 0. To illustrate the example, let's assume that we use the `ab` bigram and the `c` unigram, which are common and exist in our index used by the suggester. However, we don't have the `abc` trigram present. What the `stupid backoff` model will do is that it will use the `ab` bigram model, because `abc` doesn't exist and, of course, the `ab` bigram model will be given a discount equal to the value of the `discount` property.

The `stupid backoff` model provides a single property that we can alter: `discount`. By default, it is set to `0.4`, and it is used as a discount factor for the lower ordered n-gram model.

You can read more about n-gram smoothing models by looking at `http://en.wikipedia.org/wiki/N-gram#Smoothing_techniques` and `http://en.wikipedia.org/wiki/Katz's_back-off_model` (which is similar to the `stupid backoff` model described).

The **Laplace** smoothing model is also called additive smoothing. When used (to use it, we need to use the `laplace` value as its name), a constant value equal to the value of the `alpha` parameter (which is by `0.5` default) will be added to counts to balance the weights of frequent and infrequent n-grams. As mentioned, the Laplace smoothing model can be configured using the `alpha` property, which is set to `0.5` by default. The usual values for this parameter are typically equal or below `1.0`.

You can read more about additive smoothing at `http://en.wikipedia.org/wiki/Additive_smoothing`.

Linear interpolation, the last smoothing model, takes the values of the lambdas provided in the configuration and uses them to calculate the weights of trigrams, bigrams, and unigrams. In order to use the linear interpolation smoothing model, we need to provide the name of `linear` in the `smoothing` object in the suggester query and provide three parameters: `trigram_lambda`, `bigram_lambda`, and `unigram_lambda`. The sum of the values of the three mentioned parameters must be equal to `1`. Each of these parameters is a weight for a given type of n-gram; for example, the `bigram_lambda` parameter value will be used as a weight for bigrams.

Configuring candidate generators

In order to return possible suggestions for a term from the text provided in the `text` parameter, Elasticsearch uses so-called **candidate generators**. You can think of candidate generators as `term` suggesters although they are not exactly the same—they are similar because they are used for every single term in the query provided to the suggester. After the candidate terms are returned, they are scored in combination with suggestions for other terms from the text, and this way, the phrase suggestions are built.

Currently, **direct generators** are the only candidate generators available in Elasticsearch, although we can expect more of them to be present in the future. Elasticsearch allows us to provide multiple direct generators in a single phrase suggester request. We can do this by providing the list named `direct_generators`. For example, we could run the following command:

```
curl -XGET "http://localhost:9200/wikinews/_search?pretty" -d'
{
   "suggest": {
      "text": "chrimes in wordl",
      "generators_example_suggestion": {
         "phrase": {
            "analyzer": "standard",
            "field": "text",
            "direct_generator": [
               {
                  "field": "text",
                  "suggest_mode": "always",
                  "min_word_length": 2
               },
               {
                  "field": "text",
                  "suggest_mode": "always",
                  "min_word_length": 3
               }
            ]
         }
      }
   }
}'
```

The response should be very similar to the one previously shown, so we decided to omit it.

The completion suggester

Until now, we have read about the `term` suggester and `phrase` suggester, which are used for providing suggestions, but the `completion` suggester is completely different and is used as a prefix-based suggester allowing us to create the autocomplete (search as you type) functionality in a very performance-effective way. It does this by storing complicated structures in the index instead of calculating them during query time. This suggester is not about correcting user spelling mistakes.

In Elasticsearch 5.0, the `completion` suggester has gone through a complete rewrite. Both the syntax and data structures of the `completion` type field have been changed and so has the response structure. Many new, exciting features and speed optimizations have been introduced in the `completion` suggester. One of these features is making the `completion` suggester near real-time which allows deleted suggestions to be omitted from suggestion results as soon as they are deleted.

The logic behind the completion suggester

The prefix suggester is based on the data structure called **Finite State Transducer** (**FST**) (http://en.wikipedia.org/wiki/Finite_state_transducer). Although it is highly efficient, it may require significant resources to build on systems with large amounts of data in them: systems that Elasticsearch is perfectly suitable for. If we would like to build such a structure on the nodes after each restart or cluster state change, we may lose performance. Because of this, the Elasticsearch creators decided to use an FST-like structure during index time and store it in the index so that it can be loaded into memory when needed.

Using the completion suggester

To use a prefix-based suggester, we need to properly index our data with a dedicated field type called `completion`. It stores the FST-like structure in the index. In order to illustrate how to use this suggester, let's assume that we want to create an autocomplete feature to allow us to show book authors, which we store in an additional index. In addition to authors' names, we want to return the identifiers of the books they wrote in order to search for them with an additional query. We start with creating the `authors` index by running the following command:

```
curl -XPUT "http://localhost:9200/authors" -d'
{
"mappings": {
"author": {
"properties": {
"name": {
```

```
        "type": "keyword"
        },
        "suggest": {
        "type": "completion"
        }
        }
        }
        }
        }'
```

Our index will contain a single type called `author`. Each document will have two fields: the `name` field, which is the name of the author, and the `suggest` field, which is the field we will use for autocomplete. The `suggest` field is the one we are interested in; we've defined it using the `completion` type, which will result in storing the FST-like structure in the index.

Indexing data

Indexing data for `completion` type fields has become simpler in comparison to older Elasticsearch versions. To index the data, we need to provide some additional information in addition to what we usually provide during indexing. Let's look at the following commands that index two documents describing `authors`:

```
curl -XPOST 'localhost:9200/authors/author/1' -d '{
"name" : "Fyodor Dostoevsky",
"suggest" : {
"input" : [ "fyodor", "dostoevsky" ]
}
}'
curl -XPOST 'localhost:9200/authors/author/2' -d '{
"name" : "Joseph Conrad",
"suggest" : {
"input" : [ "joseph", "conrad" ]
}
}'
```

Notice the structure of the data for the `suggest` field. The `input` property is used inside our `completion` field to provide input information that will be used to build the FST-like structure and will be used to match the user input to decide whether the document should be returned by the suggester.

Querying data

Finally, let's look at how to query our indexed data. If we would like to find documents that have authors starting with `fyo`, we would run the following command:

```
curl -XGET "http://localhost:9200/authors/_search?pretty" -d'
{
    "suggest": {
        "authorsAutocomplete": {
            "prefix": "fyo",
            "completion": {
                "field": "suggest"
            }
        }
    }
}'
```

Before we look at the results, let's discuss the query. As you can see, we've run the command to the `_suggest` endpoint, because we don't want to run a standard query; we are just interested in autocomplete results. The rest of the query is exactly the same as the standard suggester query run against the `_suggest` endpoint, with the query type set to `completion`.

The results returned by Elasticsearch for the preceding query look as follows:

```
{
"took" : 2,
"timed_out" : false,
"_shards" : {
"total" : 5,
"successful" : 5,
"failed" : 0
},
"hits" : {
"total" : 0,
"max_score" : 0.0,
"hits" : [ ]
},
"suggest" : {
"authorsAutocomplete" : [
{
"text" : "fyo",
"offset" : 0,
"length" : 3,
"options" : [
{
"text" : "fyodor",
```

```
"_index" : "authors",
"_type" : "author",
"_id" : "1",
"_score" : 1.0,
"_source" : {
"name" : "Fyodor Dostoevsky",
"suggest" : {
"input" : [
"fyodor",
"dostoevsky"
]
}
}
}
]
}
]
}
}
```

As you can see, in response, we've got the document we were looking for and we can use the name field inside our auto suggestion field.

Similar to `fyo`, you can also search for the prefix `dos`, since we have `Dostoevsky` as the second input parameter in the first document.

Custom weights

By default, the term frequency will be used to determine the weight of the document returned by the prefix suggester. However, this may not be the best solution when you have multiple shards for your index, or when your index is composed of multiple segments. In such cases, it is useful to define the weight of the suggestion by specifying the `weight` property for the field defined as `completion`; the `weight` property should be set to a positive integer value and not a float one like the boost for queries and documents. The higher the `weight` property value, the more important the suggestion is. This gives us plenty of opportunities to control how the returned suggestions will be sorted.

For example, if we would like to specify a weight for the first document in our example, we would run the following command:

```
curl -XPOST 'localhost:9200/authors/author/1' -d '{
"name" : "Fyodor Dostoevsky",
"suggest" : {
"input" : [ "fyodor", "dostoevsky" ],
"weight" : 80
}
}'
```

Now, if we run our example query, the results would be as follows:

```
{
"took" : 7,
"timed_out" : false,
"_shards" : {
"total" : 5,
"successful" : 5,
"failed" : 0
},
"hits" : {
"total" : 0,
"max_score" : 0.0,
"hits" : [ ]
},
"suggest" : {
"authorsAutocomplete" : [
{
"text" : "fyo",
"offset" : 0,
"length" : 3,
"options" : [
{
"text" : "fyodor",
"_index" : "authors",
"_type" : "author",
"_id" : "1",
"_score" : 80.0,
"_source" : {
"name" : "Fyodor Dostoevsky",
"suggest" : {
"input" : [
"fyodor",
"dostoevsky"
],
"weight" : 80
}
```

```
      }
      }
    ]
      }
    ]
      }
      }
```

See how the score of the result changed? In our initial example, it was 1.0 and, now, it is 80.0; this is because we've set the weight parameter to 80 during the indexing.

Using fuzziness with the completion suggester

To tackle the typo in your searches, you can use the fuzziness support for the completion suggester. Let's see an example of how you can use it in your queries.

Suppose you are searching for fyo but, by mistake you have typed fio; with the following query you will still get an accurate result:

```
curl -XGET "http://localhost:9200/authors/_search?pretty" -d'
{
"suggest": {
"authorsAutocomplete": {
"text": "fio",
"completion": {
"field": "suggest",
"fuzzy": {
"fuzziness": 2
}
}
}
}
}'
```

Suggestions that share the longest prefix to the query prefix will be scored higher.

Please see the fuzzy object inside the completion request. The fuzzy object has a special attribute, fuzziness which defaults to AUTO, but you can use a desired value based on your needs and use case.

Implementing your own auto-completion

Completion suggester does have limitations..!!

The `completion` suggester has been designed to be a powerful and easily implemented solution for autocompletion but it supports only prefix queries, as we have seen in the previous section. Most of the time, autocomplete needs only to work as a prefix query, for example, if I type `elastic`, then I expect `elasticsearch` as a suggestion, but not `nonelastic`.

There are some use cases when one wants to implement more general, partial word completion. The `completion` suggester fails to fulfill this requirement.

The second limitation of the `completion` suggester is it does not allow advance queries and filters searched.

To get rid of both these limitations, we are going to implement a custom auto-complete feature based on n-grams, which works in almost all the scenarios.

Creating an index

Let's create an index, `location-suggestion` with the following settings and mappings:

```
curl -XPUT "http://localhost:9200/location-suggestion" -d'
{
"settings": {
"index": {
"analysis": {
"filter": {
"nGram_filter": {
"token_chars": [
"letter",
"digit",
"punctuation",
"symbol",
"whitespace"
],
"min_gram": "2",
"type": "nGram",
"max_gram": "20"
}
},
"analyzer": {
"nGram_analyzer": {
```

```
"filter": [
    "lowercase",
    "asciifolding",
    "nGram_filter"
],
"type": "custom",
"tokenizer": "whitespace"
},
"whitespace_analyzer": {
"filter": [
    "lowercase",
    "asciifolding"
],
"type": "custom",
"tokenizer": "whitespace"
}
}
}
}
},
"mappings": {
"locations": {
"properties": {
"name": {
"type": "text",
"analyzer": "nGram_analyzer",
"search_analyzer": "whitespace_analyzer"
},
"country": {
"type": "keyword"
}
}
}
}
}'
```

Understanding the parameters

If you look carefully at the preceding curl request for creating the index, it contains both settings and the mappings. We will see them now in detail, one by one.

Configuring settings

Our settings contain two custom analyzers: nGram_analyzer and, whitespace_analyzer. We have made a custom whitespace_analyzer using a whitespace tokenizer just for making sure that all the tokens are indexed in lowercase and asci folded form.

Our main interest is nGram_analyzer, which contains a custom filter, nGram_filter consisting of the following parameters:

- type: Specifies the type of token filters, which is N-gram in our case.
- token_chars: Specifies what kind of characters are allowed in the generated tokens. Punctuation and special characters are generally removed from the token streams but in our example, we have intended to keep them. We have kept whitespace as well, so that if any text contains United States and a user searches for u s, United States still appears in the suggestion.
- min_gram and max_gram: These two attributes set the minimum and maximum length of substrings that will be generated and added to the lookup table. For example, according to our settings for the index, the token India will generate the following tokens:

```
[ "di", "dia", "ia", "in", "ind", "indi", "india", "nd", "ndi", "ndia" ]
```

Configuring mappings

The document type of our index is locations and it has two fields, name and country. The most important thing to see is the way analyzers have been defined for the name field which will be used for autosuggestion. For this field, we have set index analyzer to our custom nGram_analyzer where the search analyzer is set to whitespace_analyzer. Very soon you will get to know the reason behind doing so.

 Please note that the index_analyzer parameter is no longer supported from Elasticsearch version 5.0 onward. Also, if you want to configure the search_analyzer property for a field, then you must configure the analyzer property the way we have shown in the example as well.

Indexing documents

Let's index some documents which consist of names of cities and countries:

```
curl -XPUT "http://localhost:9200/location-suggestion/location/1" -d'
{"name":"Bradford","country":"england"}'
curl -XPUT "http://localhost:9200/location-suggestion/location/2" -d'
{"name":"Bridport","country":"england"}'
curl -XPUT "http://localhost:9200/location-suggestion/location/3" -d'
{"name":"San Diego Country Estates","country":"usa"}'
curl -XPUT "http://localhost:9200/location-suggestion/location/4" -d'
{"name":"Ike's Point, NJ","country":"usa"}'
```

Querying documents for auto-completion

Now we have four documents in the index and we can execute search requests to test our auto-complete functionality. Our first request contains `ke's`, and it will match `Ike's Point, NJ` and return the fourth document from our index:

```
curl -XGET "http://localhost:9200/location-suggestion/location/_search"
 -d'
 {
 "query": {
 "match": {
 "name": "ke's"
 }
 }
 }'
```

Similarly, searching for `br` will return `Bradford` and `Bridport` in the response. The number of matches to be returned in response can be controlled using the `size` parameter.

In addition, you can use advance query and filters to provide suggestions in a selected context, because it works like a normal search request.

Working with synonyms

Full text searches often require synonym searches. For example, if a user is searching for equity then he would expect to get the results which contain share and stock. A user might search for `the US` and expect to find documents that contain United States, USA, U.S.A., or America. However, they wouldn't expect to see results about the states of matter or state machines.

Synonyms are used to broaden the scope matching documents and often people try to provide synonyms for every word in the language, to ensure that any document can be found with even the most remotely related terms. But they should be used only when necessary and just as with partial matching we have seen in previous sections, synonym fields should not be used alone but should be combined with a query to set the context and get better results.

Synonyms appear to be a very simple concept but they are very tricky to implement. They are prone to yield false positive or false negative results if all scenarios are not taken care of. It also very much depends on the product domain. For example, a finance domain is completely different from a recruitment domain and so the context of phrases and terms appearing in both of the domains is different.

Preparing settings for synonym search

To use synonyms in the search, the field must be pre-configured with a synonym token filter. This filter allows synonym words to be configured both inline (in the settings itself) as well as to be picked up from the file:

```
curl -XPUT "http://localhost:9200/synonyms-index" -d'
{
"settings": {
"analysis": {
"filter": {
"my_synonym_filter": {
"type": "synonym",
"synonyms": [
"shares","equity","stock"
]
}
},
"analyzer": {
"my_synonyms": {
"tokenizer": "standard",
"filter": [
"lowercase",
"my_synonym_filter"
]
}
}
}
}
}'
```

In the preceding index settings, we have created a custom analyzer using the custom filter, `my_synonym_filter` based on a synonym token filter. Additionally, using the synonyms parameter, we have used three words; `shares`, `equity`, and `stock` which belong to the same synonym group.

Instead of using these words inline, you can create a file with the name `synonyms.txt` under the Elasticsearch configuration directory which usually belongs to `/etc/elasticsearch/` and place these words inside that file. To use this file, the custom filter will look like the following:

```
"my_synonym_filter": {
  "type": "synonym",
  "synonyms_path": "synonyms.txt",
}
```

> Please do not forget to change the ownership of the file to user `Elasticsearch` with this command: `sudochown /etc/elasticsearch/synonyms.txt`

Formatting synonyms

We have already seen how we can keep synonyms in both ways: inline as well as file. Now let's see how to format multiple synonyms groups.

In the simplest form, synonyms are formatted in comma separated words, as we have seen in the previous setting file. Using this structure allows us to search for any word and find any other word. It is possible because tokens are generated in the following way:

Original term	Replaced by
Share	shares, equity, stock
Equity	shares, equity, stock
Stock	shares, equity, stock

This form is known as **simple expansion**, and using this form is quite an expensive process since each term will be replaced by a number of terms available in its synonym group and this will lead to an exponential increase in the index size.

There is an alternate syntax using =>, in which terms which appear on the left side are replaced by terms which appear on the right side. When you use only a single word on the right side, it is called **simple contraction**, whereas using only one word on the left side and more than one word on the right side is known as **genre expansion**. For example:

```
"u s a,united states =>usa"
"gb =>britain,england"
```

This format will cause terms replacement in the following way:

Original term	Replaced by
u s a	Usa
united states	Usa
gb	britain,england

Please note that according to Lucene documentation, for nested/overlapping synonyms, there is a big issue with the way this has been implemented in Lucene. The synonym token filter cannot properly handle position increments != 1, for instance, you should place this filter before filtering out stop words. Also, with the current implementation, parsing is greedy, so whenever multiple parses would apply, the rule starting the earliest and parsing the most tokens wins.
For example, if you have these rules:
a => x
a b => y
b c d => z
Then input a b c d e parses to y b c d, for instance, the 2nd rule "wins" because it started earliest and matched the most input tokens of other rules starting at that point.

Synonym expansion versus contraction

We have already seen all the expansion and contraction types in the precious section. Now let's look at the advantages and drawbacks of them.

As said earlier, **simple expansion**, if used at indexing time, has two main drawbacks. One, it leads to a much bigger index, and for existing documents, synonym rules can't be changed without re-indexing them, although the search speed will be very fast since only one term lookup needs to be done by Elasticsearch.

But if you use this technique at query time, it will give you a big performance impact on search speed since a query for a single term is rewritten to look for all the terms of its synonyms group. The biggest advantage of using simple expansion at query time is synonym rules can be updated without re-indexing the documents.

A **simple contraction**, for example, `"u s a,united states =>usa"` maps a group of synonyms from left side to a single word on the right side. This approach has many advantages though:

- First, index size will be normal since a single term replaces the complete synonym group.
- Second, the query performance will also be very good since only a single term needs to be matched.
- Third, synonym rules can be updated without re-indexing documents with the following trick.

Let's assume we have a pre-existing rule:

```
"u s a,united states =>usa"
```

And now we also want to add `america` in our synonym group. It can be done by adding `america` in both the left and right side of the `=>` as follows:

```
"u s a,united states, america =>usa, america"
```

> Please note that whenever you update any synonym rule, you need to reload the new rules into the index setting by closing the index and re-opening it.

Simple contraction has one downside though, and that is it impacts relevancy a lot. The inverse document frequencies of all the terms which belong to single synonym groups are the same so you can't differentiate between the most common and less common words.

The genre expansion expands the meaning of a term to be more generic. It is completely different as well, more confusing and requires much expertise to work with in comparison to the other two techniques we just saw. To show you an example, let's consider the following rule of genre expansion:

```
"gb =>gb,greatbritain"
"britain =>britain,gb,greatbritain"
```

When applied at the indexing time:

- A query for `britain` would find just documents about `britain`
- A query for `gb` would find documents about `gb` and `britain`
- A query for `great britain` would find documents about `gb`, `britain` or `great britain`

Dealing with the complexity of human languages in full text search is a very broad topic and a single solution never satisfies every use case or every domain. This scenario becomes more difficult to handle with the few limitations imposed by the analysis process of Lucene. For example, dealing with nested synonyms is a very big issue which will probably be handled in coming releases, and so is the issue of handling multi-word synonyms. For example, when using a rule
`online sale, online revenues =>revenue`
, you can't find a document with only the
`online`
term mentioned in it. To get rid of this situation you need to create synonym rules with each possible term separately.

Summary

In this chapter, we focused on improving the user search experience. We started with working on did-you-mean functionality which is implemented by term and phrase suggesters and then covered search-as-you-type, for instance an auto-completion feature which is implemented using the `completion` suggester. We also saw the limitations of the `completion` suggester in handling advanced queries and partial matching, which was further solved by implementing our custom `completion` using n-grams. Lastly, we discussed the synonyms implementation and the limitations of synonyms usage in some scenarios.

In the next chapter, we will discuss topics which will give you an expert idea of designing index architecture, such as choosing the right number of shards and replicas along with a detailed discussion on how routing works, how shard allocation works, and how to alter its behavior. In addition to that, the chapter discusses what query execution preference is and how it allows us to choose where the queries are going to be executed. It also covers how one can strip data on multiple path on disk.

6
The Index Distribution Architecture

In the last chapter, we focused on improving the user search experience by showing you how you can leverage the did-you-mean functionality, which is implemented by `term` and `phrase` suggesters and then covered search-as-you-type, for instance, the auto-completion feature, which is implemented using the `completion` suggester. We also saw the limitations of the `completion` suggester in handling advanced queries and partial matching, which was further solved by implementing custom completion using n-grams. At last we discussed the synonyms implementation and the limitations of synonyms usage in some scenarios.

In this chapter, we will learn about creating a multi-node cluster and then we will cover the index distribution architecture in Elasticsearch, including choosing the right number of shards and replicas along with a detailed discussion on how routing works, how shard allocation works, and how to alter the default shard allocation behavior. In addition to that, we will also discuss query execution preference. By the end of this chapter, we will have covered following topics:

- Configuring an example multi-node cluster
- Choosing the right amount of shards and replicas
- Routing and its advantages
- Shard allocation control
- Using query execution preference
- Stripping data on multiple paths
- Index versus type: revised approach for creating indices

Configuring an example multi-node cluster

Till now, we have been playing around with a single node cluster but since we are going into more detail about index architecture, it's important to know how things work in a multi-node cluster. Although we will look into detailed cluster configurations in Chapter 8, *Elasticsearch Administration*, we will start with creating a two-node cluster in this chapter to demonstrate the concepts clearly.

Let's start with installing Elasticsearch on two separate machines. Please make sure that both the machines exist on the same network and port 9200 and 9300 are open between them. Also, you need to have Java 1.8 or above installed on your machines and each machine should have at least 3 GB of RAM available since the default heap size (both min and max) used by Elasticsearch is 2 GB.

 If you have less amount of RAM available in your machines, you can alter and minimize the default Min and Max heap size after installing the Elasticsearch by editing these two parameters –Xms and –Xmx inside the jvm.options file which can be found inside the Elasticsearch config directory. For example, to set min and max heap size to 1 GB, these parameters should look like –Xms1g and–Xmx1g.

On Ubuntu machines, you can follow the given steps to download, install, and configure the cluster.

 Please follow the given URL to learn installation through the RPM package on CentOS, or on Wndows machines: https://www.elastic.co/guide/en/elasticsearch/reference/5.0/install-elasticsearch.html

1. Download Elasticsearch.

   ```
   wget
   https://artifacts.elastic.co/downloads/elasticsearch/elasticsearch-
   5.0.0.deb
   ```

2. Install Elasticsearch.

   ```
   dpkg –i elasticsearch-5.0.0.deb
   ```

3. Open the elasticsearch.yml file which you can find in the /etc/elasticsearch/ directory.

   ```
   sudo vi /etc/elasticsearch/elasticsearch.yml
   ```

4. Once the file is open, edit the following three parameters and save the file before exiting.

```
cluster.name: test-cluster
network.host: 0.0.0.0
discovery.zen.ping.unicast.hosts: ["11.0.2.15:9300",
"11.0.2.16:9300"]
```

> Inside the `discovery.zen.ping.unicast.hosts` parameter, please use the IP addresses of your machines. Also, please do not forget to uncomment these parameters after editing and make sure that there is no space existing before these parameters. Please also note that by default, Elasticsearch binds itself on localhost but if you try to modify the `network.host` parameter for binding it on a non-localhost IP address then it consider this node as a production ready node and this node should satisfy all the necessary bootstrap checks introduced inside Elasticsearch 5.0. Your node would refuse to start if anyone of those checks are not satisfied on your system. You can read more about bootstrap checks here:
> `https://www.elastic.co/guide/en/elasticsearch/reference/master/bootstrap-checks.html` and also in this article:
> `https://www.elastic.co/blog/bootstrap_checks_annoying_instead_of_devastating`

5. After configuring these three parameters, you can start both the nodes and they will join each other to form a cluster.

```
sudo service elasticsearch start
```

6. To verify, you can use following command:

```
curl -XGET localhost:9200/_cat/nodes?v
```

7. The output of the command should look like the following:

```
ip          heap.percent ram.percent cpu load_1m load_5m load_15m node.role master name
11.0.2.16            5           67   0    0.00    0.01     0.05 mdi       *      y7lLdir
11.0.2.15            7           67   0    0.05    0.05     0.05 mdi       -      Tg5Q7AX
```

Choosing the right amount of shards and replicas

In the beginning, when you started using Elasticsearch, you probably began by creating the index, importing your data to it and, after that, you started sending queries. We are pretty sure all worked well–at least in the beginning when the amount of data and the number of queries per second were not high. In the background, Elasticsearch created some shards and probably replicas as well (if you are using the default configuration, for example), and you didn't pay much attention to this part of the deployment.

When your application grows, you have to index more and more data and handle more and more queries per second. This is the point where everything changes. Problems start to appear (you can read about how we can handle the application's growth in `Chapter 10`, *Improving Performance*). It's now time to think about how you should plan your index and its configuration for your application. In this chapter, we will give you some guidelines on how to handle this. Unfortunately, there is no exact recipe; each application has different characteristics and requirements, based on which, not only does the index structure depend, but also the configuration. For example, these factors can be ones like the size of the document or the whole index, query types, and the desired throughput.

Sharding and overallocation

You already know from the *An overview of Elasticsearch* section in `Chapter 1`, *Revisiting Elasticsearch and The Changes*, what sharding is, but let's recall it. Sharding is the splitting of an Elasticsearch index to a set of smaller indices, which allows us to spread them among multiple nodes in the same cluster. While querying, the result is a sum of all the results that were returned by each shard of an index (although it's not really a sum, because a single shard may hold all the data we are interested in). By default, Elasticsearch creates five shards for every index, even in a single-node environment. This redundancy is called **overallocation**: it seems to be totally unneeded at this point and only leads to more complexity when indexing (spreading document to shards) and handling queries (querying shards and merging the results). Happily, this complexity is handled automatically, but why does Elasticsearch do this?

Let's say that we have an index that is built only of a single shard. This means that if our application grows above the capacity of a single machine, we will face a problem. In the current version of Elasticsearch, there is no possibility of splitting the index into multiple, smaller parts; we need to say how many shards the index should be built from when we create that index. What we can do is prepare a new index with more shards and reindex the data. However, such an operation requires additional time and server resources, such as CPU time, RAM, and mass storage. When it comes to the production environment, we don't always have the required time and mentioned resources. On the other hand, while using overallocation, we can just add a new server with Elasticsearch installed, and Elasticsearch will rebalance the cluster by moving parts of the index to the new machine without the additional cost of reindexing. The default configuration (which means five shards and one replica) chosen by the authors of Elasticsearch is the balance between the possibilities of growing and overhead resulting from the need to merge results from a different shard.

The default shard number of five is chosen for standard use cases. So now, this question arises: when should we start with more shards or, on the contrary, try to keep the number of shards as low as possible?

The first answer is obvious. If you have a limited and strongly defined dataset, you can use only a single shard. If you do not, however, the rule of thumb dictates that the optimal number of shards be dependent on the target number of nodes. So, if you plan to use 10 nodes in the future, you need to configure the index to have 10 shards. One important thing to remember is that for high availability and query throughput, we should also configure replicas, and it also takes up room on the nodes just like the normal shard. If you have one additional copy of each shard (`number_of_replicas` equal to one), you end up with 20 shards–10 with the main data and 10 with its replicas.

To sum up, our simple formula can be presented as follows:

```
max number of nodes = number of shards * (number of replicas + 1)
```

In other words, if you have planned to use 10 shards and you like to have two replicas, the maximum number of nodes that will hold the data for this setup will be 30.

A positive example of overallocation

If you carefully read the previous part of this chapter, you will have a strong conviction that you should use the minimal number of shards. However, sometimes, having more shards is handy, because a shard is, in fact, an Apache Lucene index, and more shards mean that every operation executed on a single, smaller Lucene index (especially indexing) will be faster. Sometimes, this is a good enough reason to use many shards. Of course, there is the possible cost of splitting a query into multiple requests to each and every shard and merging the response from it. This can be avoided for particular types of applications where the queries are always filtered by the concrete parameter. This is the case with multitenant systems, where every query is run in the context of the defined user. The idea is simple; we can index the data of this user in a single shard and use only that shard during querying. This is in place when routing should be used (we will discuss it in detail in the *Routing explained* section in this chapter).

Multiple shards versus multiple indices

You may wonder whether, if a shard is the **de-facto** of a small Lucene index, what about true Elasticsearch indices? What is the difference between having multiple small shards and having multiple indices? Technically, the difference is not that great and, for some use cases, having more than a single index is the right approach (for example, to store time-based data such as logs in time-sliced indices). When you are using a single index with many shards, you can limit your operations to a single shard when using routing, for example. When dealing with indices, you may choose which data you are interested in; for example, choose only a few of your time-based indices using the `logs_2016-10-10`,`logs_2016-10-11`, . . . notation. More differences can be spotted in the shard and index-balancing logic, although we can configure both balancing logics.

Replicas

While sharding lets us store more data than we can fit on a single node, replicas are there to handle increasing throughput and, of course, for high availability and fault tolerance. When a node with the primary shard is lost, Elasticsearch can promote one of the available replicas to be a new primary shard. In the default configuration, Elasticsearch creates a single replica for each of the shards in the index. However, the number of replicas can be changed at any time using the Settings API. This is very convenient when we are at a point where we need more query throughput; increasing the number of replicas allows us to spread the querying load on more machines, which basically allows us to handle more parallel queries.

The drawback of using more replicas is obvious: the cost of additional space used by additional copies of each shard, the cost of indexing on nodes that host the replicas, and, of course, the cost of data copy between the primary shard and all the replicas. While choosing the number of shards, you should also consider how many replicas need to be present. If you select too many replicas, you can end up using disk space and Elasticsearch resources, when in fact, they won't be used. On the other hand, choosing to have none of the replicas may result in the data being lost if something bad happens to the primary shard.

A replica can always be increased or decreased using the following command:

```
curl -XPUT 'localhost:9200/books/_settings' -d '
{
    "index" : {
        "number_of_replicas" : 2
    }
}'
```

In the preceding command, we have used the Elasticsearch `_settings` API to increase the replica to 2 for the `index` books. If you choose `number_of_replicas` as 0, there won't be any replica for this index.

Routing explained

In the *Choosing the right amount of shards and replicas* section in this chapter, we mentioned routing as a solution for the shards on which queries will be executed on a single one. Now it's time to look closer at this functionality.

Shards and data

Usually, it is not important how Elasticsearch divides data into shards and which shard holds the particular document. During query time, the query will be sent to all the shards of a particular index, so the only crucial thing is to use the algorithm that spreads our data evenly so that each shard contains similar amounts of data. We don't want one shard to hold 99 percent of the data while the other shard holds the rest—it is not efficient.

The situation complicates slightly when we want to remove or add a newer version of the document. Elasticsearch must be able to determine which shard should be updated. Although it may seem troublesome, in practice, it is not a huge problem. It is enough to use the sharding algorithm, which will always generate the same value for the same document identifier. If we have such an algorithm, Elasticsearch will know which shard to point to when dealing with a document.

However, there are times when it would be nice to be able to hit the same shard for some portion of data. For example, we would like to store every book of a particular type only on a particular shard and, while searching for that kind of book, we could avoid searching on many shards and merging results from them. Instead, because we know the value we used for routing, we could point Elasticsearch to the same shard we used during indexing. This is exactly what routing does. It allows us to provide information that will be used by Elasticsearch to determine which shard should be used for document storage and for querying; the same routing value will always result in the same shard. It's basically like saying: search for documents on the shard where you've put the documents by using the provided routing value.

Let's test routing

To show you an example that will illustrate how Elasticsearch allocates shards and which documents are placed on the particular shard, we will use the _cat API of Elasticsearch. It will help us visualize what Elasticsearch did with our data.

Let's start both our Elasticsearch nodes and create an index by running the following command:

```
    curl -XPUT 'localhost:9200/documents' -d '{
"settings": {
"number_of_replicas": 0,
"number_of_shards": 2
}
}'
```

We've created an index without replicas, which is built of two shards. To increase the number of replicas, you can see the *Choosing the right amount of shards and replicas* section of this chapter. The next operation is to index some documents; we will do that by using the following commands:

```
    curl -XPUT localhost:9200/documents/doc/1 -d '{ "title" : "Document
No. 1" }'


 curl -XPUT localhost:9200/documents/doc/2 -d '{ "title" : "Document No. 2"
 }'


 curl -XPUT localhost:9200/documents/doc/3 -d '{ "title" : "Document No. 3"
 }'
```

```
curl -XPUT localhost:9200/documents/doc/4 -d '{ "title" : "Document No. 4"
}'
```

After that, we look at the output of the following command to see our two primary shards created and assigned:

```
curl -XGET localhost:9200/_cat/shards?v
```

```
index       shard prirep state    docs store ip         node
documents 1       p     STARTED  3 6.5kb 11.0.2.15 Tg5Q7AX
documents 0       p     STARTED  1 3.3kb 11.0.2.16 y7lLdir
```

In the information about shards, we can also find the information that we are currently interested in. Each of the nodes in the cluster holds exactly two documents. This leads us to the conclusion that the sharding algorithm did its work perfectly, and we have an index that is built of shards that have evenly redistributed documents.

Now, let's create some chaos and let's shut down the second node. Now, our `cat` command would show the following output and we should see something like this:

```
index       shard prirep state      docs store ip         node
documents 1       p     STARTED    3 6.5kb 11.0.2.15 Tg5Q7AX
documents 0       p     UNASSIGNED
```

The first information we see is that the cluster is now in the red state. This means that at least one primary shard is missing, which tells us that some of the data is not available and some parts of the index are not available. Nevertheless, Elasticsearch allows us to execute queries; it is our decision as to what applications should do–inform the user about the possibility of incomplete results or block querying attempts. Let's try to run a simple query by using the following command:

```
curl -XGET 'localhost:9200/documents/_search?pretty'
```

The response returned by Elasticsearch will look as follows:

```
{
  "took" : 24,
  "timed_out" : false,
  "_shards" : {
    "total" : 2,
    "successful" : 1,
    "failed" : 0
  },
  "hits" : {
    "total" : 3,
```

```
     "max_score" : 1.0,
     "hits" : [
       {
         "_index" : "documents",
         "_type" : "doc",
         "_id" : "1",
         "_score" : 1.0,
         "_source" : {
           "title" : "Document No. 1"
         }
       },
       {
         "_index" : "documents",
         "_type" : "doc",
         "_id" : "2",
         "_score" : 1.0,
         "_source" : {
           "title" : "Document No. 2"
         }
       },
       {
         "_index" : "documents",
         "_type" : "doc",
         "_id" : "4",
         "_score" : 1.0,
         "_source" : {
           "title" : "Document No. 4"
         }
       }
     ]
   }
 }
```

As you can see, Elasticsearch returned the information about failures; we can see that one of the shards is not available. In the returned result set, we can only see the documents with identifiers of 1, 2, and 4. Other documents have been lost, at least until the failed primary shard is back online. If you start the second node, after a while (depending on the network and gateway module settings), the cluster should return to the green state and all documents should be available. Now, we will try to do the same using routing, and we will try to observe the difference in the Elasticsearch behavior.

Indexing with routing

With routing, we can control the target shard Elasticsearch will choose to send the documents to, by specifying the routing parameter. The value of the routing parameter is irrelevant; you can use whatever value you choose. The important thing is that the same value of the routing parameter should be used to place different documents together in the same shard. To say it simply, using the same routing value for different documents will ensure that these documents will be placed in the same shard.

There are a few possibilities as to how we can provide the routing information to Elasticsearch. The simplest way is to add the routing URI parameter when indexing a document, for example:

```
curl -XPUT localhost:9200/books/doc/1?routing=A -d '{ "title" :
"Document" }'
```

Of course, we can also provide the routing value when using bulk indexing. In such cases, routing is given in the metadata for each document by using the _routing property, for example:

```
curl -XPOST localhost:9200/_bulk --data-binary '
{ "index" : { "_index" : "books", "_type" : "doc", "_routing" : "A" } }
{ "title" : "Document" }'
```

Routing in practice

Now let's get back to our initial example and do the same as what we did but now using routing. The first thing is to delete the old documents. If we do not do this and add documents with the same identifier, routing may cause that same document to now be placed in the other shard. Therefore, we run the following command to delete all the documents from our index:

```
curl -XPOST "http://localhost:9200/documents/_delete_by_query" -d'
{"query": {"match_all": {}}}'
```

After that, we index our data again, but this time, we add the routing information. The commands used to index our documents now look as follows:

```
curl -XPUT localhost:9200/documents/doc/1?routing=A -d '{ "title" :
"Document No. 1" }'

curl -XPUT localhost:9200/documents/doc/2?routing=B -d '{ "title" :

"Document No. 2" }'
```

```
curl -XPUT localhost:9200/documents/doc/3?routing=A -d '{ "title" :

"Document No. 3" }'

curl -XPUT localhost:9200/documents/doc/4?routing=A -d '{ "title" :

"Document No. 4" }'
```

As we said, the routing parameter tells Elasticsearch in which shard the document should be placed. Of course, it may be that more than a single document will be placed in the same shard. That's because you usually have less shards than routing values. If we now kill one node, the cluster will go into a red state. If we query for all the documents, Elasticsearch will return the following response (of course, it depends which node you kill):

```
curl -XGET 'localhost:9200/documents/_search?q=*&pretty'
```

The response from Elasticsearch would be as follows:

```
{
  "took" : 6,
  "timed_out" : false,
  "_shards" : {
    "total" : 2,
    "successful" : 1,
    "failed" : 0
  },
  "hits" : {
    "total" : 3,
    "max_score" : 1.0,
    "hits" : [
      {
        "_index" : "documents",
        "_type" : "doc",
        "_id" : "1",
        "_score" : 1.0,
        "_routing" : "A",
        "_source" : {
          "title" : "Document No. 1"
        }
      },
      {
        "_index" : "documents",
        "_type" : "doc",
        "_id" : "3",
        "_score" : 1.0,
        "_routing" : "A",
        "_source" : {
          "title" : "Document No. 3"
```

```
          }
        },
        {
          "_index" : "documents",
          "_type" : "doc",
          "_id" : "4",
          "_score" : 1.0,
          "_routing" : "A",
          "_source" : {
            "title" : "Document No. 4"
          }
        }
      ]
    }
  }
```

In our case, the document with the identifier 2 is missing. We lost a node with the documents that had the routing value of B. If we were less lucky, we could lose three documents!

Querying

Routing allows us to tell Elasticsearch which shards should be used for querying. Why send queries to all the shards that build the index if we want to get data from a particular subset of the whole index? For example, to get the data from a shard where routing A was used, we can run the following query:

```
curl -XGET 'localhost:9200/documents/_search?pretty&q=*&routing=A'
```

We just added a routing parameter with the value we are interested in. Elasticsearch replied with the following result:

```
{
  "took" : 2,
  "timed_out" : false,
  "_shards" : {
    "total" : 1,
    "successful" : 1,
    "failed" : 0
  },
  "hits" : {
    "total" : 3,
    "max_score" : 1.0,
    "hits" : [
      {
```

```
          "_index" : "documents",
          "_type" : "doc",
          "_id" : "1",
          "_score" : 1.0,
          "_routing" : "A",
          "_source" : {
            "title" : "Document No. 1"
          }
        },
        {
          "_index" : "documents",
          "_type" : "doc",
          "_id" : "3",
          "_score" : 1.0,
          "_routing" : "A",
          "_source" : {
            "title" : "Document No. 3"
          }
        },
        {
          "_index" : "documents",
          "_type" : "doc",
          "_id" : "4",
          "_score" : 1.0,
          "_routing" : "A",
          "_source" : {
            "title" : "Document No. 4"
          }
        }
      ]
    }
  }
```

The preceding query can also be written as follows:

```
    curl -XPOST
"http://localhost:9200/documents/doc/_search?routing=A&pretty" -d'
    {
      "query": {
        "match_all": {}
      }
    }'
```

Everything works like a charm. But look closer! We forgot to start the node that holds the shard with the documents that were indexed with the routing value of B. Even though we didn't have a full index view, the reply from Elasticsearch doesn't contain information about shard failures. This is proof that queries with routing hit only a chosen shard and ignore the rest. If we run the same query with routing=B, we will get an exception like the following one:

```
{
  "error" : {
    "root_cause" : [ ],
    "type" : "search_phase_execution_exception",
    "reason" : "all shards failed",
    "phase" : "query_fetch",
    "grouped" : true,
    "failed_shards" : [ ],
    "caused_by" : {
      "type" : "no_shard_available_action_exception",
      "reason" : null,
      "index_uuid" : "ZE_gLDCzRAqyF1om7kf6sw",
      "shard" : "1",
      "index" : "documents"
    }
  },
  "status" : 503
}
```

We can test the preceding behavior by using the search shard API. For example, let's run the following command:

```
curl -XGET 'localhost:9200/documents/_search_shards?pretty&routing=A' -
d '{"query":"match_all":{}}'
```

The response from Elasticsearch would be as follows:

```
{
  "nodes" : {
    "y7lLdircSQSQLSsidfN4sg" : {
      "name" : "y7lLdir",
      "ephemeral_id" : "bsKrLgPjRLmcnck-qqRNtQ",
      "transport_address" : "11.0.2.16:9300",
      "attributes" : { }
    }
  },
  "shards" : [
    [
      {
        "state" : "STARTED",
```

```
        "primary" : true,
        "node" : "y7lLdircSQSQLSsidfN4sg",
        "relocating_node" : null,
        "shard" : 0,
        "index" : "documents",
        "allocation_id" : {
          "id" : "_KkddmPhTVuHwEaCpPnRIg"
        }
      }
    ]
  ]
}
```

As we can see, only a single node will be queried.

There is one important thing that we would like to repeat. Routing ensures us that, during indexing, documents with the same routing value are indexed in the same shard. However, you need to remember that a given shard may have many documents with different routing values. Routing allows you to limit the number of shards used during queries, but it cannot replace filtering! This means that a query with routing and without routing should have the same set of filters. For example, if we use user identifiers as routing values and we search for that user's data, we should also include filters on that identifier.

Aliases

If you work as a search engine specialist, you probably want to hide some configuration details from programmers in order to allow them to work faster and not care about search details. In an ideal world, they should not worry about routing, shards, and replicas. Aliases allow us to use shards with routing as ordinary indices. For example, let's create an alias by running the following command:

```
curl -XPOST 'http://localhost:9200/_aliases' -d '{
"actions" : [
{
"add" : {
"index" : "documents",
"alias" : "documentsA",
"routing" : "A"
}
}
]
}'
```

In the preceding example, we created a named `documentsA` alias from the `documents` index. However, in addition to that, searching will be limited to the shard used when routing value `A` is used. Thanks to this approach, you can give information about the `documentsA` alias to developers, and they may use it for querying and indexing like any other index.

Multiple routing values

Elasticsearch gives us the possibility to search with several routing values in a single query. Depending on which shard documents with given routing values are placed, it could mean searching on one or more shards. Let's look at the following query:

```
curl -XGET 'localhost:9200/documents/_search?routing=A,B'
```

After executing it, Elasticsearch will send the search request to two shards in our index (which in our case, happens to be the whole index), because the routing value of `A` covers one of two shards of our index and the routing value of `B` covers the second shard of our index.

Of course, multiple routing values are supported in aliases as well. The following example shows you the usage of these features:

```
curl -XPOST 'http://localhost:9200/_aliases' -d '{
"actions" : [
{
  "add" : {
  "index" : "documents",
  "alias" : "documentsA",
  "search_routing" : "A,B",
  "index_routing" : "A"
  }
}
]
}'
```

The preceding example shows you two additional configuration parameters we didn't talk about until now—we can define different values of routing for searching and indexing. In the preceding case, we've defined that during querying (the `search_routing` parameter) two values of routing (`A` and `B`) will be applied. When indexing (`index_routing` parameter), only one value (`A`) will be used.

Note that indexing doesn't support multiple routing values, and you should also remember proper filtering (you can add it to your alias).

Shard allocation control

One of the primary roles of the master node in an Elasticsearch cluster is allocation of shards on nodes and moving shards from one node to another for balancing the cluster state. In this section, we will see the available settings to control this allocation process.

Allocation awareness

Allocation awareness allows us to configure shards and their replicas' allocation with the use of generic parameters. This comes very handy in cases where you are running the cluster on multiple VMs on the same physical server, on multiple racks, or across multiple availability zones. In these scenarios, if more than one node on the same physical server, same rack, or same availability zone goes down, there would be a huge problem. Shard allocation awareness helps in ensuring the high availability by tagging instances, so that primaries and replicas are spread across different zones/racks.

In order to illustrate how allocation awareness works, we assume that we have a cluster built of four nodes that looks as follows:

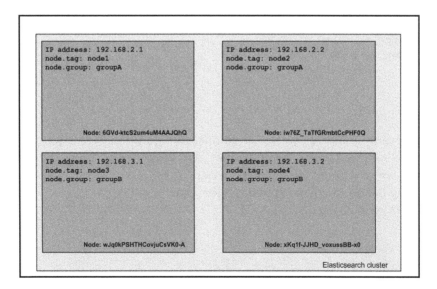

As you can see, our cluster is built of four nodes. Each node was bound to a specific IP address, and each node was given the `tag` property and a `group` property (added to `elasticsearch.yml` as `node.attr.tag` and `node.attr.group` properties). This cluster will also serve the purpose of showing you how shard allocation filtering works.

> The `node.attr` can take whatever property name you want to configure. Similar to what we have used as `node.attr.group`, you can use `node.attr.rack_id`, `node.attr.tag` or even `node.attr.party`. Also, you are free to declare multiple attributes in the same configuration file like we have shown in the previous example.

Now on all of the nodes, add the following property to the `elasticsearch.yml` file:

```
cluster.routing.allocation.awareness.attributes: group
```

This will tell Elasticsearch to use the `node.group` property as the awareness parameter.

> One can specify multiple attributes when setting the `cluster.routing.allocation.awareness.attributes` property, for example: `cluster.routing.allocation.awareness.attributes: group,node`

After this, let's start the node with the `node.group` parameter equal to `groupA`, and let's create an index by running the following command:

```
curl -XPOST 'localhost:9200/mastering' -d '{
"settings" : {
  "index" : {
    "number_of_shards" : 2,
    "number_of_replicas" : 1
  }
 }
}'
```

After this command, our two nodes' cluster will look like this:

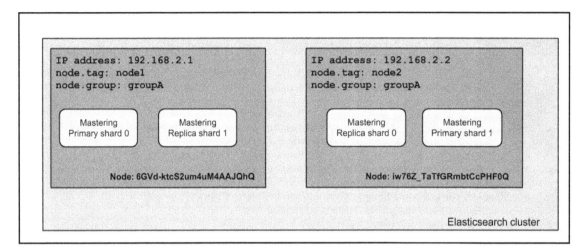

As you can see, the index was divided evenly between two nodes. Now let's see what happens when we launch the rest of the nodes (the ones with `node.attr.group` set to `groupB`):

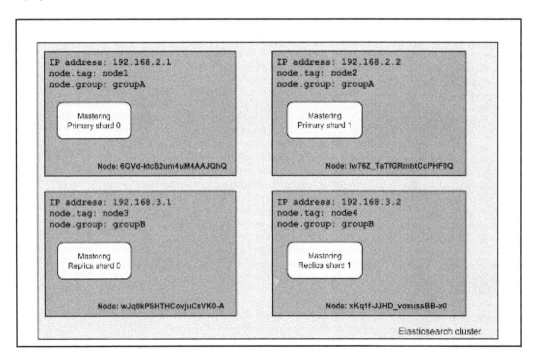

Notice the difference; the primary shards were not moved from their original allocation nodes, but the replica shards were moved to the nodes with a different `node.attr.group` value. That's exactly right—when using shard allocation awareness, Elasticsearch won't allocate shards and replicas to the nodes with the same value of the property used to determine the allocation awareness (which, in our case, is `node.attr.group`). One of the example usages of this functionality is to divide the cluster topology between virtual machines or physical locations in order to be sure that you don't have a single point of failure.

 Please remember that when using allocation awareness, shards will not be allocated to the node that doesn't have the expected attributes set. So, in our example, a node without the `node.attr.group` property set will not be taken into consideration by the allocation mechanism.

Forcing allocation awareness

Forcing allocation awareness can come in handy when we know, in advance, how many values our awareness attributes can take, and we don't want more replicas than needed to be allocated in our cluster, for example, not to overload our cluster with too many replicas. To do this, we can force allocation awareness to be active only for certain attributes. We can specify these values using the `cluster.routing.allocation.awareness.force.zone.values` property and providing a list of comma-separated values to it. For example, if we would like allocation awareness to only use the groupA and groupB values of the `node.attr.group` property, we would add the following to the `elasticsearch.yml` file:

```
cluster.routing.allocation.awareness.attributes: group
cluster.routing.allocation.awareness.force.zone.values: groupA, groupB
```

Shard allocation filtering

Elasticsearch allows us to configure the allocation for the whole cluster or for the index level. In the case of cluster allocation, we can use the properties prefixes:

```
cluster.routing.allocation.include
cluster.routing.allocation.require
cluster.routing.allocation.exclude
```

When it comes to index-specific allocation, we can use the following properties prefixes:

```
index.routing.allocation.include
index.routing.allocation.require
index.routing.allocation.exclude
```

The previously mentioned prefixes can be used with the properties that we've defined in the `elasticsearch.yml` file (our `tag` and `group` properties) and in addition there are three special properties called `_ip`, `_name` and `_host`.

The `_ip` allows us to match or exclude IPs using nodes' IP addresses, for example, like this:

```
cluster.routing.allocation.include._ip: 192.168.2.1
```

The `_name` allows us to match nodes by their names, for example:

```
cluster.routing.allocation.include._name: node-1
```

The `_host` allows us to match nodes by their hostnames, like this:

```
cluster.routing.allocation.include._host: es-host-1
```

What include, exclude, and require mean

If you look closely at the parameters mentioned previously, you will notice that there are three kinds:

- `include`: This type will result in the inclusion of all the nodes with this parameter defined. If multiple include conditions are visible, then all the nodes that match at least one of these conditions will be taken into consideration when allocating shards. For example, if we add two `cluster.routing.allocation.include.tag` parameters to our configuration, one with a property to the value of `node1` and the second with the `node2` value, we would end up with indices (actually, their shards) being allocated to the first and second node (counting from left to right). To sum up, the nodes that have the include allocation parameter type will be taken into consideration by Elasticsearch when choosing the nodes to place shards on, but that doesn't mean that Elasticsearch will put shards on them.

- `require`: This was introduced in the Elasticsearch 0.90 type of allocation filter, and it requires all the nodes to have the value that matches the value of this property. For example, if we add one `cluster.routing.allocation.require.tag` parameter to our configuration with the value of `node1` and a `cluster.routing.allocation.require.group` parameter, the value of `groupA` would end up with shards allocated only to the first node (the one with the IP address of `192.168.2.1`).

- `exclude`: This allows us to exclude nodes with given properties from the allocation process. For example, if we set `cluster.routing.allocation.include.tag` to `groupA`, we would end up with indices being allocated only to nodes with IP addresses `192.168.3.1` and `192.168.3.2` (the third and fourth node in our example).

> Property values can use simple wildcard characters. For example, if we would like to include all the nodes that have the `group` parameter value beginning with `group`, we could set the `cluster.routing.allocation.include.group` property to `group*`. In the example cluster case, it would result in matching nodes with the `groupA` and `groupBgroup` parameter values.

Runtime allocation updating

In addition to setting all discussed properties in the `elasticsearch.yml` file, we can also use the update API to update these settings in real-time when the cluster is already running.

Index level updates

In order to update settings for a given index (for example, our `mastering` index), we could run the following command:

```
curl -XPUT 'localhost:9200/mastering/_settings' -d '{
  "index.routing.allocation.require.group": "groupA"
}'
```

As you can see, the command was sent to the `_settings` endpoint for a given index. You can include multiple properties in a single call.

Cluster level updates

In order to update settings for the whole cluster, we could run the following command:

```
curl -XPUT 'localhost:9200/_cluster/settings' -d '{
"transient" : {
 "cluster.routing.allocation.require.group": "groupA"
}
}'
```

As you can see, the command was sent to the `cluster/_settings` end-point. You can include multiple properties in a single call. Please remember that the `transient` name in the preceding command means that the property will be forgotten after the cluster restart. If you want to avoid this and set this property as a permanent one, use `persistent` instead of the `transient` one. An example command, which will keep the settings between restarts, could look like this:

```
curl -XPUT 'localhost:9200/_cluster/settings' -d '{
"persistent" : {
 "cluster.routing.allocation.require.group": "groupA"
}
}'
```

 Please note that running the preceding commands, depending on the command and where your indices are located, can result in shards being moved between nodes.

Defining total shards allowed per node

In addition to the previously mentioned properties, we are also allowed to define how many shards (primaries and replicas) for an index can by allocated per node. In order to do that, one should set the `index.routing.allocation.total_shards_per_node` dynamic property to a desired value:

```
curl -XPUT 'localhost:9200/mastering/_settings' -d '{
"index.routing.allocation.total_shards_per_node": "4"
}'
```

This would result in a maximum of four shards per index being allocated to a single node.

From Elasticsearch 5.0 onward, you cannot set the `index.routing.allocation.total_shards_per_node` property inside `elasticsearch.yml`. If you try to do so, you will get the following error inside your Elasticsearch node's log file

```
Found index level settings on node level configuration.
```

Since Elasticsearch 5.x index level settings cannot be set on the node's configuration like the `elasticsearch.yml`, in system properties or command line arguments, in order to upgrade all indices, the settings must be updated via the `/${index}/_settings` API. Unless all settings are dynamic, all indices must be closed. In order to apply the upgrade, indices created in the future should use index templates to set default values.

Please ensure all required values are updated on all indices by executing:

```
    curl -XPUT
'http://localhost:9200/_all/_settings?preserve_existing=true' -d '{
        "index.routing.allocation.total_shards_per_node" : "1"
    }'
```

Defining total shards allowed per physical server

One of the properties that can be useful when having multiple nodes on a single physical server is `cluster.routing.allocation.same_shard.host`. It defaults to `false` but when set to `true`, it prevents Elasticsearch from placing a primary shard and its replica (or replicas) on the same physical host by checking the host name and host address. We really advise that you set this property to `true` if you have very powerful servers and that you go for multiple Elasticsearch nodes per physical server.

Inclusion

Now, let's use our example cluster to see how the allocation inclusion works. Let's start by deleting and recreating the `mastering` index by using the following commands:

```
    curl -XDELETE 'localhost:9200/mastering'
    curl -XPUT 'localhost:9200/mastering' -d '{
  "settings" : {
  "index" : {
   "number_of_shards" : 2,
   "number_of_replicas" : 0
```

```
        }
      }
    }'
```

After this, let's try to run the following command:

```
curl -XPUT 'localhost:9200/mastering/_settings' -d '{
"index.routing.allocation.include.tag": "node1",
"index.routing.allocation.include.group": "groupA",
"index.routing.allocation.total_shards_per_node": 1
}'
```

If we visualize the response of the index status, we would see that the cluster looks like the one in the following image:

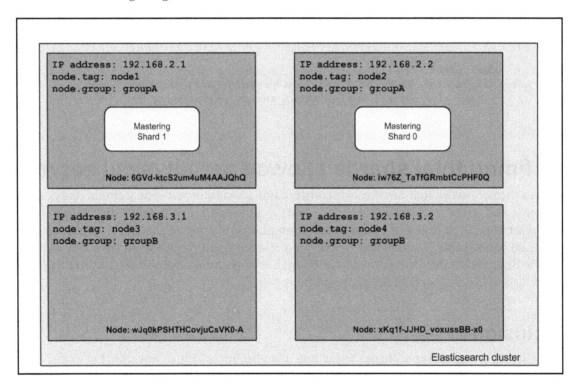

As you can see, the `mastering` index shards are allocated to nodes with the `tag` property set to `node1` or the `group` property set to `groupA`.

Requirement

Now, let's reuse our example cluster and try running the following command:

```
curl -XPUT 'localhost:9200/mastering/_settings' -d '{
"index.routing.allocation.require.tag": "node1",
"index.routing.allocation.require.group": "groupA"
}'
```

If we visualize the response of the index status command, we would see that the cluster looks like this:

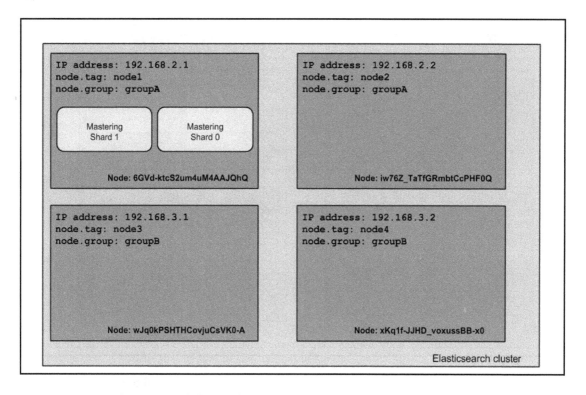

As you can see, the view is different from the one when using `include`. This is because we tell Elasticsearch to allocate shards of the `mastering` index only to the nodes that match both the `require` parameters, and in our case, the only node that matches both is the first node.

Exclusion

Let's now look at exclusions. To test it, we try to run the following command:

```
curl -XPUT 'localhost:9200/mastering/_settings' -d '{
"index.routing.allocation.exclude.tag": "node1",
"index.routing.allocation.require.group": "groupA"
}'
```

Again, let's look at our cluster now:

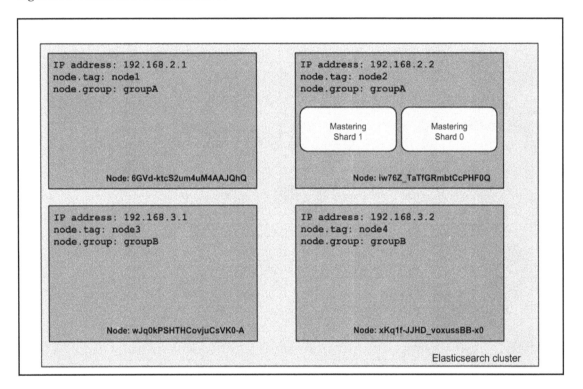

As you can see, we said that we require the `group` property to be equal to `groupA`, and we want to exclude the node with a `tag` equal to `node1`. This resulted in the shard of the `mastering` index being allocated to the node with the `192.168.2.2` IP address, which is what we wanted.

Disk-based allocation

Of course, the mentioned properties are not the only ones that can be used. With the release of Elasticsearch 1.3.0, we gained the ability to configure awareness on the basis of the disk usage. By default, disk-based allocation is turned on, and if we want, we can turn it off by setting the `cluster.routing.allocation.disk.threshold_enabled` property to `false`.

There are three additional properties that can help us configure disk-based allocation. The `cluster.routing.allocation.disk.watermark.low` cluster controls when Elasticsearch does not allow you to allocate new shards on the node. By default, it is set to 85 percent and it means that when the disk usage is equal or higher than 85 percent, no new shards will be allocated on that node. The second property is `cluster.routing.allocation.disk.watermark.high`, which controls when Elasticsearch will try to move the shards out of the node and is set to `90` percent by default. This means that Elasticsearch will try to move the shard out of the node if the disk usage is `90` percent or higher. Both `cluster.routing.allocation.disk.watermark.low` and `cluster.routing.allocation.disk.watermark.high` can be set to absolute values, for example, 10,240 MB or 10 GB.

Elasticsearch checks the disk usage on each node every `30s` by default. This interval can be updated using the `cluster.info.update.interval` parameter.

Let's see an example of how you can dynamically update these settings in a running cluster:

```
        curl -XPUT "http://localhost:9200/_cluster/settings" -d'
{
    "transient": {
        "cluster.routing.allocation.disk.watermark.low": "90%",
        "cluster.routing.allocation.disk.watermark.high": "10gb",
        "cluster.info.update.interval": "1m"
    }
}'
```

Please note that prior to version 2.0.0, when using multiple data paths, the disk threshold decider only factored in the usage across all data paths (if you had two data paths, one with 50GB out of 100GB free (50 percent used) and another with 40GB out of 50GB free (80 percent used) it would see the node's disk usage as 90GB out of 150GB). From 2.0.0 onward, the minimum and maximum disk usages are tracked separately. So it's a better practice to set the watermarks in percentage.

Query execution preference

Let's forget about the shard placement and how to configure it—at least for a moment. In addition to all the fancy stuff that Elasticsearch allows us to set for shards and replicas, we also have the possibility to specify where our queries (and other operations, for example, the real-time GET) should be executed.

Introducing the preference parameter

In order to control where the query (and other operations) we are sending will be executed, we can use the `preference` parameter, which can be set to one of the following values:

- `_primary`: Using this property, the operations we are sending will only be executed on primary shards. So, if we send a query against the `mastering` index with the preference parameter set to the _primary value, we would have it executed on the nodes with the names `node1` and `node2`. For example, if you know that your primary shards are in one rack and the replicas are in other racks, you may want to execute the operation on primary shards to avoid network traffic.

- `_primary_first`: This option is similar to the _primary value's behavior but with a failover mechanism. If we ran a query against the `mastering` index with the preference parameter set to the _primary_first value, we would have it executed on the nodes with the names `node1` and `node2`; however, if one (or more) of the primary shards fail, the query will be executed against the other shard, which in our case is allocated to a node named `node3`. As we said, this is very similar to the _primary value but with additional fallback to replicas if the primary shard is not available for some reason.

- `_replica`: When this value is used, queries are used only against replicas and not primary shards.

- `_replica_first`: This option behaves exactly like the `_primary_first` value. When we use `replica_first`, queries go first to replica shards and if the replica shard is not available then as a failover, operations are executed against the primary shards.
- `_local`: Elasticsearch will prefer to execute the operation on a local node, if possible. For example, if we send a query to `node3` with the preference parameter set to `_local`, we would end up having that query executed on that node. However, if we send the same query to `node2`, we would end up with one query executed against the primary shard numbered 1 (which is located on that node) and the second part of the query will be executed against `node1` or `node3` where the shard numbered 0 resides. This is especially useful while trying to minimize the network latency; while using the `_local` preference, we ensure that our queries are executed locally whenever possible (for example, when running a client connection from a local node or sending a query to a node).
- `_prefer_nodes:Tg5Q7AX`: This option sets the `preference` parameter to `_prefer nodes`: The value followed by a node identifier (which is `Tg5Q7AX` in our case) will result in Elasticsearch preferring the mentioned node while executing the query, but if some shards are not available on the preferred node, Elasticsearch will send the appropriate query parts to nodes where the shards are available. The `_prefer_node` can be used while choosing a particular node, with a fallback to other nodes.
- `_shards:0,1`: This is the preference value that allows us to identify which shards the operation should be executed against (in our case, it will be all the shards, because we only have shards 0 and 1 in the `mastering` index). This is the only preference parameter value that can be combined with the other mentioned values. For example, in order to locally execute our query against the 0 and 1 shard, we should concatenate the 0,1 value with `_local` using the ; character, so the final value of the `preference` parameter should look like this: 0,1;_local. Allowing us to execute the operation against a single shard can be useful for diagnostic purposes.

- `custom, string value`: Setting the `_preference` parameter to a custom value will guarantee that the query with the same custom value will be executed against the same shards. For example, if we send a query with the `_preference` parameter set to the `mastering_elasticsearch` value, we would end up having the query executed against primary shards located on nodes named `node1` and `node2`. If we send another query with the same `preference` parameter value, then the second query will again be executed against the shards located on nodes named `node1` and `node2`. This functionality can help us in cases where we have different refresh rates and we don't want our users to see different results while repeating requests. There is one more thing missing, which is the default behavior. What Elasticsearch will do by default is that it will randomize the operation between shards and replicas. If we sent many queries, we would end up having the same (or almost the same) number of queries run against each of the shards and replicas.

An example of using query execution preference

The following query shows you an example of how to use the `preference` parameter with search requests:

```
curl -XGET
"http://localhost:9200/documents/_search?preference=_primary&pretty" -d'
    {
        "query": {
            "match_all": {}
        }
    }'
```

Note that, if you pass a wrong `preference` value, Elasticsearch ignores that without throwing an error and executes the default search `preference`.

Stripping data on multiple paths

The support for stripping data on more than one path has been available for a very long time now. But since version 2.0.0, it is no longer supported. Instead of data stripping on multiple paths, Elasticsearch now allows you to allocate different shards on different paths. The reason for removing data stripping was that a file from a single segment in a shard could be spread across multiple disks and failure of a single disk could corrupt multiple shards/indices.

The data path is configured inside the `elasticsearch.yml` file using the `path.data` parameter and similar to version 1.x, you can still use multiple data paths using comma separated values shown as follows:

```
path.data: /data_path1/,/data_path2/
```

In this way, all the files belonging to a single shard will be stored at the same path. The other important change based on disk allocation we have already discussed in this chapter, in the *Disk-based allocation* section, where we mentioned how Elasticsearch now checks for free disk space on individual data paths.

Index versus type – a revised approach for creating indices

In the beginning of this chapter, we talked about strategies for choosing the right amount of shards and replicas for indices in *Choosing the right amount of shards and replicas*. Now, we will bring another factor; **document types** which can be taken into account while creating indices with a greater or fewer number of shards.

Creating too many indices or creating too many shards is always very resource demanding, since in the end every index or shard is internally a Lucene index, which has particular overhead of memory usage, file descriptors, and other resources needed. With a larger number of shards or indices, the other overhead comes at the time of search. More shards means search is executed on more shards and Elasticsearch has to combine the response returned from all the shards and merge them before sending the response back to the client. This becomes an expensive process both in terms of aggregations and normal search requests.

Document types comes to the rescue in this scenario as they are used to classify different categories of documents inside index with the help of a special `_type` field. The cost of searching across different types, even with more than one index, is not an overhead.

In the beginning of Elasticsearch, engineers tried to keep things simple as they built an analogy similar to relational databases and considered an index as a database and a type as a table. But this was not completely correct because of how documents are indexed inside Lucene segments under the hood and there are some limitations with using multiple types inside the same index. If you want to learn about these limitations and in which scenarios you can go for multiple document types, you can read this blog, `https://www.elastic.co/blog/index-vs-type` written by *Adrien Grand*.

 While creating multiple document types you must know two things, First, the same field name cannot have a different data type across multiple types and Second, you cannot delete a type from the index. The only solution is to create a new index and reindex the data.

Summary

In this chapter, we started with creating a multi-node cluster and then focused on index distribution architecture in Elasticsearch including choosing the right number of shards and replicas along with a detailed discussion on how routing works, how shard allocation works, and how to alter the default shard allocation behavior. In addition to that, we also discussed what query execution preference is and how it allows us to choose where the queries are going to be executed. We finally covered two important considerations to keep in mind that is, splitting data on multiple paths and creating multiple document types inside an Elasticsearch index.

In the next chapter, we will cover some granular details of Apache Lucene scoring and how one can alter them and can choose the right scoring algorithm. We will also cover NRT searching and indexing, the transaction logs, and then will talk about segment merging and removed merge policies inside Elasticsearch 5.0. At the end of the chapter, you will also find information about I/O throttling and Elasticsearch caching.

7
Low-Level Index Control

In the last chapter, we learned about creating a multi-node cluster and then went through index distribution architecture in Elasticsearch, including choosing the right number of shards and replicas along with a detailed discussion on how routing works, how shard allocation works, and how to alter the default shard allocation behavior. In addition to that, we also discussed what query execution preference is and how to configure it. We also saw how data stripping works and considerations for creating multiple document types inside an Elasticsearch index.

In this chapter, we will cover some granular details of **Apache Lucene** scoring and how you can alter them and can choose the right scoring algorithm. We will also cover **Near Real Time (NRT)** searching and indexing and the transaction logs. You will also get to know about segment merging and removed merge policies inside Elasticsearch 5.0. At the end of the chapter, you will also find information about IO throttling and Elasticsearch caching. By the end of this chapter, we will have covered following topics:

- Altering Apache Lucene scoring by using different similarity models
- Choosing the right directory implementation – the store module
- Near real-time indexing and querying
- Data flushing, index refresh, and transaction log handling
- Segment merge control and merge policy changes
- Elasticsearch caching

Altering Apache Lucene scoring

In `Chapter 2`, *The Improved Query DSL*, we discussed the changes in default scoring inside Elasticsearch as well as Apache Lucene. We also covered the new default text scoring algorithm, BM25, in detail. But apart from BM25 and TF-IDF, there are some additional similarity models available in Lucene since the release of Apache Lucene 4.0 in 2012, which basically allows you to alter the default algorithm and also to choose a different scoring formula for our documents. In this section, we will take a deeper look at these similarity scoring algorithms offered by Lucene and how these features were incorporated into Elasticsearch.

Available similarity models

As already mentioned, the original and default similarity model available before Apache Lucene 6.0 was the TF-IDF model but in Lucene 6.0 it is changed to BM25, which we have already discussed in detail in *The changed default text scoring in Lucene: BM25* section in `Chapter 2`, *The Improved Query DSL*.

Apart from BM25, other similarity models that we can use are:

- **TF-IDF** (classic): This similarity model is based on TF-IDF model and used to be the default similarity model before Elasticsearch 5.0. In order to use this similarity in Elasticsearch, you need to use the `classic` name.
- **Divergence from randomness** (**DFR**): This similarity model is based on the probabilistic model of the same name. In order to use this similarity in Elasticsearch, you need to use the `DFR` name. It is said that the divergence from the randomness similarity model performs well on text similar to natural language text.

- **Divergence from independence** (DFI): This similarity model is based on the probabilistic model of the same name. In order to use this similarity in Elasticsearch, you need to use the `DFI` name. You can read more about this model here: `http://trec.nist.gov/pubs/trec21/papers/irra.web.nb.pdf`.

- **Information-based**: This is very similar to the model used by DFR. In order to use this similarity in Elasticsearch, you need to use the `IB` name. Similar to the DFR similarity, it is said that the information-based model performs well on data similar to natural language text.

- **LM Dirichlet**: This similarity model uses Bayesian smoothing with Dirichlet priors. To use this similarity, we need to use the `LM Dirichlet` name. More information about it can be found at `https://lucene.apache.org/core/6_2_0/core/org/apache/lucene/search/sim ilarities/LMDirichletSimilarity.html`.

- **LM Jelinek Mercer**: This similarity model is based on the Jelinek Mercer smoothing method. To use this similarity, we need to use the `LMJelinekMercer` name. More information about it can be found at `https://lucene.apache.org/core/6_2_0/core/org/apache/lucene/search/sim ilarities/LMJelinekMercerSimilarity.html`.

Setting a per-field similarity

Since Elasticsearch 0.90, we are allowed to set a different similarity for each of the fields we have in our mappings. For example, let's assume that we have the following simple mappings that we use in order to index blog posts (stored in the `posts_no_similarity.json` file):

```
{
  "mappings" : {
    "post" : {
      "properties" : {
        "id" : { "type" : "long", "store" : "yes" },
        "name" : { "type" : "text", "store" : "yes", "index" :
          "analyzed" },
        "contents" : { "type" : "text", "store" : "no", "index" :
        "analyzed" }
      }
    }
  }
}
```

What we would like to do is use the classic similarity model for the `name` field and the `contents` field. In order to do this, we need to extend our field definitions and add the `similarity` property with the value of the chosen similarity name. Our changed mappings (stored in the `posts_similarity.json` file) would look as follows:

```
{
    "mappings" : {
        "post" : {
            "properties" : {
                "id" : { "type" : "long", "store" : "yes" },
                "name" : { "type" : "text", "store" : "yes", "index" :
                    "analyzed", "similarity" : "classic" },
                "contents" : { "type" : "text", "store" : "no", "index" :
                    "analyzed", "similarity" : "classic" }
            }
        }
    }
}
```

That's all; nothing more is needed. After the preceding change, Apache Lucene will use the classic similarity to calculate the score factor for the `name` and `contents` fields.

In the case of the divergence from randomness, divergence from independence and information-based similarities, we need to configure some additional properties to specify these similarities' behavior. How to do that is covered in the next part of the current section.

Similarity model configuration

As we now know how to set the desired similarity for each field in our index, it's time to see how to configure them if we need them, which is actually pretty easy. What we need to do is use the index settings section to provide an additional similarity section. An example is as follows (this example is stored in the `posts_custom_similarity.json` file):

```
{
    "settings" : {
        "index" : {
            "similarity" : {
                "mastering_similarity" : {
                    "type" : "classic",
                    "discount_overlaps" : false
                }
            }
        }
    }
}
```

```
    },
    "mappings" : {
     "post" : {
      "properties" : {
       "id" : { "type" : "long", "store" : "yes" },
       "name" : { "type" : "text", "store" : "yes", "index" :
  "analyzed", "similarity" : "mastering_similarity" },
        "contents" : { "type" : "text", "store" : "no", "index" :
  "analyzed" }
       }
      }
     }
    }
```

You can, of course, have more than one similarity configuration, but let's focus on the preceding example. We've defined a new similarity model named `mastering_similarity`, which is based on the classic similarity, which is the TF-IDF one. We've set the `discount_overlaps` property to `false` for this similarity, and we've used it as the similarity for the `name` field. We'll talk about what properties can be used for different similarities further in this section. Now, let's see how to change the default similarity model Elasticsearch will use.

Choosing the default similarity model

In order to change the similarity model used by default, we need to provide a configuration of a similarity model that will be called by default. For example, if we would like to use our `mastering_similarity` name as the default one, we would have to change the preceding configuration to the following one (the whole example is stored in the `posts_default_similarity.json` file):

```
 {
   "settings" : {
   "index" : {
     "similarity" : {
       "default" : {
         "type" : "classic",
         "discount_overlaps" : false
       }
     }
   }
   },
   ...
 }
```

Because of the fact that the query norm and coordination factors (which were explained in *The changed default text scoring in Lucene* section, in `Chapter 2`, *The Improved Query DSL*) are used by all similarity models globally and are taken from the default similarity, Elasticsearch allows us to change them when needed. To do this, we need to define another similarity – one called base. It is defined exactly the same as what we've shown previously, but instead of setting its name to `default`, we set it to `base`, just like as follows (the whole example is stored in the `posts_base_similarity.json` file):

```
{
  "settings" : {
    "index" : {
      "similarity" : {
        "base" : {
          "type" : "classic",
          "discount_overlaps" : false
        }
      }
    }
  },
  ...
}
```

If the base similarity is present in the index configuration, Elasticsearch will use it to calculate the query norm and coordination factors when calculating the score using other similarity models.

Configuring the chosen similarity model

Each of the newly introduced similarity models can be configured to match our needs. Elasticsearch allows us to use the default and classic similarities without any configuration, because they are preconfigured for us. In the case of DFR, DFI, and IB, we need to provide the configuration in order to use them. Now let's see what properties each of the similarity models' implementation provides.

Configuring the TF-IDF similarity

In the case of the TF-IDF similarity, we are allowed to set only a single parameter–`discount_overlaps`, which defaults to `true`. By default, the tokens that have their position increment set to `0` (and therefore, are placed at the same position as the one before them) will not be taken into consideration when calculating the score. If we want them to be taken into consideration, we need to configure the similarity with the `discount_overlaps` property set to `false`.

Configuring the BM25 similarity

In the case of the Okapi BM25 similarity, we have these parameters: we can configure `k1` (controls the saturation–nonlinear term frequency normalization) as a float value, `b` (controls how the document length affects the term frequency values) as a float value, and `discount_overlaps`, which is exactly the same as in TF-IDF similarity.

Configuring the DFR similarity

In the case of the DFR similarity, we have these parameters that we can configure: `basic_model` (which can take the value `be`, `d`, `g`, `if`, `in`, `ine`, or `p`), `after_effect` (with values of `no`, `b`, and `1`), and `normalization` (which can be `no`, `h1`, `h2`, `h3`, or `z`). If we choose a normalization other than `no`, we need to set the normalization factor. Depending on the chosen normalization, we should use `normalization.h1.c` (the float value) for the `h1` normalization, `normalization.h2.c` (the float value) for the `h2` normalization, `normalization.h3.c` (the float value) for the `h3` normalization, and `normalization.z.z` (the float value) for the `z` normalization. For example, this is what the example similarity configuration could look like:

```
"similarity" : {
  "esserverbook_dfr_similarity" : {
    "type" : "DFR",
    "basic_model" : "g",
    "after_effect" : "l",
    "normalization" : "h2",
    "normalization.h2.c" : "2.0"
  }
}
```

Configuring the IB similarity

In the case of the IB similarity, we have these parameters that we can configure: the `distribution` property (which can take the value of `ll` or `spl`) and the `lambda` property (which can take the value of `df` or `tff`). In addition to this, we can choose the normalization factor, which is the same as the one used for the DFR similarity, so we'll omit describing it for the second time. This is what the example IB similarity configuration could look like:

```
"similarity" : {
  "esserverbook_ib_similarity" : {
    "type" : "IB",
    "distribution" : "ll",
    "lambda" : "df",
```

```
      "normalization" : "z",
      "normalization.z.z" : "0.25"
    }
  }
```

Configuring the LM Dirichlet similarity

In the case of the LM Dirichlet similarity, we have the mu property that we can configure, which is by default set to 2000. An example configuration of this could look as follows:

```
"similarity" : {
  "esserverbook_lm_dirichlet_similarity" : {
    "type" : "LMDirichlet",
    "mu" : "1000"
  }
}
```

Configuring the LM Jelinek Mercer similarity

When it comes to the LM Jelinek Mercer similarity, we can configure the lambda property, which is set to 0.1 by default. An example configuration of this could look as follows:

```
"similarity" : {
  "esserverbook_lm_jelinek_mercer_similarity" : {
    "type" : "LMJelinekMercer",
    "lambda" : "0.7"
  }
}
```

 It is said that for short fields (such as the document title) the optimal lambda value is around 0.1, while for long fields the lambda value should be set to 0.7.

Choosing the right directory implementation – the store module

The store module is one of the modules that we usually don't pay much attention to when configuring our cluster; however, it is very important. It is an abstraction between the I/O subsystem and Apache Lucene itself. All the operations that Lucene do with the hard disk drive are done using the store module. Most of the store types in Elasticsearch are mapped to an appropriate Apache Lucene directory class (http://lucene.apache.org/core/6_2_0/core/org/apache/lucene/store/Directory.htm l). The directory is used to access all the files the index is built of, so it is crucial to properly configure it.

The store type

Elasticsearch exposes five store types that we can use. By default, Elasticsearch picks the best implementation based on the operating system environment. But you can override the default behavior in following ways:

- The first way, is to set for all the indices, by adding the `index.store.type` property inside the `elasticsearch.yml` file. For example, if you want to set the `niofs` store type to all the indices you can add following line inside `elasticsearch.yml` file:

```
index.store.type: niofs
```

- The second way is to set per index at the index creation time in the following way:

```
curl -XPUT "http://localhost:9200/index_name" -d' {
  "settings": {
  "index.store.type": "niofs"
  }
}'
```

Let's see what these store types provide and how we can leverage their features.

The simple file system store – simplefs

The simplest implementation of the `Directory` class that is available is implemented using a random access file (Java `RandomAccessFile`—http://docs.oracle.com/javase/8/docs/api/java/io/RandomAccessFile.html) which maps to `SimpleFSDirectory` (http://lucene.apache.org/core/6_2_0/core/org/apache/lucene/store/SimpleFSDirectory.html) in Apache Lucene. It is sufficient for very simple applications. However, the main bottleneck will be multithreaded access, which has poor performance. In the case of Elasticsearch, it is usually better to use the new I/O based system store instead of the simple filesystem store. However, if you would like to use this system store, you should set `index.store.type` to `simplefs`.

The new I/O filesystem store – niofs

This store type uses the `Directory` class implementation based on the `FileChannel` class (http://docs.oracle.com/javase/8/docs/api/java/nio/channels/FileChannel.html) from the `java.nio package` and maps to `NIOFSDirectory` in Apache Lucene (https://lucene.apache.org/core/6_2_0/core/org/apache/lucene/store/NIOFSDirectory.html). The discussed implementation allows multiple threads to access the same files concurrently without performance degradation. In order to use this store, one should set `index.store.type` to `niofs`.

The mmap filesystem store – mmapfs

This store type uses Apache Lucene's `MMapDirectory` (http://lucene.apache.org/core/6_2_0/core/org/apache/lucene/store/MMapDirectory.html) implementation. It uses the `mmap` system call (http://en.wikipedia.org/wiki/Mmap) for reading, and it uses random access files for writing. It uses a portion of the available virtual memory address space in the process equal to the size of the file being mapped. It doesn't have any locking, so it is scalable when it comes to multithread access. When using `mmap` to read index files for the operating system, it looks like it is already cached (it was mapped to the virtual space). Because of this, when reading a file from the Apache Lucene index, this file doesn't need to be loaded into the operating system cache and thus the access is faster. This basically allows Lucene, and therefore Elasticsearch, to directly access the I/O cache, which should result in fast access to index files.

It is worth noting that the mmap filesystem store works best on 64-bit environments and should only be used on 32-bit machines when you are sure that the index is small enough and the virtual address space is sufficient. In order to use this store, one should set `index.store.type` to `mmapfs`.

The default store type – fs

This is the default filesystem implementation and when set to this Elasticsearch is smart enough to pick the best implementation depending on the operating system environment: `simplefs` on Windows 32 bit, `niofs` on other 32 bit, and `mmapfs` on 64 bit systems.

In Elasticsearch version 1.x, there used to be two other store types: `Hybrid` (known as `default_fs` in version 2.x) and `Memory`. The memory store type has been removed from Elasticsearch 2.x where the `default_fs` store type has been marked as deprecated in Elasticsearch version 5.0. The `default_fs` now points internally to `fs` type for backward compatibilities and will soon be removed.

If you are looking for some information from experts on how they see which Directory implementation to use, please take a look at the following:
`http://blog.thetaphi.de/2012/07/use-lucenes-mmapdirectory-on-64b it.html` post written by Uwe Schindler and
`http://jprante.github.io/lessons/2012/07/26/Mmap-with-Lucene.htm l` by Jörg Prante.

Usually, the default store type will be the one that you want to use. However, sometimes, it is worth considering using the MMap filesystem store type, especially when you have plenty of memory and your indices are big. This is because when using `mmap` to access the index file, it will cause the index files to be cached only once and be reused both by Apache Lucene and the operating system.

NRT, flush, refresh, and transaction log

In an ideal search solution, when new data is indexed, it is instantly available for searching. When you start Elasticsearch, this is exactly how it works even in distributed environments. However, this is not the whole truth, and we will show you why it is like this.

Let's start by indexing an example document to the newly created index using the following command:

```
curl -XPOST localhost:9200/test/test/1 -d '{ "title": "test" }'
```

Now, let's replace this document, and let's try to find it immediately. In order to do this, we'll use the following command chain:

```
curl -XPOST localhost:9200/test/test/1 -d '{ "title": "test2" }' ;
curl -XGET 'localhost:9200/test/test/_search?pretty'
```

The preceding command will probably result in a response that is very similar to the following one:

```
{"_index":"test","_type":"test","_id":"1","_version":2,"result":"updated","
_shards":{"total":2,"successful":1,"failed":0},"created":false}
{
  "took" : 6,
  "timed_out" : false,
  "_shards" : {
    "total" : 5,
    "successful" : 5,
    "failed" : 0
  },
  "hits" : {
    "total" : 1,
    "max_score" : 1.0,
    "hits" : [
      {
        "_index" : "test",
        "_type" : "test",
        "_id" : "1",
        "_score" : 1.0,
        "_source" : {
          "title" : "test"
        }
      }
    ]
  }
}
```

We see two responses glued together. The first line starts with a response to the indexing command–the first command we've sent. As you can see, everything is correct–we've updated the document (look at _version). With the second command, our search query should return the document with the title field set to test2; however, as you can see, it returned the first document. What happened? Before we give you the answer to this question, we will take a step back and discuss how the underlying Apache Lucene library makes the newly indexed documents available for searching.

Updating the index and committing changes

As we already know from the *Introducing Apache Lucene* section in Chapter 1, *Revisiting Elasticsearch and the Changes,* during the indexing process, new documents are written into segments. The segments are independent indices, which means that queries that are run in parallel to indexing should add newly created segments from time to time to the set of these segments that are used for searching. Apache Lucene does this by creating subsequent (because of the write-once nature of the index) segments_N files, which list segments in the index. This process is called **committing**. Lucene can do this in a secure way–we are sure that all changes or none of them hit the index. If a failure happens, we can be sure that the index will be in a consistent state.

Let's return to our example. The first operation adds the document to the index but doesn't run the commit command to Lucene. This is exactly how it works. However, a commit is not enough for the data to be available for searching. The Lucene library uses an abstraction class called Searcher to access the index, and this class needs to be refreshed.

After a commit operation, the Searcher object should be reopened in order for it to be able to see the newly created segments. This whole process is called **refresh**. For performance reasons, Elasticsearch tries to postpone costly refreshes and, by default, refresh is not performed after indexing a single document (or a batch of them), but the Searcher is refreshed every second. This happens quite often, but sometimes, applications require the refresh operation to be performed more often than once every second. When this happens, you can consider using another technology, or the requirements should be verified. If required, there is a possibility of forcing the refresh by using the Elasticsearch API. For example, in our example, we can add the following command:

```
curl -XGET localhost:9200/test/_refresh
```

If we add the preceding command before the search, Elasticsearch would respond as we had expected.

Changing the default refresh time

The time between automatic Searcher refresh operations can be changed by using the `index.refresh_interval` parameter either in the Elasticsearch configuration file or by using the Update Settings API. For example:

```
curl -XPUT localhost:9200/test/_settings -d '{
"index" : {
"refresh_interval" : "5m"
}
}'
```

The preceding command will change the automatic refresh to be performed every five minutes. Please remember that the data that is indexed between refreshes won't be visible by queries.

As we said, the refresh operation is costly when it comes to resources. The longer the period of the refresh, the faster your indexing will be. If you are planning for a very high indexing procedure when you don't need your data to be visible until the indexing ends, you can consider disabling the refresh operation by setting the `index.refresh_interval` parameter to −1 and setting it back to its original value after the indexing is done.

The transaction log

Apache Lucene can guarantee index consistency and all or nothing indexing, which is great. However, this fact cannot ensure us that there will be no data loss when failure happens while writing data to the index (for example, when there isn't enough space on the device, the device is faulty, or there aren't enough file handlers available to create new index files). Another problem is that frequent commits are costly in terms of performance (as you may recall, a single commit will trigger a new segment creation, and this can trigger the segments to merge). Elasticsearch solves these issues by implementing the transaction log. The transaction log holds all uncommitted transactions and, from time to time, Elasticsearch creates a new log for subsequent changes. When something goes wrong, the transaction log can be replayed to make sure that none of the changes were lost. All of these tasks are happening automatically, so the user may not be aware of the fact that the commit was triggered at a particular moment. In Elasticsearch, the moment where the information from the transaction log is synchronized with the storage (which is the Apache Lucene index) and the transaction log is cleared is called **flushing**.

Please note the difference between flush and refresh operations. In most of the cases, refresh is exactly what you want. It is all about making new data available for searching. On the other hand, the flush operation is used to make sure that all the data is correctly stored in the index and the transaction log can be cleared.

In addition to automatic flushing, it can be forced manually using the Flush API. For example, we can run a command to flush all the data stored in the transaction log for all indices by running the following command:

```
curl -XGET localhost:9200/_flush
```

Or, we can run the `flush` command for the particular index, which in our case is the one called `library`:

```
curl -XGET localhost:9200/library/_flush
curl -XGET localhost:9200/library/_refresh
```

In the second example, we used it together with the refresh, which after flushing the data, opens a new searcher.

The transaction log configuration

If the default behavior of the transaction log is not enough, Elasticsearch allows us to configure its behavior when it comes to the transaction log handling. The following parameters can be configured using index settings' Update API to control the transaction log behavior:

- `index.translog.sync_interval`: This defaults to five seconds (`5s`). It controls the time of how often the translog is fsynced to disk, regardless of write operations. You cannot set it below 100 milliseconds (`100ms`).

- `index.translog.durability`: This property control whether or not to fsync and commit the translog after every index, delete, update or bulk request operation. You can set this property to either request or async. When it is set to request which is also the default behavior, fsync and commit is done after every request. In the event of hardware failure, all acknowledged writes will already have been committed to disk. But if it is set to async, the fsync and commit operations are performed in the background at every sync_interval. In the event of hardware failure, all acknowledged writes since the last automatic commit will be discarded.

- `index.translog.flush_threshold_size`: This specifies the maximum size of the transaction log. If the size of the transaction log is equal to or greater than the parameter, the flush operation will be performed. It defaults to `512 MB`.

An example of configuring these setting through the Settings Update API is shown as follows:

```
curl -XPUT localhost:9200/test/_settings -d '{
"index" : {
"translog.flush_threshold_size" : "256mb"
  }
}'
```

The previous command changes the flush threshold size to 256 MB.

Handling corrupted translogs

In some cases (such as a bad drive or user error), transaction logs can be corrupted. When this corruption is detected by Elasticsearch due to mismatching checksums in the transaction log file, Elasticsearch will fail the shard and refuse to allocate that copy of the data to the node, recovering from a replica, if available.

If there is no copy of the data from which Elasticsearch can recover successfully, for example there is no replica available for that shard, a user may can recover the data that is part of the shard at the cost of losing the data that is currently contained in the translog. This can be done easily with a script, `elasticsearch-translog.sh` which is shipped within Elasticsearch setup can be found under Elasticsearch `bin` directory.

The `elasticsearch-translog` script should not be run while Elasticsearch is running, or you will permanently lose the documents that were contained in the translog!

In order to run the `elasticsearch-translog` script, you need to specify the truncate subcommand as well as the directory for the corrupted translog with the `-d` option as shown in following example:

```
sudo /usr/share/elasticsearch/bin/elasticsearch-translog truncate -d
/var/lib/elasticsearchdata/nodes/0/indices/my_index/0/translog/
```

In above command `/var/lib/elasticsearchdata` refers to the data path on a particular node.

Near real-time GET

Transaction logs give us one more feature for free, that is, the real-time GET operation, which provides us with the possibility of returning to the previous version of the document, including non-committed versions. The real-time GET operation fetches data from the index, but first, it checks whether a newer version of this document is available in the transaction log. If there is no flushed document, the data from the index is ignored and a newer version of the document is returned–the one from the transaction log.

In order to see how it works, you can replace the search operation in our example with the following command:

```
curl -XGET localhost:9200/test/test/1?pretty
```

Elasticsearch should return a result similar to the following:

```
{
  "_index" : "test",
  "_type" : "test",
  "_id" : "1",
  "_version" : 2,
  "exists" : true, "_source" : { "title": "test2" }
}
```

If you look at the result, you will see that, again, the result was just as we expected and no trick with refresh was required to obtain the newest version of the document.

Segment merging under control

Lucene segments are written once and read many times, and data structures, apart from the information about the deleted documents that are held in one of the files, can be changed. After some time, when certain conditions are met, the contents of some segments can be copied to a bigger segment, and the original segments are discarded and thus deleted from the disk. Such an operation is called **segment merging**.

You may ask yourself, why bother about segment merging? There are a few reasons. First of all, the more segments the index is built from, the slower the search will be and the more memory Lucene will need. In addition to this, segments are immutable, so the information is not deleted from them. If you happen to delete many documents from your index, until the merge happens, these documents are only marked as deleted and are not deleted physically. So, when segment merging happens, the documents that are marked as deleted are not written into the new segment, and this way, they are removed, which decreases the final segment size.

Many small changes can result in a large number of small segments, which can lead to problems with a large number of opened files. We should always be prepared to handle such situations; for example, by having the appropriate opened files' limit set.

So, just to quickly summarize, segment merging takes place and from the user's point of view, it will result in two effects:

- It will reduce the number of segments in order to allow faster searching when a few segments are merged into a single one
- It will reduce the size of the index because of the removal of the deleted documents when the merge is finalized

However, you have to remember that segment merging comes with a price: the price of I/O operations, which can affect performance on slower systems. Because of this, Elasticsearch allows us to alter the merge policy and the store level throttling.

Merge policy changes in Elasticsearch

Segment merging is a very expensive process and sometimes it happens that segment merging falls behind data ingestion speed. In an earlier version of Elasticsearch, merges were used to throttle and indexing requests were limited to a single thread. This was necessary to avoid the index explosion problem, in which hundreds of segments are generated before they could be merged together. The problem of the default settings were that the merge throttle limit was too low (20 MB/second) especially for SSD. Although Elasticsearch used to provide settings to increase this throttle limit, it is always hard to decide the correct limit for other users. Keeping this big issue in mind, Elasticsearch now has the concept of auto-regulating feedback loops to control the merge throttling speed and balance the use of hardware resources between merging and other activities such as search. As a result, many of the old settings were removed from configurations.

The following are the removed settings for merge throttling:

- `indices.store.throttle.type`
- `indices.store.throttle.max_bytes_per_sec`
- `index.store.throttle.type`
- `index.store.throttle.max_bytes_per_sec`

In addition, two merge policies (`log_byte_size` and `log_doc`) have also been removed and a tiered merge policy is the default and the only policy remaining in Elasticsearch. As a result, the following merge policy settings are removed:

- `index.merge.policy.type`
- `index.merge.policy.min_merge_size`
- `index.merge.policy.max_merge_size`
- `index.merge.policy.merge_factor`
- `index.merge.policy.max_merge_docs`
- `index.merge.policy.calibrate_size_by_deletes`
- `index.merge.policy.min_merge_docs`
- `index.merge.policy.max_merge_docs`

Configuring the tiered merge policy

The tiered merge policy is the default and the only merge policy that Elasticsearch 5.0 uses. It merges segments of an approximately similar size, taking into account the maximum number of segments allowed per tier. It is also possible to differentiate the number of segments that are allowed to be merged at once from how many segments are allowed to be present per tier. During indexing, this merge policy will compute how many segments are allowed to be present in the index, which is called **budget**. If the number of segments the index is built from is higher than the computed budget, the tiered policy will first sort the segments by the decreasing order of their size (taking into account the deleted documents). After that, it will find the merge that has the lowest cost. The merge cost is calculated in a way that merges are reclaiming more deletions, and having a smaller size is favored.

If the merge produces a segment that is larger than the value specified by the `index.merge.policy.max_merged_segment` property, the policy will merge fewer segments to keep the segment size under the budget. This means that for indices that have large shards, the default value of the `index.merge.policy.max_merged_segment` property may be too low and will result in the creation of many segments, slowing down your queries. Depending on the volume of your data, you should monitor your segments and adjust the merge policy setting to match your needs.

With the `tiered` merge policy, the following options can be altered:

- `index.merge.policy.expunge_deletes_allowed`: This defaults to 10 and specifies the percentage of deleted documents in a segment in order for it to be considered to be merged when running `expungeDeletes`.

- `index.merge.policy.floor_segment`: This is a property that enables us to prevent the frequent flushing of very small segments. Segments smaller than the size defined by this property are treated by the merge mechanism, as they would have the size equal to the value of this property. It defaults to 2MB.

- `index.merge.policy.max_merge_at_once`: This specifies the maximum number of segments that will be merged at the same time during indexing. By default, it is set to 10. Setting the value of this property to higher values can result in multiple segments being merged at once, which will need more I/O resources.

- `index.merge.policy.max_merge_at_once_explicit`: This specifies the maximum number of segments that will be merged at the same time during the optimize operation or `expungeDeletes`. By default, this is set to 30. This setting will not affect the maximum number of segments that will be merged during indexing.

- `index.merge.policy.max_merged_segment`: This defaults to 5GB and specifies the maximum size of a single segment that will be produced during segment merging when indexing. This setting is an approximate value, because the merged segment size is calculated by summing the size of segments that are going to be merged minus the size of the deleted documents in these segments.

- `index.merge.policy.segments_per_tier`: This specifies the allowed number of segments per tier. Smaller values of this property result in less segments, which means more merging and lower indexing performance. It defaults to 10 and should be set to a value higher than or equal to `index.merge.policy.max_merge_at_once`, or you'll be facing too many merges and performance issues.

- `index.reclaim_deletes_weight`: This defaults to 2.0 and specifies how many merges that reclaim deletes are favored. When setting this value to 0.0, the reclaim deletes will not affect the merge selection. The higher the value, the more favored the merge that reclaims deletes will be.

- `index.compund_format`: This is a Boolean value that specifies whether the index should be stored in a compound format or not. It defaults to `false`. If set to `true`, Lucene will store all the files that build the index in a single file. Sometimes, this is useful for systems running constantly out of file handlers, but it will decrease the searching and indexing performance.

Merge scheduling

In addition to having control over how the merge policy is behaving, Elasticsearch allows us to define the execution of the merge policy once a merge is needed. Elasticsearch uses `ConcurrentMergeScheduler` for this purpose.

The concurrent merge scheduler

This is a merge scheduler that will use multiple threads in order to perform segments merging. This scheduler will create a new thread until the maximum number of threads is reached. If the maximum number of threads is reached and a new thread is needed (because segments merging needs to be performed), all the indexing will be paused until at least one merge is completed.

In order to control the maximum threads allowed, we can alter the `index.merge.scheduler.max_thread_count` property. By default, it is set to the value calculated by the following equation:

```
Math.max(1, Math.min(4, Runtime.getRuntime().availableProcessors() / 2))
```

You should also remember that this is especially not good for spinning disks. You want to be sure that merging won't saturate your disks' throughput. Because of this, if you see extensive merging, you should lower the number of merging threads. It is usually said that for spinning disks, the number of threads used by the concurrent merge scheduler should be set to 1.

Force merging

Elasticsearch provides a Force Merge API, which allows the force merging of one or more indices. The force merge operation can be sometime very useful as it allows you to reduce the number of segments by merging them. Especially in the scenario where you do not perform indexing frequently, you can use this API to limit the total segment in each shard to even 1, which will result in very fast searches.

This call will block until the merge is complete. If the HTTP connection is lost, the request will continue in the background, and any new requests will block until the previous force merge is complete.

It allows the following parameters to be used:

- `max_num_segments`: The number of segments to merge to. To fully merge the index, set it to 1. Defaults to simply checking if a merge needs to execute, and if so, executes it.
- `only_expunge_deletes`: This parameter controls if the merge process should only expunge segments with deletes in it. In Lucene, a document is not deleted from a segment, just marked as deleted. During a merge process of segments, a new segment is created that does not have those deletes. This flag allows you to only merge segments that have deletes. Defaults to `false`.

 Note that this won't override the `index.merge.policy.expunge_deletes_allowed` threshold.

- `flush`: This tells Elasticsearch if a flush should be performed after the forced merge. Defaults to `true`.

For example, if you want to fully merge an index, you can use following request:

```
curl -XPOST
"http://localhost:9200/library/_forcemerge?max_num_segments=1"
```

Understanding Elasticsearch caching

One of the very important parts of Elasticsearch, although not always visible to the users, is caching. It allows Elasticsearch to store commonly used data in memory and reuse it on demand. Of course, we can't cache everything; we usually have way more data than we have memory, and creating caches may be quite expensive when it comes to performance. In the *Instant aggregations in Elasticsearch 5.0* section of Chapter 5, *Improving the User Search Experience*, we discussed some major improvements done in query parsing and caching. In this chapter, we will look at the different caches exposed by Elasticsearch, and we will discuss how they are used and how we can control their usage. Hopefully, such information will allow you to better understand how this great search server works internally.

Node query cache

The query cache is responsible for caching the results of queries. There is one queries cache per node that is shared by all shards existing on that node. The cache implements an LRU (Least Recently Used) eviction policy: when a cache becomes full, the least recently used data is evicted to make way for new data.

 The query cache only caches queries which are being used in a filter context.

Configuring node query cache

You can configure the following two settings for query cache:

- `indices.queries.cache.size`: This setting controls the memory size for the filter cache. It defaults to 10%. It accepts either a percentage value, such as 5%, or an exact value, such as 512 MB. There is a node level setting which must be configured inside the `elasticsearch.yml` file on every data node in the cluster.
- `index.queries.cache.enabled`: This setting controls whether to enable query caching or not. It accepts `true` (default) or `false`. This is an index level setting that can be configured on a per-index basis. This should be configured either at the time of creating an index or can be updated dynamically using the Update Setting API.

Shard request cache

When a search request is executed against an index or against more than one index, the coordinating node that receives the search request, forwards the request to all the participating data nodes and then each involved shard on every node executes the search locally and returns its local result to the coordinating node, which combines these shard level results into a global result set.

The shard request cache module is responsible for caching the local results of each shard and it allows most frequently used (and potentially heavy) search requests almost instantly.

By using this cache, frequently used aggregations (for example, displaying on the home page of a website) can be cached for faster responses. These cached results are the same results that would be returned by an uncached aggregation; you will never get stale results.

This is also a very good fit for logging a use case, where only the most recent index is being actively updated. Results from older indices will be served directly from the cache.

 By default, the requests cache will only cache the results of search requests where `size=0`, meaning, it does not cache hits, but it caches `hits.total`, `aggregations`, and `suggestions` responses. If the requests size is greater than 0, it will not be cached even if the request cache is enabled in the index settings. To cache these requests, a complete JSON query is used as a cache key, and for this you need to make sure that keys of JSON queries are always emitted in the same order.

Enabling and disabling the shard request cache

The `index.requests.cache.enable` parameter controls the enabling or disabling of the request cache. The request cache is enabled by default, but it can be disabled at the time of index creating in the following way:

```
curl -XPUT "http://localhost:9200/library" -d'
{
  "settings": {
    "index.requests.cache.enable": false
  }
}'
```

It can also be enabled or disabled using the Update Setting API as follows:

```
curl -XPUT "http://localhost:9200/library/_settings" -d'
{ "index.requests.cache.enable": true }'
```

Elasticsearch also allows us to enable or disable the request cache per request. For example:

```
curl -XGET
"http://localhost:9200/library/_search?request_cache=true" -d'
{
  "size": 0,
  "aggs": {
    "popular_tags": {
      "terms": {
        "field": "tags"
      }
    }
  }
}'
```

Request cache settings

The cache is managed at the node level, and has a default maximum size of 1% of the heap. This can be changed in the `elasticsearch.yml` file with:

```
indices.requests.cache.size: 2%
```

Cache invalidation

Cached results are invalidated automatically whenever the shard refreshes, but only if the data in the shard has actually changed. In other words, you will always get the same results from the cache as you would for an uncached search request. The longer the refresh interval, the longer that cached entries will remain valid. If the cache is full, the least recently used cache keys will be evicted.

In addition, you can clear the cache using the `_cache` API as follows:

```
curl -XPOST
"http://localhost:9200/library/_cache/clear?request_cache=true"
```

The field data cache

The field data cache is used when we want to send queries that involve operations that work on uninverted data. What Elasticsearch needs to do is load all the values for a given field and store them in the memory; you can call this field data cache. This cache is used by Elasticsearch when we use aggregations, scripting, or sorting on the field value. When first executing an operation that requires data uninverting, Elasticsearch loads all the data for that field into the memory. Yes, that's right; all the data from a given field is loaded into the memory by default and is never removed from it. Elasticsearch does this to be able to provide fast document-based access to values in a field. Remember that the field data cache is usually expensive to build from the hardware resource's point of view, because the data for the whole field needs to be loaded into the memory, and this requires both I/O operations and CPU resources.

You can use the `indices.fielddata.cache.size` parameter inside every data node in your cluster. The value of this parameter is the max size of the field data cache, for example 30% of node heap space, or an absolute value, for example 12 GB. It defaults to unbounded.

> One should remember that for every field that we sort on or use faceting on, the data needs to be loaded into the memory each and every term. This can be expensive, especially for the fields that are high cardinality ones: the ones with numerous different terms in them.

Field data or doc values

Doc values came in Elasticsearch as an alternative to field data and now enable by default for every `not_analyzed` (keyword type field). They are calculated at indexing time and are stored in the disk in a columnar format. Doc values are not only as fast as field data cache but they require very less memory too. So with Elasticsearch 5.0, you should avoid using field data and continue with doc values without any worry.

Using circuit breakers

Because queries can put a lot of pressure on Elasticsearch resources, they allow us to use so-called circuit breakers that prevent Elasticsearch from using too much memory in certain functionalities. Elasticsearch estimates the memory usage and rejects the query execution if certain thresholds are met. Let's look at the available circuit breakers and what they can help us with.

The parent circuit breaker

The parent level circuit breaker can be set using the `indices.breaker.total.limit` parameter. The starting limit for the overall parent breaker defaults to `70%` of the JVM heap.

The field data circuit breaker

The field data circuit breaker will prevent request execution if the estimated memory usage for the request is higher than the configured values. By default, Elasticsearch sets `indices.breaker.fielddata.limit` to `60%`, which means that no more than 60% of the JVM heap is allowed to be used for the field data cache.

We can also configure the multiplier that Elasticsearch uses for estimates (the estimated values are multiplied by this property value) by using the `indices.breaker.fielddata.overhead` property. By default, it is set to `1.03`.

The request circuit breaker

Introduced in Elasticsearch 1.4.0, the request circuit breaker allows us to configure Elasticsearch to reject the execution of the request if the total estimated memory used by it will be higher than the `indices.breaker.request.limit` property (set to `60%` of the total heap memory assigned to the JVM by default).

Similar to the field data circuit breaker, we can set the overhead by using the `indices.breaker.request.overhead` property, which defaults to `1`.

In flight requests circuit breaker

The in-flight requests circuit breaker allows Elasticsearch to limit the memory usage of all currently active incoming requests on transport or the HTTP level from exceeding a certain amount of memory on a node. The memory usage is based on the content length of the request itself.

The configurable parameters are `network.breaker.inflight_requests.limit`, which defaults to `100%` of JVM heap, and `network.breaker.inflight_requests.overhead`, a constant that all in-flight request estimations are multiplied with to determine a final estimation, and it defaults to `1`.

Script compilation circuit breaker

The first time Elasticsearch sees a new script, it compiles it and stores the compiled version in a cache. Compilation can be a heavy process. This circuit breaker limits the inline script compilations within a period of time. You can use the `script.max_compilations_per_minute` parameter to limit for the number of unique dynamic scripts within a minute that are allowed to be compiled. It defaults to 15.

 Please remember that all the circuit breakers can be dynamically changed on a working cluster using the Cluster Update Settings API.

Summary

In this chapter, we started with different Apache Lucene scoring algorithms and learned about how to alter them and how to choose the right algorithm. Then we went through the store module of Elasticsearch and learned about different directory implementations for indices. We also covered near real-time searches, indexing, and learned about transaction logs configurations. Then, we looked into how segment merging works and what are all the possible ways to control the merge process. At the end, we discussed caching in Elasticsearch and the roles of circuit breakers.

Our next chapter is going to be a very important as well as interesting chapter as it focuses on Elasticsearch administration concepts. We will discuss Elasticsearch discovery, including the Amazon EC2 discovery module and the Elasticsearch recovery module, which helps users to configure them as per need. We will also cover the major changes done in Elasticsearch monitoring and then we will discuss the CAT API in detail. In the end, backup and recovery modules are covered, which will help users to understand various ways to take backups and restore them back to the cluster.

8

Elasticsearch Administration

In the last chapter, we went through various scoring algorithms provided by Apache Lucene, altering them and choosing the right one for the required use case along with Elasticsearch store module. We also discussed NRT searching and indexing and the role of transaction logs. After that we looked into how segment merging works and what are all the possible ways to control the merge process for an improved performance. Finally, we discussed Elasticsearch caching and circuit breakers.

In this chapter, we will focus around concepts of administering Elasticsearch, which include learning about discovery and recovery modules, configuring a full-blown Elasticsearch cluster with defined roles of nodes and the Cat API. We will also cover the major changes done in Elasticsearch monitoring parameters and in the end you will learn about how to perform backups and restore tasks of Elasticsearch indices. By the end of this chapter, we will have covered following topics:

- Node types in Elasticsearch
- Configuring the discovery and recovery modules
- Using the cat API that allows a human-readable insight into the cluster status
- The backup and restore functionality

Node types in Elasticsearch

In Elasticsearch you can configure five types of nodes:

- Data node
- Master node

- Ingest node
- Tribe node
- Coordinating node

Let us see how these nodes differ from each other and how to configure them.

Data node

A data node in Elasticsearch is responsible for holding the data, segment merging, and query executions. Data nodes are the real work horses of your cluster and need higher configuration than any other type of node in the cluster.

By default, every node is eligible to be a data node. A dedicated data node can be configured by adding the following lines in the `/etc/elasticsearch/elasticsearch.yml` file:

```
node.data: true
node.master: false
node.ingest: false
```

The main benefit of having a dedicated data node is the separation between data and master node.

Master node

A master node is responsible for management of the complete cluster. It hold the states of all the nodes and periodically distributes the cluster state to all other nodes in the cluster, to make them aware of which new node has joined the cluster and which node has left in between. The master node periodically sends the ping to all other nodes to see if they are alive (Other nodes also send ping to the master node). One final major task of the master node is that of configuration management. It holds the complete metadata and mapping of all the indexes in the cluster. If a master leaves, a new master node is chosen from the rest of the eligible master nodes.

By default, every node is eligible to be a master node. A dedicated master node can be configured by adding the following lines in the `/etc/elasticsearch/elasticsearch.yml` file:

```
node.data: false
node.master: true
node.ingest: false
```

Ingest node

An ingest node helps in per-processing of data pipelines which are composed of one or more ingest processors. Depending of the processing required by the ingest node, they may require a good amount of resources and sometimes it makes sense to have dedicated ingest nodes in the cluster.

By default, every node is eligible to be an ingest node. A dedicated ingest node can be configured by adding the following lines in the `/etc/elasticsearch/elasticsearch.yml` file:

```
node.data: false
node.data: false
node.master: false
node.ingest: true
```

We will look at the functionalities of ingest nodes in detail in `Chapter 9`, *Data Transformation and Federated Search*.

Tribe node

A tribe node is a special type of coordinating node that can connect to multiple clusters and perform a search and other operations across all connected clusters.

We will cover tribe nodes in the *Federated search* section of `Chapter 9`, *Data Transformation and Federated Search*.

Coordinating nodes/Client nodes

In Elasticsearch, every search request is executed under two phases: the **scatter phase** and **gather phase**. Both of these phases are managed by a coordinating node which receives the search request. They also behave as load balancers in a cluster.

In the scatter phase, the coordinating node forwards the request to the data nodes which hold the data. Each data node executes the request locally and returns its results to the coordinating node.

In the gather phase, the coordinating node reduces each data node's results into a single global result set.

By default, every node is implicitly a coordinating node. Such a node needs to have enough memory and CPU in order to deal with the gather phase. In a big cluster, adding a dedicated coordinating node is always beneficial, since it takes off the load from data and master nodes.

A dedicated coordinating node can be configured by adding the following lines in the `/etc/elasticsearch/elasticsearch.yml` file:

```
node.data: false
node.master: false
node.ingest: false
```

> It is important to know that adding too many coordinating nodes increases the burden on the cluster since the elected master node must wait and acknowledge all the cluster state updates to all the nodes in the cluster.

Discovery and recovery modules

When an Elasticsearch node is started, it looks out for an initial list of hosts which are master eligible to perform discovery of other nodes in the cluster. The default list of master eligible hosts is `["127.0.0.1", "[::1]"]`, which means by default that each Elasticsearch node can only discover itself and cannot find another node. This behavior was introduced in Elasticsearch version 2.0. Before that, Elasticsearch, by default, used to assume that the cluster was automatically formed by the nodes that declare the same `cluster.name` setting and can communicate with each other using multicast requests.

The process of forming a cluster and finding nodes is called **discovery**. The module responsible for discovery has two main purposes: electing a master and discovering new nodes within a cluster.

After the cluster is formed, a process called **recovery** is started. During the recovery process, Elasticsearch reads the metadata and the indices from the gateway, and prepares the shards that are stored there to be used. After the recovery of the primary shards is done, Elasticsearch should be ready for work and should continue with the recovery of all the replicas (if they are present).

In this section, we will take a deeper look at these two modules and discuss the possibilities of configuration that Elasticsearch gives us and what the consequences of changing them are.

Discovery configuration

As we have already mentioned multiple times, Elasticsearch was designed to work in a distributed environment. This is the main difference when comparing Elasticsearch to other open source search and analytics solutions available. With such assumptions, Elasticsearch is very easy to set up in a distributed environment, and we are not forced to set up additional software to make it work like this.

There are a few implementations of the discovery module that we can use, so let's see what the options are.

Zen discovery

Zen discovery is the default mechanism that's responsible for discovery in Elasticsearch and is available by default. The default Zen discovery configuration uses unicast to find other nodes in the cluster. In unicast discovery, a node that is not a part of the cluster will send a ping request to all the addresses specified in the configuration using the `discovery.zen.ping.unicast.hosts` parameter. By doing this, it informs all the specified nodes that it is ready to be a part of the cluster and can be either joined to an existing cluster or can form a new one. Of course, after the node joins the cluster, it gets the cluster topology information, but the initial connection is only done to the specified list of hosts. Remember that unicast Zen discovery, requires all the Elasticsearch nodes to have the same cluster name as the other nodes.

The unicast Zen discovery configuration

The unicast part of Zen discovery provides the following configuration options:

- `discovery.zen.ping.unicats.hosts`: This is the initial list of nodes in the cluster. The list can be defined as a list or as an array of hosts. Every host can be given a name (or an IP address) or have a port or port range added. For example, the value of this property can look like this: `["master1", "master2:9300", "master3[9300-9305]"]`. So, basically, the hosts' list for the unicast discovery doesn't need to be a complete list of Elasticsearch nodes in your cluster, because once the node is connected to one of the mentioned nodes, it will be informed about all the others that form the cluster. But all the nodes mentioned in this list must be master eligible nodes.

If you specify a `host-port` combination in the initial hosts list, then the `port` must be a transport port which defaults to `9300`.

- `discovery.zen.minimum_master_nodes` (the default: 1): This is the maximum number of concurrent connections unicast discoveries will use. If you have a lot of nodes that the initial connection should be made to, it is advised that you increase the default value. This property is also useful for preventing the split-brain situation in a cluster.

The master election configuration

Imagine that you have a cluster that is built of 10 nodes which are all master eligible. Everything is working fine until, one day, your network fails and three of your nodes are disconnected from the cluster, but they still see each other. Because of the Zen discovery and the master election process, the nodes that got disconnected elect a new master and you end up with two clusters with the same name with two master nodes. Such a situation is called a **split-brain** and you must avoid it as much as possible. When a split-brain happens, you end up with two (or more) clusters that won't join each other until the network (or any other) problems are fixed. If you index your data during this time, you may end up with data loss and unrecoverable situations when the nodes get joined together after the network split.

In order to prevent split-brain situations, or at least minimize the possibility of their occurrences, Elasticsearch provides a `discovery.zen.minimum_master_nodes` property. This property defines a minimum amount of master eligible nodes that should be connected to each other in order to form a cluster. So now let's get back to our cluster; if we set the `discovery.zen.minimum_master_nodes` property to 50% of the total master nodes available plus one (which is six, in our case), we would end up with a single cluster. Why is that? Before the network failure, we would have 10 nodes, which is more than six nodes, and these nodes would form a cluster. After the disconnections of the three nodes, we would still have the first cluster up and running. However, because only three nodes disconnected and three is less than six, these three nodes wouldn't be allowed to elect a new master and they would wait for reconnection with the original cluster.

Zen discovery fault detection and configuration

Elasticsearch runs two detection processes while it is working. The first process is to send ping requests from the current master node to all the other nodes in the cluster to check whether they are operational. The second process is a reverse of that: each of the nodes sends ping requests to the master in order to verify that it is still up and running and performing its duties. However, if we have a slow network or our nodes are in different hosting locations, the default configuration may not be sufficient. Because of this, the Elasticsearch discovery module exposes three properties that we can change:

- `discovery.zen.fd.ping_interval`: This defaults to `1s` and specifies the interval of how often the node will send ping requests to the target node.
- `discovery.zen.fd.ping_timeout`: This defaults to `30s` and specifies how long the node will wait for the sent ping request to be responded to. If your nodes are 100% utilized or your network is slow, you may consider increasing that property value.
- `discovery.zen.fd.ping_retries`: This defaults to `3` and specifies the number of ping request retries before the target node will be considered not operational. You can increase this value if your network has a high number of lost packets (or you can fix your network).

There is one more thing that we would like to mention. The master node is the only node that can change the state of the cluster. To achieve a proper cluster state updates sequence, Elasticsearch master nodes process single cluster state update requests one at a time, make the changes locally, and send the request to all the other nodes so that they can synchronize their state. The master nodes wait for the given time for the nodes to respond, and if the time passes or all the nodes are returned, with the current acknowledgment information, they proceed with the next cluster state update request processing. To change the time, the master node waits for all the other nodes to respond, and you should modify the default `30` seconds time by setting the `discovery.zen.publish_timeout` property. Increasing the value may be needed for huge clusters working in an overloaded network. This property can also be updated dynamically in a running cluster through the cluster update setting API.

No Master Block

To be fully operational, a cluster must have an active master and the number of running master eligible nodes must satisfy the `discovery.zen.minimum_master_nodes` setting if set. If this condition is not satisfied, then all the operations to the cluster will be rejected. If you want to allow some operations to be active, even in the absence of a desired active master node, then you can control this behavior using the `discovery.zen.no_master_block` setting. This setting can take two values from the following:

- `all`: All operations on the node, that is both read and writes, will be rejected. This also applies for the API cluster state read or write operations, such as the get index settings, put mapping, and the cluster state API.
- `write`: This is the default value and allows only write operations to be rejected. Read operations will succeed, based on the last known cluster configuration. This may result in partial reads of stale data as this node may be isolated from the rest of the cluster.

The Amazon EC2 discovery

If you are running your Elasticsearch cluster on Amazon **Elastic Compute Cloud** (**EC2**), then you must be aware that due to the nature of the environment, some features may work slightly differently. One of these features that works differently is discovery, because Amazon EC2 doesn't support multicast discovery. Of course, we can switch to unicast discovery, but sometimes we want to be able to automatically discover nodes and, with unicast, we need to at least provide the initial list of hosts. However, there is an alternative: we can use the Amazon EC2 discovery plugin.

 Make sure that during the setup of EC2 instances, you set up communication between them (on port `9200` and `9300` by default). This is crucial in order to have Elasticsearch nodes communicate with each other and, thus, cluster functioning is required. Of course, this communication depends on `network.bind_host` and `network.publish_host` (or `network.host`) settings.

The EC2 plugin installation

The installation of the EC2 plugin is as simple as most other plugins. In order to install it, we should run the following command on every node and must restart all the nodes after installation of the plugin:

```
sudo bin/elasticsearch-plugin install discovery-ec2
```

The EC2 plugin's generic configuration

This plugin provides several configuration settings that we need to provide in order for the EC2 discovery to work:

- `cluster.aws.access_key`: Amazon access key, one of the credential values you can find in the Amazon configuration panel.
- `cluster.aws.secret_key`: Amazon secret key, which is similar to the previously mentioned `access_key` setting. It can be found in the EC2 configuration panel.

The last thing is to inform Elasticsearch that we want to use a new discovery type by setting the `discovery.type` property to `ec2` value.

Optional EC2 discovery configuration options

The previously mentioned settings are sufficient to run the EC2 discovery, but in order to control the EC2 discovery plugin behavior, Elasticsearch exposes additional settings:

- `cloud.aws.region`: If you are not using the default AWS region then you must configure this property too. This region will be used to connect with Amazon EC2 Web Services. You can choose a region that's adequate for the region where your instance resides: for example, `eu-west-1` for Ireland.
- `cloud.aws.ec2.endpoint`: If you are using EC2 API services, instead of defining a region, you can provide an address of the AWS endpoint: for example, `ec2.eu-west-1.amazonaws.com`.

- `cloud.aws.protocol`: This is the protocol that should be used by the plugin to connect to AWS endpoints. By default, Elasticsearch will use the HTTPS protocol (which means setting the value of the property to `https`). We can also change this behavior and set the property to `http` for the plugin to use HTTP without encryption. We are also allowed to overwrite the `cloud.aws.protocol` settings for each service by using the `cloud.aws.ec2.protocol` and `cloud.aws.s3.protocol` properties (the possible values are the same: `https` and `http`).

- `cloud.aws.proxy.host`: Elasticsearch allows us to define a proxy that will be used to connect to AWS endpoints. The `cloud.aws.proxy.host` property should be set to the address to the proxy that should be used.

- `cloud.aws.proxy.port`: This property is related to the AWS endpoints proxy and allows us to specify the port on which the proxy is listening. The `cloud.aws.proxy.port` property should be set to the port on which the proxy listens.

- `cloud.aws.proxy.username`: The property specifies the username to be used with the proxy.

- `cloud.aws.proxy.password`: The second property specifies the password to be used with the proxy.

The EC2 nodes scanning configuration

The last group of settings we want to mention allows us to configure a very important thing when building a cluster working inside the EC2 environment: the ability to filter available Elasticsearch nodes in our Amazon EC2 network. The Elasticsearch EC2 plugin exposes the following properties that can help us configure its behavior:

- `discovery.ec2.host_type`: This allows us to choose the host type that will be used to communicate with other nodes in the cluster. The values we can use are `private_ip` (the default one; the private IP address will be used for communication), `public_ip` (the public IP address will be used for communication), `private_dns` (the private hostname will be used for communication), and `public_dns` (the public hostname will be used for communication).

- `discovery.ec2.groups`: This is a comma-separated list of security groups. Only nodes that fall within these groups can be discovered and included in the cluster.(NOTE: You could provide either security group NAME or group ID.)

- `discovery.ec2.availability_zones`: This is an array or command-separated list of availability zones. Only nodes with the specified availability zones will be discovered and included in the cluster.
- `discovery.ec2.node_cache_time`: Specifies, how long the list of hosts is cached to prevent further requests to the AWS API. Defaults to `10s`.
- `discovery.ec2.any_group` (this defaults to `true`): Setting this property to `false` will force the EC2 discovery plugin to discover only those nodes that reside in an Amazon instance that falls into all of the defined security groups. The default value requires only a single group to be matched.

Other discovery implementations

The Zen discovery and EC2 discovery are not the only discovery types that are available. There are two more discovery types that are developed and maintained by the Elasticsearch team. Covering all of them is beyond the scope of this book, so please refer to the following URLs of their official documentation to read about them:

- **Azure discovery**:
  `https://www.elastic.co/guide/en/elasticsearch/plugins/5.0/discovery-az ure-classic.html`
- **Google compute engine discovery**:
  `https://www.elastic.co/guide/en/elasticsearch/plugins/5.0/discovery-gc e.html`
- **File based discovery**:
  `https://www.elastic.co/guide/en/elasticsearch/plugins/5.0/discovery-fi le.html`

The gateway and recovery configuration

The gateway module allows us to store all the data that is needed for Elasticsearch to work properly. This means that not only is the data in Apache Lucene indices stored, but also all the metadata (for example, index allocation settings), along with the mappings configuration for each index. Whenever the cluster state is changed, for example, when the allocation properties are changed, the cluster state will be persisted by using the gateway module. When the cluster is started up, its state will be loaded using the gateway module and applied.

The gateway recovery process

Let's say explicitly that the recovery process is used by Elasticsearch to load the data stored with the use of the gateway module, in order for Elasticsearch to work. Whenever a full cluster restart occurs, the gateway process kicks in to load all the relevant information we've mentioned–the metadata, the mappings, and of course, all the indices. When the recovery process starts, the primary shards are initialized first, and then, depending on the replica state, they are initialized using the gateway data, or the data is copied from the primary shards if the replicas are out of sync.

Elasticsearch allows us to configure when the cluster data should be recovered using the gateway module. We can tell Elasticsearch to wait for a certain number of master eligible or data nodes to be present in the cluster before starting the recovery process. However, one should remember that when the cluster is not recovered, all the operations performed on it will not be allowed. This is done in order to avoid modification conflicts.

Configuration properties

Before we continue with the configuration, we would like to say one more thing. As you know, Elasticsearch nodes can play different roles: they can have a role of data nodes, the ones that hold data; they can have a master role; or they can be only used for request handing, which means not holding data and not being master eligible. Remembering all this, let's now look at the gateway configuration properties that we are allowed to modify:

- `gateway.recover_after_nodes`: This is an integer number that specifies how many nodes should be present in the cluster for the recovery to happen. For example, when set to 5, at least five nodes (it doesn't matter whether they are data or master eligible nodes) must be present for the recovery process to start.
- `gateway.recover_after_data_nodes`: This is an integer number that allows us to set how many data nodes should be present in the cluster for the recovery process to start.
- `gateway.recover_after_master_nodes`: This is another gateway configuration option that allows us to set how many master eligible nodes should be present in the cluster for the recovery to start.
- `gateway.recover_after_time`: This allows us to set how much time to wait before the recovery process starts after the conditions defined by the preceding properties are met. If we set this property to `5m`, we tell Elasticsearch to start the recovery process five minutes after all the defined conditions are met. The default value for this property is `5m`.

Let's imagine that we have six nodes in our cluster, out of which four are data eligible. We also have an index that is built of three shards, which are spread across the cluster. The last two nodes are master eligible and they don't hold the data. What we would like to configure is the recovery process to be delayed for 3m after the four data nodes are present. Our gateway configuration could look like this:

```
gateway.recover_after_data_nodes: 4
gateway.recover_after_time: 3m
```

The local gateway

The local gateway uses a local storage available on a node to store the metadata, mappings, and indices. The writes to this gateway are done in a synchronous manner in order to ensure that no data will be lost during the write process.

Local gateway module allows configuring following _static_ settings, which must be set on every master node. These settings control how long a freshly elected master should wait before it tries to recover the cluster state and the cluster's data:

- `gateway.expected_nodes`: The number of (data or master) nodes that are expected to be in the cluster. Recovery of local shards will start as soon as the expected number of nodes have joined the cluster. Defaults to 0.

- `gateway.expected_master_nodes`: The number of master nodes that are expected to be in the cluster. Recovery of local shards will start as soon as the expected number of master nodes have joined the cluster. Defaults to 0.

- `gateway.expected_data_nodes`: The number of data nodes that are expected to be in the cluster. Recovery of local shards will start as soon as the expected number of data nodes have joined the cluster. Defaults to 0.

- `gateway.recover_after_time`: If the expected number of nodes is not achieved, the recovery process waits for the configured amount of time before trying to recover regardless. Defaults to 5m if one of the `expected_nodes` settings is configured. If this duration is timed out then, recovery is done based on the generic settings we discussed in the previous section, which are `gateway.recover_after.*`.

 All these settings are static (they must be configured inside the `elasticsearch.yml` file on each of the master nodes) and will take effect only after the full cluster restart.

Low-level recovery configuration

We discussed that we can use the gateway to configure the behavior of the Elasticsearch recovery process, but in addition to that, Elasticsearch allows us to configure the recovery process itself. These settings are very helpful in the scenarios where your cluster has a very large dataset and recovery is very slow.

Cluster-level recovery configuration

The recovery configuration is specified mostly on the cluster level and allows us to set general rules for the recovery module to work with. These settings are:

- `indices.recovery.max_bytes_per_sec`: By default, this is set to `40MB` and specifies the maximum number of data that can be transferred during shard recovery per second. In order to disable data transfer limiting, one should set this property to `0`. Similar to the number of concurrent streams, this property allows us to control the network usage of the recovery process. Setting this property to higher values may result in higher network utilization and a faster recovery process.
- `indices.recovery.compress`: This is set to `true` by default and allows us to define whether Elasticsearch should compress the data that is transferred during the recovery process. Setting this to `false` may lower the pressure on the CPU, but it will also result in more data being transferred over the network.
- `indices.recovery.translog_ops`: This defaults to `1000` and specifies how many transaction log lines should be transferred between shards in a single request during the recovery process.
- `indices.recovery.translog_size`: This is the chunk size used to copy the shard transaction log data from the source shard. By default, it is set to `512KB` and is compressed if the `indices.recovery.compress` property is set to `true`.

All the previously mentioned settings can be updated on a live cluster using the Cluster Update API. For example, the following command will set the recovery speed to 2000 MB per second:

```
curl -XPUT localhost:9200/_cluster/settings -d '{
"transient" : {
"indices.recovery.max_bytes_per_sec": "2000mb"}
}'
```

Please note that we have used the `transient` setting so a cluster restart will lose this property; to make it permanent you need to use persistent.

The indices recovery API

With the introduction of the indices recovery API, we are no longer limited to only looking at the cluster state and the output similar to the following one:

```
curl 'localhost:9200/_cluster/health?pretty'
{
  "cluster_name" : "mastering_elasticsearch",
  "status" : "red",
  "timed_out" : false,
  "number_of_nodes" : 10,
  "number_of_data_nodes" : 10,
  "active_primary_shards" : 9,
  "active_shards" : 9,
  "relocating_shards" : 0,
  "initializing_shards" : 0,
  "unassigned_shards" : 1
}
```

By running an HTTP GET request to the _recovery endpoint (for all the indices or for a particular one), we can get the information about the state of the indices' recovery. For example, let's look at the following request:

```
curl -XGET 'localhost:9200/_recovery?pretty'
```

The preceding request will return information about ongoing and finished recoveries of all the shards in the cluster. In our case, the response was as follows (we had to cut it):

```
{
"test_index" : {
"shards" : [ {
"id" : 3,
"type" : "GATEWAY",
"stage" : "START",
"primary" : true,
"start_time_in_millis" : 1414362635212,
"stop_time_in_millis" : 0,
"total_time_in_millis" : 175,
"source" : {
"id" : "3M_ErmCNTR-huTqOTv5smw",
"host" : "192.168.1.10",
"transport_address" : "inet[/192.168.1.10:9300]",
"ip" : "192.168.10",
"name" : "node1"
},
"target" : {
"id" : "3M_ErmCNTR-huTqOTv5smw",
```

```
"host" : "192.168.1.10",
"transport_address" : "inet[/192.168.1.10:9300]",
"ip" : "192.168.1.10",
"name" : "node1"
},
"index" : {
"files" : {
"total" : 400,
"reused" : 400,
"recovered" : 400,
"percent" : "100.0%"
},
"bytes" : {
"total" : 2455604486,
"reused" : 2455604486,
"recovered" : 2455604486,
"percent" : "100.0%"
},
"total_time_in_millis" : 28
},
"translog" : {
"recovered" : 0,
"total_time_in_millis" : 0
},
"start" : {
"check_index_time_in_millis" : 0,
"total_time_in_millis" : 0
}
}, {
"id" : 9,
"type" : "GATEWAY",
"stage" : "DONE",
"primary" : true,
"start_time_in_millis" : 1414085189696,
"stop_time_in_millis" : 1414085189729,
"total_time_in_millis" : 33,
"source" : {
"id" : "nNw_k7_XSOivvPCJLHVE5A",
"host" : "192.168.1.11",
"transport_address" : "inet[/192.168.1.11:9300]",
"ip" : "192.168.1.11",
"name" : "node3"
},
"target" : {
"id" : "nNw_k7_XSOivvPCJLHVE5A",
"host" : "192.168.1.11",
"transport_address" : "inet[/192.168.1.11:9300]",
"ip" : "192.168.1.11",
```

```
"name" : "node3"
},
"index" : {
"files" : {
"total" : 0,
"reused" : 0,
"recovered" : 0,
"percent" : "0.0%"
},
"bytes" : {
"total" : 0,
"reused" : 0,
"recovered" : 0,
"percent" : "0.0%"
},
"total_time_in_millis" : 0
},
"translog" : {
"recovered" : 0,
"total_time_in_millis" : 0
},
"start" : {
"check_index_time_in_millis" : 0,
"total_time_in_millis" : 33
},
.
.
.
]
}
}
```

The preceding response contains information about two shards for test_index (the information for the rest of the shards was removed for clarity). We can see that one of the shards is during the recovery process ("stage" : "START") and the second one already finished the recovery process ("stage" : "DONE"). We can see a lot of information about the recovery process, and the information is provided on the index shard level, which allows us to clearly see at what stage our Elasticsearch cluster is. We can also limit the information to only shards that are currently being recovered by adding the active_only=true parameter to our request, so it would look as follows:

```
curl -XGET 'localhost:9200/_recovery?active_only=true&pretty'
```

If we want to get even more detailed information, we can add the detailed=true parameter to our request, so it would look like this:

```
curl -XGET 'localhost:9200/_recovery?detailed=true&pretty'
```

In addition, you can use the Elasticsearch cat API to get the recovery details of indices. We are going to discuss the cat API in the next section.

The human-friendly status API – using the cat API

The Elasticsearch admin API is quite extensive and covers almost every part of its architecture–from low-level information about Lucene to high-level information about the cluster nodes and their health. All this information is available both using the Elasticsearch Java API as well as using the REST API; however, the data is returned in the JSON format. What's more, the returned data can sometimes be hard to analyze without further parsing. For example, try to run the following request on your Elasticsearch cluster:

```
curl -XGET 'localhost:9200/_stats?pretty'
```

On our local, single node cluster, Elasticsearch returns the following information (we cut it down drastically):

```
{
"_shards" : {
"total" : 144,
"successful" : 77,
"failed" : 0
},
"_all" : {
"primaries" : {
.

.

.

},
"total" : {
.

.

.

}
},
"indices" : {
.

.

.

}
}
```

If you look at the complete output of this command, you would see that the response is more than 1,000 lines long. This isn't quite convenient for analysis by a human without additional parsing. Because of this, Elasticsearch provides us with a more human-friendly API: the cat API. The special cat API returns data in a simple text, tabular format, and what's more, it provides aggregated data that is usually usable without any further processing.

 Remember that we've told you that Elasticsearch allows you to get information not just in the JSON format? If you don't remember this, please try to add the `format=yaml` request parameter to your request.

The basics of cat API

The base endpoint for the cat cat API is quite obvious: it is `/_cat`. Without any parameters, it shows us all the available endpoints for that API. We can check this by running the following command:

```
curl -XGET 'localhost:9200/_cat'
```

The response returned by Elasticsearch should be similar or identical (depending on your Elasticsearch version) to the following one:

```
=^.^=
/_cat/tasks
/_cat/segments
/_cat/segments/{index}
/_cat/allocation
/_cat/fielddata
/_cat/fielddata/{fields}
/_cat/recovery
/_cat/recovery/{index}
/_cat/repositories
/_cat/nodeattrs
/_cat/indices
/_cat/indices/{index}
/_cat/snapshots/{repository}
/_cat/plugins
/_cat/aliases
/_cat/aliases/{alias}
/_cat/nodes
/_cat/master
/_cat/health
/_cat/pending_tasks
/_cat/thread_pool
```

```
/_cat/thread_pool/{thread_pools}
/_cat/count
/_cat/count/{index}
/_cat/shards
/_cat/shards/{index}
```

So, looking for the top Elasticsearch allows us to get the following information using the cat API:

- Current running tasks in the cluster
- Segments' statistics
- Segments' statistics (limited to a given index)
- Shard allocation-related information
- The field data cache size
- The field data cache sizes for individual fields
- Recovery information
- Recovery information (limited to a given index)
- Snapshot repositories information registered in the cluster
- Information about custom node attributes
- Indices' statistics
- Indices' statistics (limited to a given index)
- Information about all the snapshots which belong to a specific repository
- Plugins installed on each node
- Index aliases and indices for a given alias
- Nodes information, including elected master indication
- Master node information
- Cluster health
- Tasks pending execution
- Cluster wise the thread pool information per node
- Cluster wise the thread pool information about single or multiple thread pool per node
- Document count of entire cluster or individual index
- All shard-related information (limited to a given index)

Using the cat API

Let's start using the Cat API through an example. We can start with checking the cluster health of our Elasticsearch cluster. To do this, we just run the following command:

```
curl -XGET 'localhost:9200/_cat/health'
```

The response returned by Elasticsearch to the preceding command should be similar to the following one:

```
1480256137 19:45:37 elasticsearch yellow 1 1 15 15 0 0 15 0 - 50.0%
```

It is clean and nice. Because it is in a tabular format, it is also easier to use the response in tools such as grep, awk, or sed–a standard set of tools for every administrator. It is also more readable once you know what it is all about. To add a header describing each column purpose, we just need to add an additional v parameter just like this:

```
curl -XGET 'localhost:9200/_cat/health?v'
```

The response is very similar to what we've seen previously, but it now contains a header describing each column:

```
    epoch       timestamp cluster        status node.totalnode.data shards
 prireloinitunassignpending_tasksmax_task_wait_timeactive_shards_percent
    1480256174 19:46:14  elasticsearch yellow           1          1       15
15   0   0       15           0             -
50.0%
```

Cat API common arguments

Every cat API endpoint has its own arguments, but there are a few common options that are shared among all of them:

- v: This adds a header line to response with names of presented items.
- h: This allows us to show only chosen columns (refer to the next section).
- help: This lists all possible columns that this particular endpoint is able to show. The command shows the name of the parameter, its abbreviation, and the description.

- `bytes`: This is the format for information representing values in bytes. As we said, the cat API is designed to be used by humans and, because of that, these values are represented in a human-readable form by default: for example, `3.5kB` or `40GB`. The bytes option allows us to set the same base for all numbers, so sorting or numerical comparison will be easier. For example, `bytes=b` presents all values in bytes, `bytes=k` in kilobytes, and so on.

 For the full list of arguments for each Cat API endpoint, refer to the official Elasticsearch documentation available at `http://www.elasticsearch.org/guide/en/elasticsearch/reference/current/cat.html`.

The examples of cat API

At the time of writing this book, the cat API has 25 endpoints. We don't want to describe them all, as it would be a repetition of information contained in the documentation or chapters about the administration API. However, we didn't want to leave this section without any example regarding the usage of the cat API. Because of this, we decided to show you how easily you can get information using the cat API compared to the standard JSON API exposed by Elasticsearch.

Getting information about the master node

The first example shows you how easy it is to get information about which node in our cluster is the master node. By calling the `/_cat/master` REST endpoint, we can get information about the nodes and which one of them is currently being elected as a master. For example, let's run the following command:

```
curl -XGET 'localhost:9200/_cat/master?v'
```

The response returned by Elasticsearch for my local two nodes cluster looks as follows:

```
id            host      ip          node
1NhLoN37S-OvF9QdqD4OmA 127.0.0.1 127.0.0.1 node-1
```

As you can see in the response, we've got the information about which node is currently elected as the master. We can see its identifier, IP address, and name.

Getting information about the nodes

The `/_cat/nodes` REST endpoint provides information about all the nodes in the cluster. Let's see what Elasticsearch will return after running the following command:

```
curl -XGET 'localhost:9200/_cat/nodes?v&h=name,node.role,load,uptime'
```

In the preceding example, we have used the possibility of choosing what information we want to get from the approximately 76 options for this endpoint. We have chosen to get only the node name, its role (whether a node is a master (m), data (a), ingest (i), or a client (–) node), node load (`load_1m`, `load_5m` or `load_15m`), and its uptime.

The response returned by Elasticsearch looks as follows:

```
namenode.role load_1m uptime
node-1 mdi          0.27      6m
```

As you can see the `/_cat/nodes` REST endpoint provides all requested information about the nodes in the cluster.

> You can check out the full list of options for node-related information at the following URL:
> https://www.elastic.co/guide/en/elasticsearch/reference/current/cat-nodes.html

Changes in cat API – Elasticsearch 5.0

If you have been using the Elasticsearch cat API for long, then you must be aware about the changes which the cat API has gone through. The following are the changes done in this API.

Host field removed from the cat nodes API

The `host` field has been removed from the Cat nodes API, as its value is always equal to the `ip` field. The `name` field is available in the Cat nodes API and should be used instead of the `host` field.

Changes to cat recovery API

The recovery API has seen following changes:

- The `fieldsbytes_recovered` and `files_recovered` have been added to the Cat recovery API. These fields, respectively, indicate the total number of bytes and files that have been recovered.
- The `fieldstotal_files` and `total_bytes` have been renamed as `files_total` and `bytes_total`, respectively.
- The field `translog` has been renamed as `translog_ops_recovered`, the field `translog_total` to `translog_ops`, and the field `translog_percent` to `translog_ops_percent`. The short aliases for these fields are tor, to, and top, respectively.

Changes to cat nodes API

The nodes API has become more informative because of the following new information added in the response:

The Cat nodes endpoint returns m for master eligible, `d` for data, and `i` for ingest. A node with no explicit roles will be a coordinating only node and marked with -. A node can have multiple roles. The master column has been adapted to return only whether a node is the current master (*) or not (–).

Changes to cat field data API

This is one of the major change you need to consider in your monitoring if you have been using Elasticsearch for a long time. The field data section used to take most of the heap in earlier versions of Elasticsearch but because of `doc_values`, this problem does not exist anymore.

- The cat field data endpoint adds a row per field instead of a column per field.
- The total field has been removed from the field data API. Total field data usage per node can be attained by the Cat nodes API.

Backing up

One of the most important tasks for the administrator is to make sure that no data will be lost in the case of a system failure. Elasticsearch, in its assumptions, is a resistant and well-configured cluster of nodes and can survive even a few simultaneous disasters. However, even the most properly configured cluster is vulnerable to network splits and network partitions, which in some very rare cases can result in data corruption or loss. In such cases, being able to get data restored from the backup is the only solution that can save us from recreating our indices. You probably already know what we want to talk about: the snapshot/restore functionality provided by Elasticsearch. Although we have covered the basics of the snapshot and restore functionality in previous editions of this book, we are going to cover it yet again in this chapter along with the cloud capabilities of the Elasticsearch backup functionality.

The snapshot API

The snapshot API, which is exposed by Elasticsearch on the _snapshot endpoint, allows you to create snapshots of individual indices or entire clusters into a remote repository. A Repository is a place where the data–our indices and the related meta information–is safely stored (assuming that the storage is reliable and highly available). The assumption is that every node that is a part of the cluster has access to the repository and can both write to it and read from it. Elasticsearch allows you to create snapshots on shared filesystems, HDFS, or in the cloud (Amazon S3, Microsoft Azure, or Google cloud storage). We will first see how to create snapshots in a shared filesystem and then we will cover how snapshots can be created on the cloud services.

Saving backups on a filesystem

Creating snapshots using filesystem repositories ("type": "fs") requires the repository to be accessible from all the data and master nodes in the cluster. So this type of repository can only be created using shared filesystems which can be created using the **Network File System** (**NFS**) drive.

Creating snapshot

The following sub-sections cover the various steps performed for creating a snapshot:

- Registering a repository path
- Registering a shared filesystem repository in Elasticsearch
- Creating snapshots
- Getting snapshot information
- Deleting snapshots

Let us take a closer look at each step.

Registering repository path

Add the following line inside the `elasticsearch.yml` file to register the `path.repo` setting on all the master and data nodes:

```
path.repo: ["/mnt/nfs"]
```

After that, restart the nodes one by one to reload the configuration.

Registering shared file system repository in Elasticsearch

Register the shared file system repository with the name `es-backup` as follows:

```
curl -XPUT 'http://localhost:9200/_snapshot/es-backup' -d '{
"type": "fs",
"settings": {
"location": "/mnt/nfs/es-backup",
"compress": true
}
}'
```

While registering a repository, the following parameters are supported:

- `location`: Location of the snapshots. This is a mandatory parameter.
- `compress`: Turns on compression of the snapshot files. Compression is applied only to metadata files (index mapping and settings). Data files are not compressed. It defaults to `true`.
- `chunk_size`: Big files can be broken down into chunks during snapshotting if needed. The chunk size can be specified in bytes or by using size value notation: `1g`, `10m`, `5k`. Defaults to null (unlimited chunk size).

- `max_restore_bytes_per_sec`: Throttles per node restore rate. Defaults to `40mb` per second.
- `max_snapshot_bytes_per_sec`: Throttles per node snapshot rate. Defaults to `40mb` per second.
- `readonly`: Makes the repository read-only. Defaults to `false`.

Creating snapshots

You can create multiple snapshots of the same cluster within a repository. The following is the command which is used to create a snapshot, `snapshot_1`, inside the `es-snapshot` repository:

```
curl -XPUT
'http://localhost:9200/_snapshot/es-backup/snapshot_1?wait_for_completion=t
rue'
```

The `wait_for_completion` parameter tells if a request should return immediately after the snapshot initialization (defaults to `true`) or wait for the snapshot's completion. During the snapshot initialization, information about all the previous snapshots is loaded into the memory, which means that in large repositories it may take several seconds (or even minutes) for this command to return even if the `wait_for_completion` parameter is set to `false`.

By default, a snapshot of all open and started indices in the cluster is created. This behavior can be changed by specifying the list of indices in the body of the snapshot request:

```
curl -XPUT
'http://localhost:9200/_snapshot/es-backup/snapshot_1?wait_for_completion=t
rue' -d '{
    "indices": "index_1,index_2",
    "ignore_unavailable": "true",
    "include_global_state": false
    }'
```

The following are the settings that you can specify in the request body while creating a snapshot:

- `indices`: The list of indices that should be included in the snapshot.
- `ignore_unavailable`: Setting it to `true` will cause indices that do not exist to be ignored during the snapshot creation. By default, when the `ignore_unavailable` option is not set and an index is missing, the snapshot request will fail.

- include_global_state: By setting it to false, it's possible to prevent the cluster global state to be stored as part of the snapshot. By default, the entire snapshot will fail if one or more indices participating in the snapshot don't have all the primary shards available. This behavior can be changed by setting it partially to true. Besides creating a copy of each index, the snapshot process can also store global cluster metadata, which includes persistent cluster settings and templates.

Getting snapshot information

To get details of a single snapshot you can run the following command:

```
curl -XPUT 'http://localhost:9200/_snapshot /es-backup/snapshot_1
```

Use comma-separated snapshot names to get details of more than one snapshot:

```
curl -XPUT 'http://localhost:9200/_snapshot /es-backup/snapshot_1
```

To get the details of all the snapshots, use the _all at the end like the following:

```
curl -XPUT 'http://localhost:9200/_snapshot /es-backup/_all
```

Deleting snapshots

Deleting a snapshot not only deletes the existing snapshots but also helps in stopping the current executing snapshot process. This is helpful in if you have executed a snapshot creation by mistake. A snapshot can be deleted using the following command:

```
curl -XDELETE 'http://localhost:9200/_snapshot /es-backup/snapshot_1
```

The index snapshot process is incremental in nature. This means that Elasticsearch analyzes the list of the index files that are already stored in the repository and copies only files that were created or changed since the last snapshot. This allows multiple snapshots to be preserved in the repository in a compact form. The snapshotting process is executed in a non-blocking fashion. All indexing and searching operations can continue to be executed against the index that is being snapshotted. However, a snapshot represents the point-in-time view of the index at the moment when the snapshot was created, so no records that were added to the index after the snapshot process was started will be present in the snapshot. The snapshot process starts immediately for the primary shards that have been started and are not currently relocating. Before version 1.2.0, the snapshot operation fails if the cluster has any relocating or initializing primaries of indices participating in the snapshot. Starting with version 1.2.0, Elasticsearch waits for relocation or initialization of shards to complete before snapshotting them.

Only one snapshot process can be executed in the cluster at any time. While a snapshot of a particular shard is being created, this shard cannot be moved to another node, which can interfere with the rebalancing process and allocation filtering. Elasticsearch will only be able to move a shard to another node (according to the current allocation filtering settings and rebalancing algorithm) once the snapshot is finished.

Saving backups in the cloud

Elasticsearch, with the help of additional plugins, allows us to push our data outside of the cluster to the cloud. There are three possibilities where our repository can be located, at least using officially supported plugins:

- **The S3 repository**: AWS
- **The HDFS repository**: Hadoop clusters
- **The GCS repository**: Google cloud services
- **The Azure repository**: Microsoft's cloud platform

Let's go through these repositories to see how we can push our backup data on the cloud services.

The S3 repository

The S3 repository is a part of the Elasticsearch AWS plugin, so to use S3 as the repository for snapshotting, we need to install the plugin first on every node of the cluster and each node must be restarted after the plugin installation:

```
sudo bin/elasticsearch-plugin install repository-s3
```

After installing the plugin on every Elasticsearch node in the cluster, we need to alter their configuration (the elasticsearch.yml file) so that the AWS access information is available. The example configuration can look like this:

```
cloud:
aws:
access_key: YOUR_ACCESS_KEY
secret_key: YOUT_SECRET_KEY
```

To create the S3 repository that Elasticsearch will use for snapshotting, we need to run a command similar to the following one:

```
curl -XPUT 'http://localhost:9200/_snapshot/my_s3_repository' -d '{
"type": "s3",
"settings": {
"bucket": "bucket_name"
}
}'
```

The following settings are supported when defining an S3-based repository:

- `bucket`: This is the required parameter describing the Amazon S3 bucket to which the Elasticsearch data will be written and from which Elasticsearch will read the data.
- `region`: This is the name of the AWS region where the bucket resides. By default, the US Standard region is used.
- `base_path`: By default, Elasticsearch puts the data in the root directory. This parameter allows you to change it and alter the place where the data is placed in the repository.
- `server_side_encryption`: By default, encryption is turned off. You can set this parameter to `true` in order to use the AES256 algorithm to store data.
- `chunk_size`: By default, this is set to `1GB` and specifies the size of the data chunk that will be sent. If the snapshot size is larger than the `chunk_size`, Elasticsearch will split the data into smaller chunks that are not larger than the size specified in the `chunk_size`. The chunk size can be specified in size notations such as `1GB`, `100mb`, and `1024kB`.
- `buffer_size`: The size of this buffer is set to `100mb` by default. When the chunk size is greater than the value of the `buffer_size`, Elasticsearch will split it into `buffer_size` fragments and use the AWS multipart API to send it. The buffer size cannot be set lower than 5 MB because it disallows the use of the multipart API.
- `endpoint`: This defaults to AWS's default S3 endpoint. Setting a region overrides the endpoint setting.
- `protocol`: Specifies whether to use `http` or `https`. It default to `cloud.aws.protocol` or `cloud.aws.s3.protocol`.
- `compress`: Defaults to `false` and when set to `true`. This option allows snapshot metadata files to be stored in a compressed format. Please note that index files are already compressed by default.
- `read_only`: Makes a repository to be read only. It defaults to `false`.

- `max_retries`: This specifies the number of retries Elasticsearch will take before giving up on storing or retrieving the snapshot. By default, it is set to 3.

In addition to the preceding properties, we are allowed to set two additional properties that can overwrite the credentials stored in `elasticserch.yml`, which will be used to connect to S3. This is especially handy when you want to use several S3 repositories, each with its own security settings:

- `access_key`: This overwrites `cloud.aws.access_key` from `elasticsearch.yml`
- `secret_key`: This overwrites `cloud.aws.secret_key` from `elasticsearch.yml`

AWS instances resolve S3 endpoints to a public IP. If the Elasticsearch instances reside in a private subnet in an AWS VPC then all traffic to S3 will go through that VPC's NAT instance. If your VPC's NAT instance is a smaller instance size (for example, a `t1.micro`) or is handling a high volume of network traffic, your bandwidth to S3 may be limited by that NAT instance's networking bandwidth limitations. So, if you running your Elasticsearch cluster inside a VPC then make sure that you are using instances with a high networking bandwidth and there is no network congestion.

Instances residing in a public subnet in an AWS VPC will connect to S3 via the VPC's Internet gateway and not be bandwidth limited by the VPC's NAT instance.

The HDFS repository

If you use Hadoop and its HDFS (`http://wiki.apache.org/hadoop/HDFS`) filesystem, a good alternative to back up the Elasticsearch data is to store it in your Hadoop cluster. As with the case of S3, there is a dedicated plugin for this. To install it, we can use the following command:

```
sudo bin/elasticsearch-plugin install repository-hdfs
```

The HDFS snapshot/restore plugin is built against the latest Apache Hadoop 2.x (currently 2.7.1). If your Hadoop distribution is not protocol compatible with Apache Hadoop, you can replace the Hadoop libraries inside the plugin folder with your own (you might have to adjust the security permissions required).

 Even if Hadoop is already installed on the Elasticsearch nodes, for security reasons, the required libraries need to be placed under the plugin folder. Note that in most cases, if the distribution is compatible, one simply needs to configure the repository with the appropriate Hadoop configuration files.

After installing the plugin on each node in the cluster and restarting every node, we can use the following command to create a repository in our Hadoop cluster:

```
curl -XPUT 'http://localhost:9200/_snapshot/es_hdfs_repository' -d
'{
   "type": "hdfs"
   "settings": {
   "uri": "hdfs://namenode:8020/",
   "path": "elasticsearch_snapshots/es_hdfs_repository"
   }
}'
```

The available settings that we can use are as follows:

- `uri`: This is a required parameter that tells Elasticsearch where HDFS resides. It should have a format like `hdfs://HOST:PORT/`.
- `path`: This is the information about the path where snapshot files should be stored. It is a required parameter.
- `load_default`: This specifies whether the default parameters from the Hadoop configuration should be loaded and set to `false` if the reading of the settings should be disabled. This setting is enabled by default.
- `chunk_size`: This specifies the size of the chunk that Elasticsearch will use to split the snapshot data. If you want the snapshotting to be faster, you can use smaller chunks and more streams to push the data to HDFS. By default, it is disabled.
- `conf.<key>`: This is an optional parameter and tells where a `key` is in any Hadoop argument. The value provided using this property will be merged with the configuration.

As an alternative, you can define your HDFS repository and its settings inside the `elasticsearch.yml` file of each node as follows:

```
repositories:
hdfs:
uri: "hdfs://<host>:<port>/"
path: "some/path"
load_defaults: "true"
conf.<key> : "<value>"
compress: "false"
chunk_size: "10mb"
```

The Azure repository

Just like Amazon S3, we are able to use a dedicated plugin to push our indices and metadata to Microsoft cloud services. To do this, we need to install a plugin on every node of the cluster, which we can do by running the following command:

```
sudo bin/elasticsearch-plugin install repository-azure
```

The configuration is also similar to the Amazon S3 plugin configuration. Our `elasticsearch.yml` file should contain the following section:

```
cloud:
azure:
storage:
my_account:
account: your_azure_storage_account
key: your_azure_storage_key
```

Do not forget to restart all the nodes after installing the plugin.

After Elasticsearch is configured, we need to create the actual repository, which we do by running the following command:

```
curl -XPUT 'http://localhost:9200/_snapshot/azure_repository' -d '{
"type": "azure"
}'
```

The following settings are supported by the Elasticsearch Azure plugin:

- `account`: Microsoft Azure account settings to be used.
- `container`: As with the bucket in Amazon S3, every piece of information must reside in the `container`. This setting defines the name of the `container` in the Microsoft Azure space. The default value is `elasticserch-snapshots`.

- `base_path`: This allows us to change the place where Elasticsearch will put the data. By default, the value for this setting is empty which causes Elasticsearch to put the data in the `root` directory.
- `compress`: This defaults to `false` and when enabled it allows us to compress the metadata files during the snapshot creation.
- `chunk_size`: This is the maximum chunk size used by Elasticsearch (set to `64m` by default, and this is also the maximum value allowed). You can change it to change the size when the data should be split into smaller chunks. You can change the chunk size using size value notations such as, `1g`, `100m`, or `5k`.

An example of creating a repository using the settings follows:

```
curl -XPUT "http://localhost:9205/_snapshot/azure_repository" -d'
{
"type": "azure",
"settings": {
"container": "es-backup-container",
"base_path": "backups",
"chunk_size": "100m",
"compress": true
}
}'
```

The Google cloud storage repository

Similar to Amazon S3 and Microsoft Azure, we can use a GCS repository plugin for snapshotting and restoring of our indices. The settings for this plugin are almost similar to other cloud plugins. To know how to work with the Google cloud repository plugin please refer to the following URL:
https://www.elastic.co/guide/en/elasticsearch/plugins/5.0/repository-gcs.html

Restoring snapshots

Restoring a snapshot is very easy. A snapshot can be restored to other clusters to provide the cluster in which you are restoring it its compatible version.

You cannot restore a snapshot to a lower version of Elasticsearch.

While restoring snapshots, if the index does not already exist, a new index will be created with same index name and all the mappings for that index that were there before creating the snapshot. If the index already exists, then it must be in the closed state and must have the same number of shards as the index snapshot. The restore operation automatically opens the indexes after successful completion.

Example – restoring a snapshot

To take an example of restoring a snapshot from a repository es-backup and a snapshot name, snapshot_1, run the following command against the _restore endpoint on the client node:

```
curl -XPOST localhost:9200/_snapshot/es-backup/snapshot_1/_restore
```

This command will restore all the indices of the snapshot.

Elasticsearch offers several options while restoring the snapshots. The following are some important ones.

Restoring multiple indices

There might be a scenario in which you do not want to restore all the indices of a snapshot and only a few indices. For this you can use the following command:

```
curl -XPOST
"http://localhost:9200/_snapshot/es-backup/snapshot_1/_restore" -d'
    {
       "indices": "index_1,index_2",
       "ignore_unavailable": "true"
    }'
```

Renaming indices

Elasticsearch does not have any option to rename an index once created, apart from setting aliases. But it provides you an option to rename indices while restoring from the snapshot. For example:

```
curl -XPOST
"http://localhost:9200/_snapshot/es-backup/snapshot_1/_restore" -d'
    {
    "indices": "index_1",
    "ignore_unavailable": "true",
```

```
    "rename_replacement": "restored_index"
    }'
```

Partial restore

Partial restore is a very useful feature. It comes in handy in scenarios such as creating snapshots, if the snapshot could not be created for some of the shards. In this case the entire restore process will fail if one or more indices do not have a snapshot of all the shards. In this case, you can use the following command to restore such indices back into the cluster:

```
    curl -XPOST
"http://localhost:9200/_snapshot/es-backup/snapshot_1/_restore" -d'
    {
    "partial": true
    }'
```

Missing shards will be created as empty ones after this process.

Changing index settings during restore

During restoration, many of the index settings can be changed, such as the number of replica and refresh intervals. For example, to restore an index named my_index, with a replica size of 0 (for a faster restore process), and using a default refresh interval rate, you can run the following command:

```
    curl -XPOST
"http://localhost:9200/_snapshot/es-backup/snapshot_1/_restore" -d'
    {
    "indices": "my_index",
    "index_settings": {
    "index.number_of_replicas": 0
    },
    "ignore_index_settings": [
    "index.refresh_interval"
    ]
    }'
```

The indices parameter can contain a comma-separated index name more than once.

Once restored, replicas can be increased with the following command:

```
curl -XPUT "http://localhost:9200/my_index/_settings" -d'
{
"index": {
"number_of_replicas": 1
}
}'
```

Restoring to different cluster

To restore a snapshot to a different cluster, you first need to register the repository from where snapshots need to be restored to a new cluster.

There are some additional considerations you need to take in this process.

- The version of the new cluster must be the same or greater than the cluster from which the snapshot had been taken (only one major version greater). For example, you can restore a 1.x snapshot to a 2.x cluster, but not a 1.x snapshot to a 5.x cluster.
- Index settings can be applied during the snapshot restoration.
- The new cluster need not be the same size (number of nodes, and so on) as the old cluster.
- The appropriate disk size and memory must be available for restoration.
- All the node settings must be same (such as synonyms and hunspell files) and plugins (for example, attachment plugins) on all the nodes which existed during creation of the snapshot.
- If indices in the original cluster were assigned to particular nodes using shard allocation filtering, the same rules will be enforced in the new cluster. Therefore, if the new cluster doesn't contain nodes with the appropriate attributes that a restored index can be allocated on, such an index will not be successfully restored unless these index allocation settings are changed during the restoration operation.

Summary

In this chapter, we covered most of the topics related to the administration of Elasticsearch. We started with describing different types of nodes and how to configure them and then looked into Elasticsearch discovery and recovery modules in detail. Next, we covered the cat API of Elasticsearch, which is very useful in finding out node/cluster/index stats in a very readable format. Finally, we discussed snapshot and restore APIs, which allow you to perform an incremental backup of various repositories, such as shared filesystems or clouds, and to restore the snapshots back into the cluster.

In the next chapter, we will cover one of the most exciting features introduced in Elasticsearch: the ingest node, which allows us to preprocess the data into the Elasticsearch cluster itself before indexing. We will also look into how a federated search works with different clusters using tribe nodes.

9
Data Transformation and Federated Search

In the last chapter, we covered most of the topics related to Elasticsearch cluster administration. We started with describing different types of nodes and how to configure them, and then looked into Elasticsearch discovery and recovery modules in detail. Next, we covered the cat API of Elasticsearch, which is very useful for finding out node/cluster/index stats in a very readable format. Finally, we discussed snapshot and restore APIs which allow you to perform incremental backups to various repositories like shared file systems or the cloud, and to restore the snapshots back into the cluster.

In this chapter, we will cover one of the most exciting features introduced in Elasticsearch: ingest nodes. These allow us to preprocess the data into an Elasticsearch cluster itself before indexing. We will also look into how federated search works among different clusters using tribe nodes. By the end of this chapter, we will have covered following topics:

- Preprocessing data within Elasticsearch with ingest nodes
- What federated search is and how to use it with tribe nodes

Preprocessing data within Elasticsearch with ingest nodes

We gave you a brief overview about ingest nodes under the *Node types in Elasticsearch* section of Chapter 8, *ElasticSearch Administration*. In this section, we are going to cover ingest node functionalities in detail.

Ingest nodes, which are introduced in Elasticsearch 5.0, help in preprocessing the data and enriching them before they are actually indexed. This helps a lot in scenarios where you have to use a custom parser or Logstash for processing documents and enriching them, before sending to Elasticsearch. Now you can do all those things within Elasticsearch itself. This preprocessing is achieved with the help of defining a pipeline and a series of one or more processors. Each processor transforms the document in some way. For example, you can add a new field with a custom value or remove a field completely.

Working with ingest pipeline

An ingest pipeline has the following structure:

```
{
  "description" : "...",
  "processors" : [ ... ]
}
```

Here, the `description` parameter contains any text which describes what this pipeline does and the `processors` parameter is a list of one or more processors which are always executed in the order as they are declared. In the following sections we will see lots of examples of how you can use various processors available in Elasticsearch.

The ingest APIs

Elasticsearch provides a dedicated `_ingest` API for creating a pipeline, getting the already registered pipeline details, deleting the pipeline, and debugging a pipeline.

Creating a pipeline

A pipeline ca be added or updated in the following way:

```
n be added or updated in the following way:

curl -XPUT "localhost:9200/_ingest/pipeline/pipeline-id" -d'
{
   "description": "pipeline description",
   "processors": [
      {
         "set": {
            "field": "foo",
            "value": "bar"
         }
      }
```

```
        ]
    }'
```

Getting pipeline details

To get the details of an already registered pipeline, you can use following command:

```
curl -XGET 'localhost:9200/_ingest/pipeline/pipeline-id?pretty'
```

You can use comma-separated IDs to return more than one pipeline in a single request. You may also use wildcards in IDs.

Deleting a pipeline

Similar to deleting a document from Elasticsearch index, you can delete a pipeline with the following command:

```
curl -XDELETE 'localhost:9200/_ingest/pipeline/pipeline-id'
```

You can use comma-separated IDs to return more than one pipeline in a single request. You may also use wildcards in IDs.

Simulating pipelines for debugging purposes

In addition to the _ingest API, Elasticsearch also provides a _simulate API, which is used for investigating the pipelines. This helps you in ensuring exactly what a processor will do and what errors will be thrown if the processors fail.

The simulate API can be used to run pipelines against a set of input documents. Please note that these input documents are never indexed and are only used for testing of pipelines.

The structure of a simulate request looks as follows:

```
curl -XPOST "localhost:9200/_ingest/pipeline/_simulate" -d'
{
    "pipeline": {},
    "docs": []
}'
```

The `pipeline` parameter contains the definition of pipeline and the `docs` parameter contains the array of JSON documents which are to be tested against the given pipeline.

For example, look at the following simulate request in which we are simply adding a new field, category and its value as search engine using a set processor:

```
curl -XPOST "http://localhost:9200/_ingest/pipeline/_simulate?pretty" -d'
  {
    "pipeline" :
    {
      "description": "adding a new field and value to the each document",
      "processors": [
        {
          "set" : {
            "field" : "category",
            "value" : "search engine"
          }
        }
      ]
    },
    "docs": [
      {
        "_index": "index",
        "_type": "type",
        "_id": "id",
        "_source": {
          "name": "lucene"
        }
      },
      {
        "_index": "index",
        "_type": "type",
        "_id": "id",
        "_source": {
          "name": "elasticsearch"
        }
      }
    ]
  }'
```

Now look at the response of the preceding request:

```
{
  "docs" : [
    {
      "doc" : {
        "_id" : "id",
        "_index" : "index",
```

```
          "_type" : "type",
          "_source" : {
            "name" : "lucene",
            "category" : "search engine"
          },
          "_ingest" : {
            "timestamp" : "2016-12-25T19:48:10.542+0000"
          }
        }
      },
      {
        "doc" : {
          "_id" : "id",
          "_index" : "index",
          "_type" : "type",
          "_source" : {
            "name" : "elasticsearch",
            "category" : "search engine"
          },
          "_ingest" : {
            "timestamp" : "2016-12-25T19:48:10.542+0000"
          }
        }
      }
    ]
  }
```

You can see both of our documents contain a new field, `category`.

You can use the `verbose` parameter in a simulate request to see how each processor affects the document as it passes through the pipeline. For example, let's make another simulate request which contains two processors, each adding a new field to each of the ingest documents:

```
curl -XPOST
"http://localhost:9200/_ingest/pipeline/_simulate?pretty&verbose" -d'

{
  "pipeline" :
  {
    "description": "adding a new field and value to the each document",
    "processors": [
      {
        "set" : {
          "field" : "category",
          "value" : "search engine"
        }
      },
```

```
        {
          "set" : {
            "field" : "field3",
            "value" : "value3"
          }
        }
      ]
    },
    "docs": [
      {
        "_index": "index",
        "_type": "type",
        "_id": "id",
        "_source": {
          "name": "lucene"
        }
      },
      {
        "_index": "index",
        "_type": "type",
        "_id": "id",
        "_source": {
          "name": "elasticsearch"
        }
      }
    ]
  }'
```

The output response of the preceding request will look as follows:

```
{
  "docs" : [
    {
      "processor_results" : [
        {
          "doc" : {
            "_type" : "type",
            "_index" : "index",
            "_id" : "id",
            "_source" : {
              "name" : "lucene",
              "category" : "search engine"
            },
            "_ingest" : {
              "timestamp" : "2016-12-25T19:56:50.599+0000"
            }
          }
        },
```

```
      {
        "doc" : {
          "_type" : "type",
          "_index" : "index",
          "_id" : "id",
          "_source" : {
            "name" : "lucene",
            "category" : "search engine",
            "field3" : "value3"
          },
          "_ingest" : {
            "timestamp" : "2016-12-25T19:56:50.599+0000"
          }
        }
      }
    ]
  },
  {
    "processor_results" : [
      {
        "doc" : {
          "_type" : "type",
          "_index" : "index",
          "_id" : "id",
          "_source" : {
            "name" : "elasticsearch",
            "category" : "search engine"
          },
          "_ingest" : {
            "timestamp" : "2016-12-25T19:56:50.599+0000"
          }
        }
      },
      {
        "doc" : {
          "_type" : "type",
          "_index" : "index",
          "_id" : "id",
          "_source" : {
            "name" : "elasticsearch",
            "category" : "search engine",
            "field3" : "value3"
          },
          "_ingest" : {
            "timestamp" : "2016-12-25T19:56:50.599+0000"
          }
        }
      }
    }
```

```
        ]
      }
    ]
  }
```

If you want use the simulate API with an existing pipeline then you can simply use the following request structure:

```
curl -XPOST
"http://localhost:9200/_ingest/pipeline/my-pipeline-id/_simulate" -d'
    {
      "docs" : [
        { /** first document **/ },
        { /** second document **/ },
        // ...
      ]
    }'
```

Handling errors in pipelines

We have already discussed that an ingest pipeline is a list of processors that are executed sequentially in the order that they are defined, and processing halts at the first exception. This behavior may not be desirable when failures are expected. For example, you may have logs that don't match the specified `grok` expression. Instead of halting execution, you may want to index such documents into a separate index.

To enable this behavior, you can use the `on_failure` parameter while defining the pipeline. The `on_failure` parameter defines a list of processors to be executed immediately following the failed processor. You can specify this parameter at the pipeline level, as well as at the processor level. If a processor specifies an `on_failure` configuration, whether it is empty or not, any exceptions that are thrown by the processor are caught, and the pipeline continues executing the remaining processors. Because you can define further processors within the scope of an `on_failure` statement, you can nest failure handling.

Tagging errors within the same document and index

Let's see an example, in which we define a pipeline that renames the `name` field in the processed document to `technology_name`. If the document does not contain the `category` field, the processor attaches an error message to the document for later analysis within Elasticsearch:

```
curl -XPUT "http://localhost:9200/_ingest/pipeline/pipeline1" -d'
    {
```

```
    "description" : "my first pipeline with handled exceptions",
    "processors" : [
      {
        "rename" : {
          "field" : "name",
          "target_field" : "technology_name",
          "on_failure" : [
            {
              "set" : {
                "field" : "error",
                "value" : "field "name" does not exist, cannot rename to
  "technology_name""
              }
            }
          ]
        }
      }
    ]}'
```

With previous request we have registered a pipeline, and now let's index a document using this pipeline. Please note that this document does not contain a name field but this document will be indexed:

```
curl -XPOST "http://localhost:9200/my_index/doc/1?pipeline=pipeline1" -
d'
  {
    "message": "learning ingest APIs"
  }'
```

But when you retrieve this document from Elasticsearch, you will see that it contains an additional field error with our custom error message contained as a value:

```
curl -XGET "http://localhost:9200/my_index/doc/1"
```

The output looks as follows:

```
  {
    "_index": "my_index",
    "_type": "doc",
    "_id": "1",
    "_version": 1,
    "found": true,
    "_source": {
        "message": "learning ingest APIs",
        "error": "field "name" does not exist, cannot rename to
  "technology_name""
    }
  }
```

Indexing error prone documents in a different index

You have already seen how we can tag errors inside the documents in the same index, but if you want to send all these error-prone documents into a different index, then you can define your `on_failure` block as follows:

```
"on_failure": [
            {
                "set": {
                    "field": "_index",
                    "value": "failed-{{ _index }}"
                }
            }
        ]
```

Please note that the previous syntax will create a new index with the name, `failed-my_index` and will index for indexing all those documents which throw an error.

Ignoring errors altogether

If you neither want to take any action on the errors, nor want indexing to be interrupted then you can simply ignore the errors by setting the `ignore_failure` parameter to `true`:

```
{
  "description" : "pipleline which ignore errors",
  "processors" : [
    {
      "rename" : {
        "field" : "name",
        "target_field" : "technology_name",
        "ignore_failure" : true
      }
    }
  ]
}
```

Working with ingest processors

At the time of writing this book, there are 23 built-in processors available inside Elasticsearch listed as follows:

- Append processor
- Convert processor

- Date processor
- Date index name processor
- Fail processor
- Foreach processor
- Grok processor
- Gsub processor
- Join processor
- JSON processor
- KV processor
- Lowercase processor
- Remove processor
- Rename processor
- Script processor
- Set processor
- Split processor
- Sort processor
- Trim processor
- Uppercase processor
- Dot expander processor

We have already shown you examples of using `set` (used for setting a field and adding a value for that field) and the `rename` processor (for renaming a field) in the previous section. Let's take a look at some more processors and their usage.

Append processor

This processor appends one or more values to an existing array if the field already exists and it is an array. It can also convert a scalar to an array and append one or more values to it if the field exists and it is a scalar. In addition, it can create an array containing the provided values if the field doesn't exist. This processor accepts a single value or an array of values. For example:

```
{
  "append": {
    "field": "tags"
    "value": ["tag1", "tag2", "tag3"]
  }
}
```

Convert processor

This processor can be used for converting the value of a field to a different type, such as converting an integer value in string format to an integer. For example:

```
{
    "convert": {
        "field" : "field1",
        "type": "integer"
    }
}
```

This processor can convert "33" into 33, but if the field contains non-integer text then it will throw a number format exception.

Optionally, you can use two other parameters with this processor, `target_field` which is the field to assign the converted value to, by default, the field is updated in-place, and `ignore_missing` which defaults to `false` and if set to `true` and the field does not exist or is null, the processor quietly exits without modifying the document.

Grok processor

This is one of the most powerful processors available and is able to extract structured fields out of a single text field within a document. You choose which field to extract matched fields from, as well as the `grok` pattern you expect will match. A grok pattern is like a regular expression that supports aliased expressions that can be reused.

If you have ever used Logstash then you must be aware of `grok` filters which are used for a similar purpose.

This tool is widely used with logs such as syslogs, web server logs, and so on to extract valuable information out of them and index them in a structured format. The best part of this processor is that it comes packaged with over 120 `grok` patterns which you can directly use. You can get a full list of patterns here:
`https://github.com/elastic/elasticsearch/tree/master/modules/ingest-common/src/main/resources/patterns`

The following is an example of using a `grok` processor in combination with a `convert` processor.

First, register a pipeline using the following command:

```
curl -XPUT "http://localhost:9200/_ingest/pipeline/grok-pipeline" -d'
{
    "description": "my pipeline for extracting info from logs",
    "processors": [
        {
            "grok": {
                "field": "message",
                "patterns": [
                    "%{IP:client} %{WORD:method} %{URIPATHPARAM:req}
%{NUMBER:bytes} %{NUMBER:duration}"
                ]
            }
        },
        {
            "convert": {
                "field": "duration",
                "type": "integer"
            }
        }
    ]
}'
```

Next, index a document using the pipeline we have just created:

```
curl -XPOST "http://localhost:9200/logs/doc/1?pipeline=grok-pipeline" -
d'
{
    "message": "127.0.0.1 POST /fetch_docs 200 10"
}'
```

Now, let's retrieve the document to see what it contains:

```
curl -XGET "http://localhost:9200/logs/doc/1"
```

The above command will return the following output:

```
{
        "_index": "logs",
        "_type": "doc",
        "_id": "1",
        "_version": 1,
        "found": true,
        "_source": {
            "duration": 10,
            "method": "POST",
            "bytes": "200",
            "client": "127.0.0.1",
```

```
      "message": "127.0.0.1 POST /fetch_docs 200 10",
      "req": "/fetch_docs"
    }
  }
```

In addition to using built-in `grok` patterns, you can define your custom `grok` patterns too, using the `pattern_definition` option as shown in the following example:

```
curl -XPOST "http://localhost:9200/_ingest/pipeline/_simulate" -d'
{
  "pipeline": {
  "description" : "parse custom patterns",
  "processors": [
    {
      "grok": {
        "field": "message",
        "patterns": ["%{LOVE:hobbies} about %{TOPIC:topic}"],
        "pattern_definitions" : {
          "LOVE" : "reading",
          "TOPIC" : "databases"
        }
      }
    }
  ]
},
"docs":[
  {
    "_source": {
      "message": "I like reading about databases"
    }
  }
  ]
}'
```

We have defined two custom patterns in the previous request and used them in the `patterns` parameter. The output of the request looks as follows:

```
{
    "docs": [
      {
        "doc": {
          "_type": "_type",
          "_index": "_index",
          "_id": "_id",
          "_source": {
            "topic": "databases",
            "message": "I like reading about databases",
            "hobbies": "reading"
```

```
        },
        "_ingest": {
            "timestamp": "2016-12-25T21:42:20.930+0000"
        }
    }
  }
 ]
}
```

 To get a full list of processors provided by Elasticsearch, you can look at the official documentation at this URL: https://www.elastic.co/guide/en/elasticsearch/reference/master/ingest-processors.html.

Federated search

Sometimes, having data in a single cluster is not enough. Imagine a situation where you have multiple locations where you need to index and search your data–for example, local company divisions that have their own clusters for their own data. The main center of your company would also like to search the data–not in each location but all at once. Of course, in your search application, you can connect to all these clusters and merge the results manually, but from Elasticsearch 1.0, it is also possible to use the so-called **tribe node** that works as a federated Elasticsearch client and can provide access to more than a single Elasticsearch cluster. What the tribe node does, is fetch all the cluster states from the connected clusters and merge these states into one global cluster state available on the tribe node. In this section, we will take a look at tribe nodes and how to configure and use them.

The test clusters

For the purpose of showing you how tribe nodes work, we will create two clusters that hold data. The first cluster is named `mastering_one` (as you may remember, to set the cluster name, you need to specify the `cluster.name` property in the `elasticsearch.yml` file) and the second cluster is named `mastering_two`. To keep it as simple as it can get, each of the clusters contain only a single Elasticsearch node. The node in the cluster named `mastering_one` is available at the `11.0.7.102` IP address and the cluster named `mastering_two` is available at the `11.0.7.104` IP address.

Please note that, you need to replace the IPs (11.0.7.102, 11.0.7.103 and 11.0.7.104) of Elasticsearch nodes as per your actual IP address.

Cluster one was indexed with the following documents:

```
curl -XPOST '11.0.7.102:9200/index_one/doc/1' -d '{"name" : "Test document
1 cluster 2"}'

curl -XPOST '11.0.7.102:9200/index_one/doc/2' -d '{"name" : "Test document
2 cluster 2"}'
```

For the second cluster the following data was indexed:

```
curl -XPOST '11.0.7.104:9200/index_two/doc/1' -d '{"name" : "Test document
1 cluster 2"}'

curl -XPOST '11.0.7.104:9200/index_two/doc/2' -d '{"name" : "Test document
2 cluster 2"}'
```

Creating the tribe node

Now, let's try to create a simple tribe node that will use the unicast discovery by default. To do this, we need a new Elasticsearch node. We also need to provide a configuration for this node that will specify which clusters our tribe node should connect together–in our case, these are our two clusters that we created earlier. To configure our tribe node, we need the following configuration in the elasticsearch.yml file:

```
cluster.name: tribe_cluster
tribe.mastering_one.cluster.name: mastering_one
tribe.mastering_one.discovery.zen.ping.unicast.hosts: ["11.0.7.102"]
tribe.mastering_two.cluster.name: mastering_two
tribe.mastering_two.discovery.zen.ping.unicast.hosts: ["11.0.7.104"]
node.name: tribe_node_1
```

All the configurations for the tribe node are prefixed with the tribe prefix. In the preceding configuration, we told Elasticsearch that we will have two tribes: one named mastering_one and the second one named mastering_two. These are arbitrary names that are used to distinguish the clusters that are a part of the tribe cluster. We also have configured the discovery.zen.ping.unicast.hosts property for each of the clusters so that our tribe node can connect to both the clusters using unicasting discovery.

Do not forget to configure the `network.host` property for each node in each cluster so that nodes can be bound to addresses and are available on the network. In a secured VPC, you can safely bind them to `0.0.0.0`.

We can start our tribe node, which we will start on a server with the `11.0.7.103` IP address. After starting the Elasticsearch tribe node, you should see the following in the logs of the tribe node:

```
    [[2016-12-25T12:40:16,341][INFO ][o.e.n.Node               ]
[tribe_node_1] initialized
    [2016-12-25T12:40:16,342][INFO ][o.e.n.Node               ]
[tribe_node_1] starting ...
    [2016-12-25T12:40:16,621][INFO ][o.e.t.TransportService   ]
[tribe_node_1] publish_address {11.0.7.103:9300}, bound_addresses
{[::]:9300}
    [2016-12-25T12:40:16,627][INFO ][o.e.b.BootstrapCheck     ]
[tribe_node_1] bound or publishing to a non-loopback or non-link-local
address, enforcing bootstrap checks
    [2016-12-25T12:40:16,695][INFO ][o.e.h.HttpServer         ]
[tribe_node_1] publish_address {11.0.7.103:9200}, bound_addresses
{[::]:9200}
    [2016-12-25T12:40:16,697][INFO ][o.e.n.Node               ]
[tribe_node_1/mastering_one] starting ...
    [2016-12-25T12:40:17,022][INFO ][o.e.t.TransportService   ]
[tribe_node_1/mastering_one] publish_address {11.0.7.103:9301},
bound_addresses {[::]:9301}
    [2016-12-25T12:40:20,183][INFO ][o.e.c.s.ClusterService   ]
[tribe_node_1/mastering_one] detected_master
{mastering_one_node_1}{1b4Splc6ThCNY2BCf4Ww-
A}{rRu-1h4wQAGJhCgsVnFhow}{11.0.7.102}{11.0.7.102:9300}, added
{{mastering_one_node_1}{1b4Splc6ThCNY2BCf4Ww-
A}{rRu-1h4wQAGJhCgsVnFhow}{11.0.7.102}{11.0.7.102:9300},}, reason: zen-
disco-receive(from master [master
{mastering_one_node_1}{1b4Splc6ThCNY2BCf4Ww-
A}{rRu-1h4wQAGJhCgsVnFhow}{11.0.7.102}{11.0.7.102:9300} committed version
[5]])
    [2016-12-25T12:40:20,195][INFO ][o.e.n.Node               ]
[tribe_node_1/mastering_one] started
    [2016-12-25T12:40:20,195][INFO ][o.e.n.Node               ]
[tribe_node_1/mastering_two] starting ...
    [2016-12-25T12:40:20,200][INFO ][o.e.t.TribeService       ]
[tribe_node_1] [mastering_one] adding node
[{tribe_node_1/mastering_one}{Ii9HdyG6RHSYRtYu32qA_w}{frKhVo-
fTxyq4VJUL5W8GA}{11.0.7.103}{11.0.7.103:9301}{tribe.name=mastering_one}]
    [2016-12-25T12:40:20,200][INFO ][o.e.t.TribeService       ]
[tribe_node_1] [mastering_one] adding node
```

```
[{mastering_one_node_1}{lb4Splc6ThCNY2BCf4Ww-
A}{rRu-1h4wQAGJhCgsVnFhow}{11.0.7.102}{11.0.7.102:9300}{tribe.name=masterin
g_one}]
    [2016-12-25T12:40:20,214][INFO ][o.e.c.s.ClusterService    ]
[tribe_node_1] added
{{tribe_node_1/mastering_one}{Ii9HdyG6RHSYRtYu32qA_w}{frKhVo-
fTxyq4VJUL5W8GA}{11.0.7.103}{11.0.7.103:9301}{tribe.name=mastering_one},{ma
stering_one_node_1}{lb4Splc6ThCNY2BCf4Ww-
A}{rRu-1h4wQAGJhCgsVnFhow}{11.0.7.102}{11.0.7.102:9300}{tribe.name=masterin
g_one},}, reason: cluster event from mastering_one[zen-disco-receive(from
master [master {mastering_one_node_1}{lb4Splc6ThCNY2BCf4Ww-
A}{rRu-1h4wQAGJhCgsVnFhow}{11.0.7.102}{11.0.7.102:9300} committed version
[5]])]
    [2016-12-25T12:40:20,506][INFO ][o.e.t.TransportService    ]
[tribe_node_1/mastering_two] publish_address {11.0.7.103:9302},
bound_addresses {[::]:9302}
    [2016-12-25T12:40:23,580][INFO ][o.e.c.s.ClusterService    ]
[tribe_node_1/mastering_two] detected_master
{mastering_two_node_1}{kLoK49a7Sc2COFJc1i-21A}{zyCqnk79R2KIeucUdMc2Ug}{11.0
.7.104}{11.0.7.104:9300}, added
{{mastering_two_node_1}{kLoK49a7Sc2COFJc1i-21A}{zyCqnk79R2KIeucUdMc2Ug}{11.
0.7.104}{11.0.7.104:9300},}, reason: zen-disco-receive(from master [master
{mastering_two_node_1}{kLoK49a7Sc2COFJc1i-21A}{zyCqnk79R2KIeucUdMc2Ug}{11.0
.7.104}{11.0.7.104:9300} committed version [6]])
    [2016-12-25T12:40:23,581][INFO ][o.e.t.TribeService    ]
[tribe_node_1] [mastering_two] adding node
[{tribe_node_1/mastering_two}{dlqAZKckQwCnhCtDw4veDg}{CWadKcbqTn24fl5qJlvOj
A}{11.0.7.103}{11.0.7.103:9302}{tribe.name=mastering_two}]
    [2016-12-25T12:40:23,581][INFO ][o.e.t.TribeService    ]
[tribe_node_1] [mastering_two] adding node
[{mastering_two_node_1}{kLoK49a7Sc2COFJc1i-21A}{zyCqnk79R2KIeucUdMc2Ug}{11.
0.7.104}{11.0.7.104:9300}{tribe.name=mastering_two}]
    [2016-12-25T12:40:23,582][INFO ][o.e.c.s.ClusterService    ]
[tribe_node_1] added
{{tribe_node_1/mastering_two}{dlqAZKckQwCnhCtDw4veDg}{CWadKcbqTn24fl5qJlvOj
A}{11.0.7.103}{11.0.7.103:9302}{tribe.name=mastering_two},{mastering_two_no
de_1}{kLoK49a7Sc2COFJc1i-21A}{zyCqnk79R2KIeucUdMc2Ug}{11.0.7.104}{11.0.7.10
4:9300}{tribe.name=mastering_two},}, reason: cluster event from
mastering_two[zen-disco-receive(from master [master
{mastering_two_node_1}{kLoK49a7Sc2COFJc1i-21A}{zyCqnk79R2KIeucUdMc2Ug}{11.0
.7.104}{11.0.7.104:9300} committed version [6]])]
    [2016-12-25T12:40:23,583][INFO ][o.e.n.Node    ]
[tribe_node_1/mastering_two] started
    [2016-12-25T12:40:23,583][INFO ][o.e.n.Node    ]
[tribe_node_1] started
```

Reading data with the tribe node

We said in the beginning that the tribe node fetches the cluster state from all the connected clusters and merges it into a single cluster state. This is done in order to enable read and write operations on all the clusters when using the tribe node. Because the cluster state is merged, almost all operations work in the same way as they would on a single cluster, for example, searching.

Let's try to run a single query against our tribe now to see what we can expect. To do this, we use the following command:

```
curl -XGET '11.0.7.103:9200/_search?pretty'
```

The results of the preceding query look as follows:

```
{
  "took" : 12,
  "timed_out" : false,
  "_shards" : {
    "total" : 10,
    "successful" : 10,
    "failed" : 0
  },
  "hits" : {
    "total" : 4,
    "max_score" : 1.0,
    "hits" : [
      {
        "_index" : "index_one",
        "_type" : "doc",
        "_id" : "2",
        "_score" : 1.0,
        "_source" : {
          "name" : "Test document 2 cluster 2"
        }
      },
      {
        "_index" : "index_two",
        "_type" : "doc",
        "_id" : "2",
        "_score" : 1.0,
        "_source" : {
          "name" : "Test document 2 cluster 2"
        }
      },
      {
        "_index" : "index_one",
```

```
        "_type" : "doc",
        "_id" : "1",
        "_score" : 1.0,
        "_source" : {
          "name" : "Test document 1 cluster 2"
        }
      },
      {
        "_index" : "index_two",
        "_type" : "doc",
        "_id" : "1",
        "_score" : 1.0,
        "_source" : {
          "name" : "Test document 1 cluster 2"
        }
      }
    ]
  }
}
```

As you can see, we have documents coming from both clusters–yes, that's right; our tribe node was about to automatically get data from all the connected tribes and return the relevant results. We can, of course, do the same with more sophisticated queries; we can use percolation functionality, suggesters, and so on.

Master-level read operations

Read operations that require the master to be present, such as reading the cluster state or cluster health, will be performed on the tribe cluster. For example, let's look at what cluster health returns for our tribe node. We can check this by running the following command:

```
curl -XGET '11.0.7.103:9200/_cluster/health?pretty'
```

The results of the preceding command will be similar to the following one:

```
{
  "cluster_name" : "tribe_cluster",
  "status" : "yellow",
  "timed_out" : false,
  "number_of_nodes" : 5,
  "number_of_data_nodes" : 2,
  "active_primary_shards" : 10,
  "active_shards" : 10,
  "relocating_shards" : 0,
  "initializing_shards" : 0,
  "unassigned_shards" : 10,
```

```
    "delayed_unassigned_shards" : 0,
    "number_of_pending_tasks" : 0,
    "number_of_in_flight_fetch" : 0,
    "task_max_waiting_in_queue_millis" : 0,
    "active_shards_percent_as_number" : 50.0
}
```

As you can see, our tribe node reported five nodes present. We have a single node for each of the connected clusters: one tribe node and two internal nodes that are used to provide connectivity to the connected clusters. This is why there are five nodes and not three of them.

Writing data with the tribe node

We talked about querying and master-level read operations, so it is time to write some data to Elasticsearch using the tribe node. We won't say much; instead of talking about indexing, let's just try to index additional documents to one of our indices that are present on the connected clusters. We can do this by running the following command:

```
curl -XPOST '11.0.7.103:9200/index_one/doc/3' -d '{"name" : "Test
document 3 cluster 1"}'
```

The execution of the preceding command will result in the following response:

```
{"_index":"index_one","_type":"doc","_id":"3","_version":1,"result":"create
d","_shards":{"total":2,"successful":1,"failed":0},"created":true}
```

As we can see, the document has been created and, what's more, it was indexed in the proper cluster. The tribe node just did its work by forwarding the request internally to the proper cluster. All the write operations that don't require the cluster state to change, such as indexing, will be properly executed using the tribe node.

Master-level write operations

Master-level write operations can't be executed on the tribe node–for example, we won't be able to create a new index using the tribe node. Operations such as index creation will fail when executed on the tribe node, because there is no global master present. We can test this easily by running the following command:

```
curl -XPUT '11.0.7.103:9200/index_three'
```

The preceding command will return the following error after about 30 seconds of waiting:

```
{"error":{"root_cause":[{"type":"master_not_discovered_exception","reason":
null}],"type":"master_not_discovered_exception","reason":null},"status":503
}
```

As we can see, the index was not created. We should run the master-level write commands on the clusters that are a part of the tribe.

Handling indices conflicts

One of the things that the tribe node can't handle properly is indices with the same names present in multiple connected clusters. What the Elasticsearch tribe node will do by default is that it will choose one and only one index with the same name. So, if all your clusters have the same index, only a single one will be chosen.

Let's test this by creating the index called `test_conflicts` on the `mastering_one` cluster and the same index on the `mastering_two` cluster. We can do this by running the following commands:

```
curl -XPUT '11.0.7.102:9200/test_conflicts'
curl -XPUT '11.0.7.104:9200/test_conflicts'
```

In addition to this, let's index two documents–one to each cluster. We do this by running the following commands:

```
curl -XPOST '11.0.7.102:9200/test_conflicts/doc/11' -d '{"name" : "Test
conflict cluster 1"}'
curl -XPOST '11.0.7.104:9200/test_conflicts/doc/21' -d '{"name" : "Test
conflict cluster 2"}'
```

Now, let's run our tribe node and try to run a simple search command:

```
curl -XGET '11.0.7.103:9200/test_conflicts/_search?pretty'
```

The output of the command will be as follows:

```
{
  "took" : 5,
  "timed_out" : false,
  "_shards" : {
    "total" : 5,
    "successful" : 5,
    "failed" : 0
  },
  "hits" : {
```

```
        "total" : 1,
        "max_score" : 1.0,
        "hits" : [
          {
            "_index" : "test_conflicts",
            "_type" : "doc",
            "_id" : "11",
            "_score" : 1.0,
            "_source" : {
              "name" : "Test conflict cluster 1"
            }
          }
        ]
      }
    }
```

As you can see, we only got a single document in the result. This is because the Elasticsearch tribe node can't handle indices with the same names coming from different clusters and will choose only one index. This is quite dangerous, because we don't know what to expect.

The good thing is that we can control this behavior by specifying the `tribe.on_conflict` property in `elasticsearch.yml` (introduced in Elasticsearch 1.2.0). We can set it to one of the following values:

- `any`: This is the default value that results in Elasticsearch choosing one of the indices from the connected tribe clusters.
- `drop`: Elasticsearch will ignore the index and won't include it in the global cluster state. This means that the index won't be visible when using the cluster node (both for write and read operations) but will still be present on the connected clusters themselves.
- `prefer_TRIBE_NAME`: Elasticsearch allows us to choose the tribe cluster from which the indices should be taken. For example, if we set our property to `prefer_mastering_one`, it would mean that Elasticsearch will load the conflicting indices from the cluster named `mastering_one`.

Blocking write operations

The tribe node can also be configured to block all write operations and all the metadata change requests. To block all the write operations, we need to set the `tribe.blocks.write` property to `true`. To disallow metadata change requests, we need to set the `tribe.blocks.metadata` property to `true`. By default, these properties are set to `false`, which means that write and metadata altering operations are allowed. Disallowing these operations can be useful when our tribe node should only be used for searching and nothing else.

In addition to this, Elasticsearch 1.2.0 introduced the ability to block write operations on defined indices. We do this by using the `tribe.blocks.indices.write` property and setting its value to the name of the indices. For example, if we want our tribe node to block write operations on all the indices starting with `test` and `production`, we set the following property in the `elasticsearch.yml` file of the tribe node:

```
tribe.blocks.indices.write: test*, production*
```

Summary

In this chapter, we discussed ingest nodes which help us to preprocess and enrich the data within the Elasticsearch cluster itself before the actual indexing takes place. We also covered the concept of federated search in Elasticsearch and how it can be achieved with the help of tribe nodes.

Our next chapter is dedicated to Elasticsearch performance improvements under different loads and the right way of scaling production clusters along with covering insights into garbage collection and hot thread issues and how to deal with them. We will also talk about query profiling and query benchmarking to know which part of the query is taking more time to execute. In the end, we will talk about general Elasticsearch cluster tuning advice under high query rate scenarios versus high indexing throughput scenarios.

10
Improving Performance

In the last chapter, we focused on two special kinds of nodes in Elasticsearch: ingest nodes and tribe nodes. We read about how one can do preprocessing and enrichment of data within Elasticsearch itself, and then we saw how to use a tribe node to enable cross cluster searching and called a **federated search**.

In this chapter, we are going to focus primarily on performance improvements of Elasticsearch clusters and how to scale them under different loads and scenarios. Additionally, we will also see how to work with query profiling and query benchmarking to know which part of the query takes more time to execute. In the end, we will also discuss general Elasticsearch cluster tuning considerations, under high query rate scenarios versus high indexing throughput scenarios. By the end of this chapter we will have covered the following topics:

- Validating queries and using the query profiler to measure performance
- What the hot threads API is and how it can help you with diagnosing problems
- How to scale Elasticsearch and what to look for when doing it
- Preparing Elasticsearch for high querying throughput use cases
- Preparing Elasticsearch for high indexing throughput use cases
- Managing time-based indices efficiently using shrink and rollover APIs

Query validation and profiling

In this section, we are going to learn two important features related to queries. First, the query validation, which will help you in finding out if your queries, can be executed or is bugged. Second, getting the full execution time information of a query so that you can check out which component of your query is taking how much and eventually it will help you in diagnosis of your slow queries.

Validating expensive queries before execution

While writing a new query, it's better to be sure that the query you have formed has the correct syntax and does not have any other issues such as data type conflicts with respect to any field. Elasticsearch provides a dedicated `_validate` REST endpoint for validating the queries without executing them. Let's look at an example to see how to use this API.

First of all, let's create and index some sample documents inside it:

```
    curl -XPUT
"http://localhost:9200/elasticsearch_books/books/_bulk?refresh" -d'
    {"index":{"_id":1}}
    {"author" : "d_bharvi", "publishing_date" : "2009-11-15T14:12:12",
"title" : "Elasticsearch Essentials"}
    {"index":{"_id":2}}
    {"author" : "d_bharvi", "publishing_date" : "2009-11-15T14:12:13",
"title" : "Mastering Elasticsearch 5.0"}'
```

Now we can build a simple query and validate it against our newly created index as follows:

```
    curl -XGET
"http://localhost:9200/elasticsearch_books/books/_validate/query?explain=tr
ue" -d'
    {
      "query" : {
        "bool" : {
          "must" : [{
           "query_string": {
              "default_field": "title",
              "query": "elasticsearch AND essentials"
           }
          }],
          "filter" : {
            "term" : { "author" : "d_bharvi" }
          }
        }
      }
    }'
```

The response of the mentioned request looks as follows. Please note that there are three main attributes shown in the response:

- `valid`: `true` if the query is valid and safe to be executed against the index; `false` otherwise
- `_shards`: The validate API is randomly executed against a single shard so it always contains the number of total shards as `1`
- `explanations`: Contains the low level re-written queries which are actually executed if the query is valid, else it contains a detailed explanation of why the query is not valid:

```
{
  "valid": true,
  "_shards": {
   "total": 1,
   "successful": 1,
   "failed": 0
  },
  "explanations": [
  {
   "index": "elasticsearch_books",
   "valid": true,
   "explanation": "+(+(+title:elasticsearch +title:essentials)
#author:d_bharvi) #(#_type:books)"
  }
  ]
}
```

Now let's execute another query, in which we are going to match a string against a `date` field:

```
curl -XGET
"http://localhost:9200/elasticsearch_books/books/_validate/query?explain=tr
ue" -d'
    {
        "query": {
            "bool": {
                "must": [
                    {
                        "query_string": {
                            "default_field": "publishing_date",
                            "query": "elasticsearch AND essentials"
                        }
                    }
                ],
                "filter": {
```

```
                "term": {
                    "author": "d_bharvi"
                }
            }
        }
    }
}'
```

And see the response which says that this query is not valid along with explanation of the error:

```
{
    "valid": false,
    "_shards": {
        "total": 1,
        "successful": 1,
        "failed": 0
    },
    "explanations": [
        {
            "index": "elasticsearch_books",
            "valid": false,
            "error": "[elasticsearch_books/vVEFyx1xSwidd4AcdGqU7A]
QueryShardException[failed to create query: .....
ElasticsearchParseException[failed to parse date field [elasticsearch] with
format [strict_date_optional_time||epoch_millis]]; nested:
IllegalArgumentException[Parse failure at index [0] of [elasticsearch]];;
ElasticsearchParseException[failed to parse date field [elasticsearch] with
format [strict_date_optional_time||epoch_millis]]; ......"
        }
    ]
}
```

Query profiling for detailed query execution reports

We just saw how we can use the validate API to avoid executing unwanted buggy queries to Elasticsearch. There is another awesome feature available in Elasticsearch to get detailed timing information of query execution. It is available through the `profile` API. This API gives the user insight into how search requests are executed at a low level so that the user can understand why certain requests are slow, and take steps to improve them:

```
curl -XGET "http://localhost:9200/elasticsearch_books/_search" -d'
{
    "profile": true,
```

```
    "query" : {
      "match" : { "title" : "mastering elasticsearch" }
    }
  }'
```

 The output of the profile API is very verbose and we can't show the
complete output here, though you can find the output along with the code
bundle of the book inside the `profile_api_response.json` file.

The partial output of the request looks as follows:

```
{
  "took": 2,
  "timed_out": false,
  "_shards": {
    "total": 5,
    "successful": 5,
    "failed": 0
  },
  "hits": {
    "total": 2,
    "max_score": 0.5063205,
    "hits": [.......................]
  },
  "profile": {
    "shards": [
      {
        "id": "[1NhLoN37S-OvF9QdqD4OmA][elasticsearch_books][3]",
        "searches": [
          {
            "query": [
              {
                "type": "BooleanQuery",
                "description": "title:masteringtitle:elasticsearch",
                "time": "0.2596310000ms",
                "breakdown": {
                  "score": 2730,
                  "build_scorer_count": 1,
                  "match_count": 0,
                  "create_weight": 201283,
                  "next_doc": 5341,
                  "match": 0,
                  "create_weight_count": 1,
                  "next_doc_count": 2,
                  "score_count": 1,
                  "build_scorer": 50272,
                  "advance": 0,
```

```
                        "advance_count": 0
                    },
                    "children": [
                      {
                        "type": "TermQuery",
                        "description": "title:mastering",
                        "time": "0.09245300000ms",
                        "breakdown": {
                          "score": 0,
                          "build_scorer_count": 1,
                          "match_count": 0,
                          "create_weight": 90642,
                          "next_doc": 0,
                          "match": 0,
                          "create_weight_count": 1,
                          "next_doc_count": 0,
                          "score_count": 0,
                          "build_scorer": 1809,
                          "advance": 0,
                          "advance_count": 0
                        }
                      },
                      {
                        "type": "TermQuery",
                        "description": "title:elasticsearch",
                        "time": "0.1238730000ms",
                        "breakdown": {
                          "score": 1875,
                          "build_scorer_count": 1,
                          "match_count": 0,
                          "create_weight": 80743,
                          "next_doc": 3058,
                          "match": 0,
                          "create_weight_count": 1,
                          "next_doc_count": 2,
                          "score_count": 1,
                          "build_scorer": 38192,
                          "advance": 0,
                          "advance_count": 0
                        }
                      }
                    ]
                  }
                ],
                "rewrite_time": 10025,
                "collector": [
                  {
                    "name": "SimpleTopScoreDocCollector",
```

```
        "reason": "search_top_hits",
        "time": "0.00735500000ms"
      }
    ]
  }
],
"aggregations": []
  }
]
}
}
```

Understanding the profile API response

If you look carefully at the response, you will see it has a profile object with the following structure:

- `profile.shard.id`: A unique ID which is the identifier of each shard involved in the response
- `profile.shard.searches`: An array which contains the details about the query execution
- `profile.shard. rewrite_time`: Total time (in nanoseconds) taken for a complete query re-writing process
- `profile.shard.collector`: This portion of the response tells us about Lucene collectors which run the search

 Lucene works by defining a collector which is responsible for coordinating the traversal, scoring, and collection of matching documents. Collectors are also how a single query can record aggregation results, execute unscoped global queries, execute post-query filters, and so on.

If you want to understand each parameter available inside the response of the profile API, please read the official documentation of Elasticsearch which beautifully describes each parameter in detail at the following URL:
https://www.elastic.co/guide/en/elasticsearch/reference/master/_profiling_queries.html

Consideration for profiling usage

As you saw, profiling enables you to have very specific details of each component in your queries. To get all these details, many low-level methods, calls such as `collect`, `advance`, and `next_doc` are called, which can be fairly expensive and introduce a non-negligible overhead on the Elasticsearch cluster. Therefore, profiling should not be enabled in production settings by default, and should not be compared against non-profiled query times. Profiling is just a diagnostic tool and should be used wisely.

There is another thing you need to know; that profiling statistics are currently not available for `suggestions`, `highlighting`, `dfs_query_then_fetch` and profiling of the reduce phase of aggregation.

 In *Mastering Elasticsearch, second edition*, we covered a detailed section on benchmarking queries using the `_bench` API. This API was an experimental work and has been completely removed from Elasticsearch. If you are keen to run some benchmarks on your Elasticsearch node, you can either use Jmeter, or you can check out Rally, a tool which was recently open-sourced by Elastic. Rally is Elastic's internal benchmarking tool which provides functionality specifically tailored to Elasticsearch and offers a number of improvements versus using a standard benchmarking tool. You can take an overview of Rally on this URL `https://www.elastic.co/blog/announcing-rally-benchmarking-for-elasticsearch`.

Very hot threads

When you are in trouble and your cluster works slower than usual and uses large amounts of CPU power, you know you need to do something to make it work again. This is when the hot threads API can give you the information necessary to find the root cause of your problems. A hot thread in this case is a Java thread that uses a high CPU volume and executes for longer periods of time. Such a thread doesn't mean that there is something wrong with Elasticsearch itself; it gives you information on what can be a possible hotspot and allows you to see which part of your deployment you need to look more deeply at, such as query execution or Lucene segments merging. The hot threads API returns information about which parts of the Elasticsearch code are hot spots from the CPU side or where Elasticsearch is stuck for some reason.

When using the hot threads API, you can examine all nodes, a selected few of them, or a particular node using the `/_nodes/hot_threads` or `/_nodes/{node or nodes}/hot_threads` endpoints. For example, to look at hot threads on all the nodes, we would run the following command:

```
curl 'localhost:9200/_nodes/hot_threads'
```

The API supports the following parameters:

- `threads` (the default: `3`): This is the number of threads that should be analyzed. Elasticsearch takes the specified number of the hottest threads by looking at the information determined by the `type` parameter.
- `interval` (the default: `500ms`): Elasticsearch checks threads twice to calculate the percentage of time spent in a particular thread on an operation defined by the `type` parameter. We can use the `interval` parameter to define the time between these checks.
- `type` (the default: `cpu`): This is the type of thread state to be examined. The API can check the CPU time taken by the given thread (`cpu`), the time in the blocked state (`block`), or the time in the waiting (`wait`) state. If you would like to know more about the thread states, refer to `http://docs.oracle.com/javase/8/docs/api/java/lang/Thread.State.html`.
- `snapshots` (the default: `10`): This is the number of stack traces (a nested sequence of method calls at a certain point of time) snapshots to take.

Using the hot threads API is very simple; for example, to look at hot threads on all the nodes that are in the waiting state with check intervals of one second, we would use the following command:

```
curl 'localhost:9200/_nodes/hot_threads?type=wait&interval=1s'
```

Usage clarification for the hot threads API

Unlike other Elasticsearch API responses where you can expect JSON to be returned, the hot threads API returns formatted text, which contains several sections. Before we discuss the response structure itself, we would like to tell you a bit about the logic that is responsible for generating this response. Elasticsearch takes all the running threads and collects various information about the CPU time spent in each thread, the number of times the particular thread was blocked or was in the waiting state, how long it was blocked or was in the waiting state, and so on. The next thing is to wait for a particular amount of time (specified by the `interval` parameter), and after that time passes, collect the same information again. After this is done, threads are sorted on the basis of time each particular thread was running. The sort is done in descending order so that the threads running for the longest period of time are on top of the list. Of course, the mentioned time is measured for a given operation type specified by the `type` parameter. After this, the first N threads (where N is the number of threads specified by the `threads` parameter) are analyzed by Elasticsearch. Elasticsearch takes a few snapshots (the number of snapshots is specified by the `snapshot` parameter) of stack traces of the threads that were selected in the previous step, every few milliseconds. The last thing that needs to be done is the grouping of stack traces in order to visualize changes in the thread state and return the response to the caller.

The hot threads API response

Now, let's go through the sections of the response returned by the Hot Threads API. For example, the following screenshot is a fragment of the Hot Threads API response generated for Elasticsearch that was just started:

```
::: {node-1}{1NhLoN37S-OvF9QdqD4OmA}{MFliun0hRbCWtOe755PtmQ}{127.0.0.1}{127.0.0.1:9300}
  Hot threads at 2016-12-31T21:31:52.890Z, interval=500ms, busiestThreads=3, ignoreIdleThreads=true:

  4.4% (22.1ms out of 500ms) cpu usage by thread 'elasticsearch[node-1][search][T#2]'
    2/10 snapshots sharing following 36 elements
      java.lang.Throwable.fillInStackTrace(Native Method)
      java.lang.Throwable.fillInStackTrace(Throwable.java:783)
      java.lang.Throwable.<init>(Throwable.java:265)
      java.lang.Exception.<init>(Exception.java:66)
      java.io.IOException.<init>(IOException.java:58)
      org.apache.lucene.queryparser.classic.FastCharStream.refill(FastCharStream.java:72)
      org.apache.lucene.queryparser.classic.FastCharStream.readChar(FastCharStream.java:45)
      org.apache.lucene.queryparser.classic.FastCharStream.BeginToken(FastCharStream.java:80)
      org.apache.lucene.queryparser.classic.QueryParserTokenManager.getNextToken(QueryParserTokenManager.java:1055)
      org.apache.lucene.queryparser.classic.QueryParser.jj_ntk(QueryParser.java:834)
      org.apache.lucene.queryparser.classic.QueryParser.Term(QueryParser.java:401)
      org.apache.lucene.queryparser.classic.QueryParser.Clause(QueryParser.java:327)
      org.apache.lucene.queryparser.classic.QueryParser.Query(QueryParser.java:216)
      org.apache.lucene.queryparser.classic.QueryParser.TopLevelQuery(QueryParser.java:187)
      org.apache.lucene.queryparser.classic.QueryParserBase.parse(QueryParserBase.java:111)
      org.apache.lucene.queryparser.classic.MapperQueryParser.parse(MapperQueryParser.java:860)
      org.elasticsearch.index.query.QueryStringQueryBuilder.doToQuery(QueryStringQueryBuilder.java:911)
      org.elasticsearch.index.query.AbstractQueryBuilder.toQuery(AbstractQueryBuilder.java:95)
      org.elasticsearch.index.query.QueryShardContext.lambda$toQuery$1(QueryShardContext.java:311)
      org.elasticsearch.index.query.QueryShardContext$$Lambda$1339/1877300117.apply(Unknown Source)
      org.elasticsearch.index.query.QueryShardContext.toQuery(QueryShardContext.java:328)
      org.elasticsearch.index.query.QueryShardContext.toQuery(QueryShardContext.java:310)
      org.elasticsearch.search.SearchService.parseSource(SearchService.java:661)
      org.elasticsearch.search.SearchService.createContext(SearchService.java:536)
      org.elasticsearch.search.SearchService.createAndPutContext(SearchService.java:502)
      org.elasticsearch.search.SearchService.executeQueryPhase(SearchService.java:243)
      org.elasticsearch.action.search.SearchTransportService.lambda$registerRequestHandler$6(SearchTransportService.java:276)
      org.elasticsearch.action.search.SearchTransportService$$Lambda$1030/788877168.messageReceived(Unknown Source)
      org.elasticsearch.transport.TransportRequestHandler.messageReceived(TransportRequestHandler.java:33)
      org.elasticsearch.transport.RequestHandlerRegistry.processMessageReceived(RequestHandlerRegistry.java:69)
      org.elasticsearch.transport.TransportService$6.doRun(TransportService.java:548)
      org.elasticsearch.common.util.concurrent.ThreadContext$ContextPreservingAbstractRunnable.doRun(ThreadContext.java:504)
      org.elasticsearch.common.util.concurrent.AbstractRunnable.run(AbstractRunnable.java:37)
      java.util.concurrent.ThreadPoolExecutor.runWorker(ThreadPoolExecutor.java:1142)
      java.util.concurrent.ThreadPoolExecutor$Worker.run(ThreadPoolExecutor.java:617)
      java.lang.Thread.run(Thread.java:745)
    2/10 snapshots sharing following 10 elements
      sun.misc.Unsafe.park(Native Method)
      java.util.concurrent.locks.LockSupport.park(LockSupport.java:175)
      java.util.concurrent.LinkedTransferQueue.awaitMatch(LinkedTransferQueue.java:737)
      java.util.concurrent.LinkedTransferQueue.xfer(LinkedTransferQueue.java:647)
      java.util.concurrent.LinkedTransferQueue.take(LinkedTransferQueue.java:1269)
      org.elasticsearch.common.util.concurrent.SizeBlockingQueue.take(SizeBlockingQueue.java:161)
      java.util.concurrent.ThreadPoolExecutor.getTask(ThreadPoolExecutor.java:1067)
      java.util.concurrent.ThreadPoolExecutor.runWorker(ThreadPoolExecutor.java:1127)
      java.util.concurrent.ThreadPoolExecutor$Worker.run(ThreadPoolExecutor.java:617)
      java.lang.Thread.run(Thread.java:745)

  4.1% (20.3ms out of 500ms) cpu usage by thread 'elasticsearch[node-1][search][T#3]'
    3/10 snapshots sharing following 2 elements
      java.util.concurrent.ThreadPoolExecutor$Worker.run(ThreadPoolExecutor.java:617)
      java.lang.Thread.run(Thread.java:745)
```

Now, let's discuss the sections of the response. To do that, we will use a slightly different response compared to the one shown previously. We do this to better visualize what is happening inside Elasticsearch. However, please remember that the general structure of the response will not change.

The first section of the hot threads API response shows us which node the thread is located on. For example, the first line of the response can look as follows:

```
::: {node-1}{1NhLoN37S-
OvF9QdqD4OmA}{MF1iun0hRbCWtOe755PtmQ}{127.0.0.1}{127.0.0.1:9300}
```

Thanks to it, we can see which node the hot threads API returns information about and which node is very handy for when the hot threads API call goes to many nodes.

The next lines of the hot threads API response can be divided into several sections, each starting with a line similar to the following one:

```
4.4% (21.1ms out of 500ms) cpu usage by thread
'elasticsearch[node-1][search][T#2]'
```

In our case, we see a thread named `search`, which takes `4.4` percent of all the CPU time at the time when the measurement was done. The `cpu usage` part of the preceding line indicates that we are using `type` equal to `cpu` (other values you can expect here are `block usage` for threads in the blocked state and `wait usage` for threads in the waiting states). The thread name is very important here, because by looking at it, we can see which Elasticsearch functionality is the hot one. In our example, we see that this thread is all about searching (the `search` value). Other example values that you can expect to see are `recovery_stream` (for recovery module events), `cache` (for caching events), `merge` (for segments merging threads), `index` (for data indexing threads), and so on.

The next part of the hot threads API response is the section starting with the following information:

```
2/10 snapshots sharing following 36 elements
```

This information will be followed by a stack trace. In our case, `2/10` means that `10` snapshots have been taken for the same stack trace. In general, this means that all the examination time was spent in the same part of the Elasticsearch code.

Scaling Elasticsearch

As we already know, Elasticsearch is a highly scalable search and analytics platform. We can scale it both horizontally and vertically.

Vertical scaling

When we talk about **vertical scaling**, we often mean adding more resources to the server Elasticsearch is running on; we can add memory and we can switch to a machine with better CPU or faster disk storage. Of course, with better machines, we can expect increase in performance; depending on our deployment and its bottleneck, there can be smaller or higher improvement. However, there are limitations when it comes to vertical scaling. For example, one is the maximum amount of physical memory available for your servers or the total memory required by the JVM to operate. When you have large enough data and complicated queries, you can very soon run into memory issues, and adding new memory may not be helpful at all.

For example, you may not want to go beyond 31 GB of physical memory given to the JVM because of garbage collection and the inability to use compressed ops, which basically means that to address the same memory space, JVM will need to use twice the memory. Even though it seems like a very big issue, vertical scaling is not the only solution we have.

Horizontal scaling

The other solution available to us Elasticsearch users is **horizontal scaling**. To give you a comparison, vertical scaling is like building a skyscraper, while horizontal scaling is like having many houses in a residential area. Instead of investing in hardware and having powerful machines, we choose to have multiple machines and our data split between them. Horizontal scaling gives us virtually unlimited scaling possibilities. Even with the most powerful hardware, a single machine is not enough to handle the data, the queries, or both. If a single machine is not able to handle the amount of data, we have cases where we divide our indices into multiple shards and spread them across the cluster, just like what is shown in the following figure:

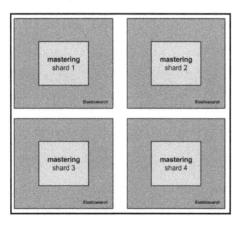

When we don't have enough processing power to handle queries, we can always create more replicas of the shards we have. We have our cluster: four Elasticsearch nodes with the `mastering` index created and running on it and built of four shards. The command for creating this index with four shards is as follows:

```
curl -XPUT "http://localhost:9200/mastering" -d'
{
 "settings": {
 "number_of_shards": 4
 }
}'
```

If we want to increase the querying capabilities of our cluster, we would just add additional nodes; for example, four of them. After adding new nodes to the cluster, we can either create new indices that will be built of more shards to spread the load more evenly, or add replicas to already existing shards. Both options are viable. We should go for more primary shards when our hardware is not enough to handle the amount of data it holds. In such cases, we usually run into out-of-memory situations, long shard query execution time, swapping, or high I/O waits. The second option–having replicas–is the way to go when our hardware is happily handling the data we have, but the traffic is so high that the nodes just can't keep up. The first option is simple, but let's look at the second case: having more replicas. So, with four additional nodes, our cluster would look as follows:

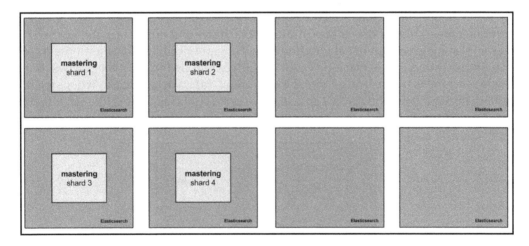

Now, let's run the following command to add a single replica:

```
curl -XPUT 'localhost:9200/mastering/_settings' -d '
{
 "index" : {
  "number_of_replicas" : 1
```

```
    }
}'
```

Our cluster view would look more or less as follows:

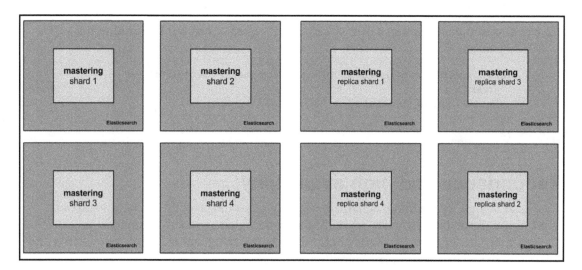

As you can see, each of the initial shards building the **mastering** index has a single replica stored on another node. Because of this, Elasticsearch is able to round-robin the queries between the shard and its replicas so that the queries don't always hit one node. Because of this, we are able to handle almost double the query load compared to our initial deployment.

Automatically creating replicas

Elasticsearch allows us to automatically expand replicas when the cluster is big enough. You might wonder where such functionality can be useful. Imagine a situation where you have a small index that you would like to be present on every node, so that your plugins don't have to run distributed queries just to get data from it. In addition to this, your cluster is dynamically changing; you add and remove nodes from it. The simplest way to achieve such a functionality is to allow Elasticsearch to automatically expand replicas. To do this, we would need to set index.auto_expand_replicas to 0-all, which means that the index can have 0 replicas or be present on all the nodes. So, if our small index is called mastering_meta and we would like Elasticsearch to automatically expand its replicas, we would use the following command to create the index:

```
curl -XPUT 'localhost:9200/mastering_meta/' -d '{
"settings" : {
```

```
  "index" : {
   "auto_expand_replicas" : "0-all"
  }
 }
}'
```

We can also update the settings of that index if it is already created by running the following command:

```
curl -XPUT 'localhost:9200/mastering_meta/_settings' -d '{
"index" : {
 "auto_expand_replicas" : "0-all"
}
}'
```

Redundancy and high availability

The Elasticsearch replication mechanism not only gives us the ability to handle higher query throughput, but also gives us redundancy and high availability. Imagine an Elasticsearch cluster hosting a single index called **mastering** that is built of two shards and zero replicas. Such a cluster could look as follows:

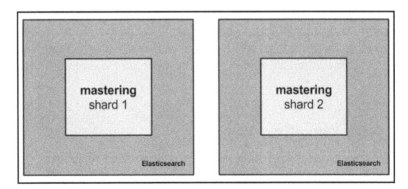

Now, what would happen when one of the nodes fails? The simplest answer is that we lose about 50 percent of the data, and if the failure is fatal, we lose that data forever. Even when having backups, we would need to spin up another node and restore the backup; this takes time. If your business relies on Elasticsearch, downtime means money loss.

Now let's look at the same cluster but with one replica:

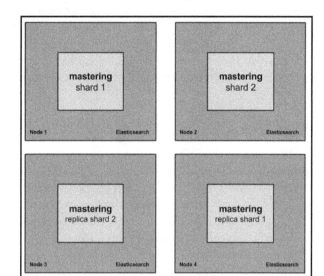

Now, losing a single Elasticsearch node means that we still have the whole data available and we can work on restoring the full cluster structure without downtime. What's more, with such deployment, we can live with two nodes failing at the same time in some cases, for example, **Node 1** and **Node 3** or **Node 2** and **Node 4**. In both the mentioned cases, we would still be able to access all the data. Of course, this will lower performance because of less nodes in the cluster, but this is still better than not handling queries at all.

Because of this, when designing your architecture and deciding on the number of nodes, how many nodes indices will have, and the number of shards for each of them, you should take into consideration how many failing nodes you want to live with. Of course, you can't forget about the performance part of the equation, but redundancy and high availability should be one of the factors of the scaling equation.

Cost and performance flexibility

The default distributed nature of Elasticsearch and its ability to scale horizontally allow us to be flexible when it comes to performance and costs that we have when running our environment. First of all, high-end servers with highly performant disks, numerous CPU cores, and a lot of RAM are expensive. In addition to this, cloud computing is getting more and more popular and it not only allows us to run our deployment on rented machines, but it also allows us to scale on demand. We just need to add more machines, which are a few clicks away, or can even be automated with some degree of work.

Getting this all together, we can say that having a horizontally scalable solution, such as Elasticsearch, allows us to bring down the costs of running our clusters and solutions. What's more, we can easily sacrifice performance if costs are the most crucial factor in our business plan. Of course, we can also go the other way. If we can afford large clusters, we can push Elasticsearch to hundreds of terabytes of data stored in the indices and still get decent performance (of course, with proper hardware and properly distributed).

Continuous upgrades

High availability, cost, performance flexibility, and virtually endless growth are not the only things worth saying when discussing the scalability side of Elasticsearch. At some point in time, you will want to have your Elasticsearch cluster upgraded to a new version. It might be because of bug fixes, performance improvements, new features, or anything that you can think of. The thing is that when having a single instance of each shard, an upgrade without replicas means the unavailability of Elasticsearch (or at least its parts), and that may mean downtime of the applications that use Elasticsearch. This is another reason why horizontal scaling is so important; you can perform upgrades, at least to the point where software such as Elasticsearch is supported. For example, you could take Elasticsearch 5.0 and upgrade it to Elasticsearch 5.1 with only rolling restarts, thus having all the data still available for searching and indexing happening at the same time.

Multiple Elasticsearch instances on a single physical machine

Although we previously said that you shouldn't go for the most powerful machines for different reasons (such as RAM consumption after going above 31 GB JVM heap), we sometimes don't have much choice. This is out of the scope of the book, but because we are talking about scaling, we thought it may be a good thing to mention what can be done in such cases.

In cases such as the ones we are discussing, when we have high-end hardware with a lot of RAM memory, a lot of high speed disks, and numerous CPU cores, among others, we should think about dividing the physical server into multiple virtual machines and running a single Elasticsearch server on each of the virtual machines.

There is also a possibility of running multiple Elasticsearch servers on a single physical machine without running multiple virtual machines. Which road to take–virtual machines or multiple instances–is really your choice; however, we like to keep things separate and, because of that, we are usually going to divide any large server into multiple virtual machines. When dividing a large server into multiple smaller virtual machines, remember that the I/O subsystem will be shared across these smaller virtual machines. Because of this, it may be good to wisely divide the disks between virtual machines.

To illustrate such a deployment, please look at the following provided figure. It shows how you could run Elasticsearch on three large servers, each divided into four separate virtual machines. Each virtual machine would be responsible for running a single instance of Elasticsearch:

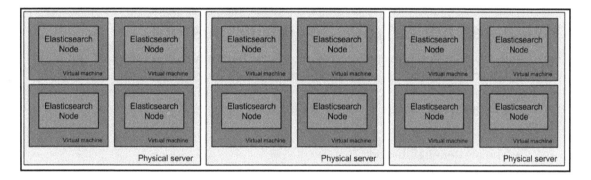

Preventing the shard and its replicas from being on the same node

There is one additional thing worth mentioning. When having multiple physical servers divided into virtual machines, it is crucial to ensure that the shard and its replica won't end up on the same physical machine. This will be tragic if a server crashes or is restarted. We can tell Elasticsearch to separate shards and replicas using cluster allocation awareness. In our preceding case, we have three physical servers; let's call them `server1`, `server2`, and `server3`.

Now for each Elasticsearch on a physical server, we define the `node.attr.server_name` property and we set it to the identifier of the server. So, for our example of all Elasticsearch nodes on the first physical server, we would set the following property in the `elasticsearch.yml` configuration file:

```
node.attr.server_name: server1
```

In addition to this, each Elasticsearch node (no matter on which physical server) needs to have the following property added to the `elasticsearch.yml` configuration file:

```
cluster.routing.allocation.awareness.attributes: server_name
```

It tells Elasticsearch not to put the primary shard and its replicas on the nodes with the same value in the `node.attr.server_name` property. This is enough for us, and Elasticsearch will take care of the rest.

Designated nodes' roles for larger clusters

There is one more thing that we wanted to tell you; to have a fully fault-tolerant and highly available cluster, we should divide the nodes and give each node a designated role. We have already seen how many nodes can be configured with an Elasticsearch cluster. Let's have a look at those roles again. The roles we can assign to each Elasticsearch node are as follows:

- The master eligible node
- The data node
- The ingest node
- The query aggregator node

By default, each Elasticsearch node is master eligible (it can serve as a master node), can hold data, can ingest data, and can work as a query aggregator node, which means that it can send partial queries to other nodes, gather and merge the results, and respond to the client sending the query. You may wonder why this is needed. Let's give you a simple example: if the master node is under a lot of stress, it may not be able to handle the cluster state-related command fast enough and the cluster can become unstable. This is only a single, simple example, and you can think of numerous others.

Because of this, most Elasticsearch clusters that are larger than a few nodes usually look like the one presented in the following figure:

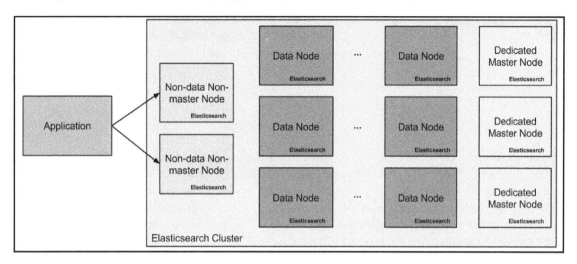

As you can see, our hypothetical cluster contains two aggregator nodes (because we know that there will not be too many queries, but we want redundancy), a dozen of data nodes because the amount of data will be large, and at least three master eligible nodes that shouldn't be doing anything else. Why three master nodes when Elasticsearch will only use a single one at any given time? Again, this is because of redundancy and to be able to prevent split brain situations by setting the `discovery.zen.minimum_master_nodes` to `2`, which would allow us to easily handle the failure of a single master eligible node in the cluster.

Let's now give you snippets of the configuration for each type of node in our cluster. We already talked about this in the *Discovery and recovery modules* section in `Chapter 8, Elasticsearch Administration`, but we would like to mention it once again.

Query aggregator nodes

The query aggregator nodes' configuration is quite simple. To configure them, we just need to tell Elasticsearch that we don't want these nodes to be master eligible and hold data. This corresponds to the following configuration in the `elasticsearch.yml` file:

```
node.data: false
node.master: false
node.ingest: false
```

Data nodes

Data nodes are also very simple to configure; we just need to say that they should not be master eligible. However, we are not big fans of default configurations (because they tend to change) and, thus, our Elasticsearch data nodes' configuration looks as follows:

```
node.data: true
node.master: false
node.ingest: false
```

Master eligible nodes

We've left the master eligible nodes for the end of the general scaling section. Of course, such Elasticsearch nodes shouldn't be allowed to hold data, but in addition to that, it is good practice to disable the HTTP protocol on such nodes. This is done in order to avoid accidentally querying these nodes. Master eligible nodes can be smaller in resources compared to data and query aggregator nodes, and because of that, we should ensure that they are only used for master-related purposes. So, our configuration for master eligible nodes looks more or less as follows:

```
node.data: false
node.master: true
node.ingest: false
```

Using Elasticsearch for high load scenarios

Now that we know the theory (and some examples of Elasticsearch scaling), we are ready to discuss the different aspects of Elasticsearch preparation for high load. We decided to split this part of the chapter into three sections: one dedicated to preparing Elasticsearch for a high indexing load, one dedicated for the preparation of Elasticsearch for a high query load, and one that can be taken into consideration in both cases. This should give you an idea of what to think about when preparing your cluster for your use case.

Please consider that performance testing should be done after preparing the cluster for production use. Don't just take the values from the book and go for them; try them with your data and your queries and try altering them, and see the differences. Remember that giving general advice that works for everyone is not possible, so treat the next two sections as general advice instead of ready-for-use recipes.

General Elasticsearch-tuning advice

In this section, we will look at the general advice related to tuning Elasticsearch. They are not connected to indexing performance only or querying performance only, but to both of them.

The index refresh rate

The second thing we should pay attention to is the index refresh rate. We know that the refresh rate specifies how fast documents will be visible for search operations. The equation is quite simple: the faster the refresh rate, the slower the queries will be and the lower the indexing throughput. If we can allow ourselves to have a slower refresh rate, such as 10s or 30s, it may be a good thing to set it. This puts less pressure on Elasticsearch, as the internal objects will have to be reopened at a slower pace and, thus, more resources will be available both for indexing and querying. Remember that, by default, the refresh rate is set to 1s, which basically means that the index searcher object is reopened every second.

To give you a bit of an insight into what performance gains we are talking about, we did some performance tests, including Elasticsearch and a different refresh rate. With a refresh rate of 1s, we were able to index about 1,000 documents per second using a single Elasticsearch node. Increasing the refresh rate to 5s gave us an increase in the indexing throughput of more than 25 percent, and we were able to index about 1280 documents per second. Setting the refresh rate to 25s gave us about 70 percent of throughput, more compared to a 1s refresh rate, which was about 1,700 documents per second on the same infrastructure. It is also worth remembering that increasing the time indefinitely doesn't make much sense, because after a certain point (depending on your data load and the amount of data you have), the increase in performance is negligible.

Thread pools tuning

This is one of the things that is very dependent on your deployment. By default, Elasticsearch comes with a very good default when it comes to all thread pools' configuration. However, there are times when these defaults are not enough. You should remember that tuning the default thread pools' configuration should be done only when you really see that your nodes are filling up the queues and they still have processing power left that could be designated to the processing of the waiting operations.

For example, if you did your performance tests and you see your Elasticsearch instances not being saturated 100 percent, but on the other hand, you've experienced rejected execution errors, then this is a point where you should start adjusting the thread pools. You can either increase the amount of threads that are allowed to be executed at the same time, or you can increase the queue. Of course, you should also remember that increasing the number of concurrently running threads to very high numbers will lead to many CPU context switches (http://en.wikipedia.org/wiki/Context_switch), which will result in a drop in performance. Of course, having massive queues is also not a good idea; it is usually better to fail fast rather than overwhelm Elasticsearch with several thousands of requests waiting in the queue. However, this all depends on your particular deployment and use case. We would really like to give you a precise number, but in this case, giving general advice is rarely possible.

Data distribution

As we know, each index in the Elasticsearch world can be divided into multiple shards, and each shard can have multiple replicas. In cases where you have multiple Elasticsearch nodes and indices divided into shards, proper data distribution may be crucial to even the load of the cluster and not have some nodes doing more work than the other ones.

Let's take the following example–imagine that we have a cluster that is built of four nodes, and it has a single index built of three shards and one replica allocated. Such a deployment could look as follows:

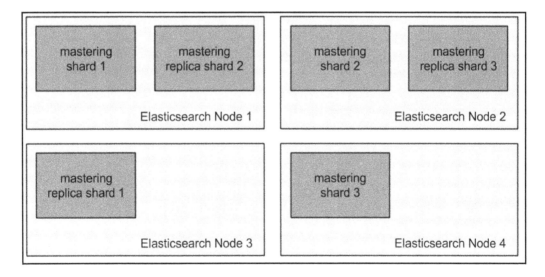

As you can see, the first two nodes have two physical shards allocated to them, while the last two nodes have one shard each. So, the actual data allocation is not even. When sending the queries and indexing data, we will have the first two nodes do more work than the other two; this is what we want to avoid. We could make the **mastering** index have two shards and one replica so that it would look like this:

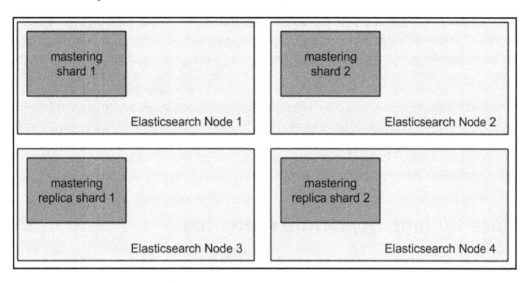

Or, we could have the **mastering** index divided into four shards and have one replica:

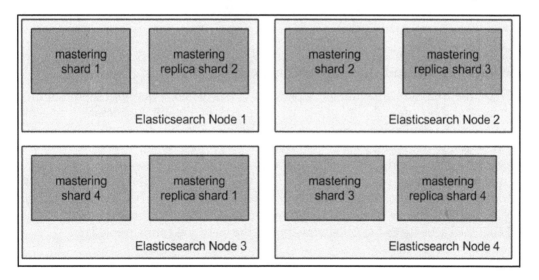

In both cases, we will end up with an even distribution of shards and replicas, with Elasticsearch doing a similar amount of work on all the nodes. Of course, with more indices (such as having daily indices), it may be trickier to get the data evenly distributed, and it may not be possible to have evenly distributed shards, but we should try to get to such a point.

One more thing to remember when it comes to data distribution, shards, and replicas is that when designing your index architecture, you should remember what you want to achieve. If you are going for a very high indexing use case, you may want to spread the index into multiple shards to lower the pressure that is put on the CPU and the I/O subsystem of the server. This is also true in order to run expensive queries, because with more shards, you can lower the load on a single server. However, with queries, there is one more thing: if your nodes can't keep up with the load caused by queries, you can add more Elasticsearch nodes and increase the number of replicas so that physical copies of the primary shards are placed on these nodes. This will make the indexing a bit slower but will give you the capacity to handle more queries at the same time.

Advice for high query rate scenarios

One of the great features of Elasticsearch is its ability to search and analyze the data that was indexed. However, sometimes, the user is needed to adjust Elasticsearch and our queries to not only get the results of the query, but also get them fast (or in a reasonable amount of time). In this section, we will not only look at the possibilities but also prepare Elasticsearch for high query throughput use cases. We will also look at general performance tips when it comes to querying.

Node query cache and shard query cache

The first cache that can help with query performance is the node query cache (if our queries use filters, and if not, they should probably use filters). By default, Elasticsearch uses the node query cache implementation that is shared among all the indices on a single node, and we can control its size using the `indices.queries.cache.size` property. It defaults to `10` percent by default and specifies the total amount of memory that can be used by the node query cache on a given node. In general, if your queries are already using filters, you should monitor the size of the cache and evictions. If you see that you have many evictions, then you probably have a cache that's too small, and you should consider having a larger one. Having a cache that's too small may impact the query performance in a bad way.

The second cache that has been introduced in Elasticsearch is the shard query cache. It was added to Elasticsearch in version 1.4.0, and its purpose is to cache aggregations, suggester results, and the number of hits (it will not cache the returned documents and, thus, it only works when our queries use `size=0`). When your queries are using aggregations or suggestions, Elasticsearch can reuse the data stored there. The best thing about the cache is that it promises the same, near real-time search as search that is not cached.

To enable the shard query cache, we need to set the `index.requests.cache.enable`property to `true`. For example, to enable the cache for our mastering index, we could issue the following command:

```
curl -XPUT 'localhost:9200/mastering/_settings' -d '{
"index.requests.cache.enable": true
}'
```

Please remember that using the shard query cache doesn't make sense if we don't use aggregations or suggesters.

One more thing to remember is that, by default, the shard query cache is allowed to take no more than one percent of the JVM heap given to the Elasticsearch node. To change the default value, we can use the `indices.requests.cache.size` property. By using the `indices.requests.cache.expire` property, we can specify the expiration date of the cache, but it is not needed, and in most cases, results stored in the cache are invalidated with every index refresh operation.

Think about the queries

This is the most general advice we can actually give: you should always think about optimal query structure, filter usage, and so on. From Elasticsearch version 2.0 onward, filters and queries are considered the same thing, but they still have a difference based on which context they are being used for. To understand the difference, let's look at the following query:

```
{
  "query" : {
  "bool" : {
    "must" : [
      {
      "query_string" : {
        "query" : "name:mastering AND department:it AND  category:book"
      }
      },
      {
      "term" : {
```

```
        "tag" : "popular"
      }
    },
    {
      "term" : {
        "tag" : "2014"
      }
    }
  ]
 }
 }
}
```

It returns the book name that matches a few conditions. However, there are a few things we can improve in the preceding query. For example, we could move a few things to filtering, so that the next time we use some parts of the query, we save CPU cycles and reuse the information stored in the cache. For example, this is what the optimized query could look like:

```
{
    "query": {
        "bool": {
            "must": [
                {
                    "query_string": {
                        "query": "name:mastering AND department:it AND
category:book"
                    }
                }
            ],
            "filter": [
                {
                    "term": {
                        "tag": "popular"
                    }
                },
                {
                    "term": {
                        "tag": "2014"
                    }
                }
            ]
        }
    }
}
```

As you can see, there are a few things that we did. First of all, we used the `filter` clause to introduce filters and we moved most of the static, non-analyzed fields to filters. This allows us to easily reuse the filters in the next queries that we execute and also avoided scoring on those fields. Because of such query restructuring, we were able to simplify the main query, so we changed `query_string_query` to the `match` query, because it is enough for our use case. This is exactly what you should be doing when optimizing your queries or designing them—have optimization and performance in mind and try to keep them as optimal as they can be. This will result in faster query execution, lower resource consumption, and better health of the whole Elasticsearch cluster.

However, performance is not the only difference when it comes to the outcome of queries. As you know, filters don't affect the score of the documents returned and are not taken into consideration when calculating the score. Because of this, if you compare the scores returned by the preceding queries for the same documents, you would notice that they are different. This is worth remembering.

Using routing

If your data allows routing, you should consider using it. The data with the same routing value will always end up in the same shard. Because of this, we can save ourselves the need to query all the shards when asking for certain data. For example, if we store the data of our clients, we may use a client identifier as the routing value. This will allow us to store the data of a single client inside a single shard. This means that during querying, Elasticsearch needs to fetch data from only a single shard, as shown in the following figure:

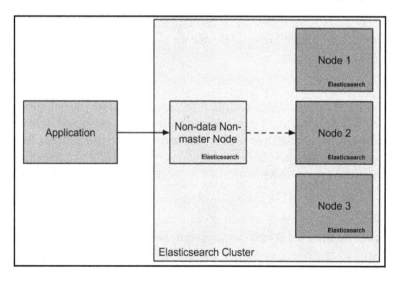

If we assume that the data lives in a shard allocated to **Node 2**, we can see that Elasticsearch only needed to run the query against that one particular node to get all the data for the client. If we don't use routing, the simplified query execution could look as follows:

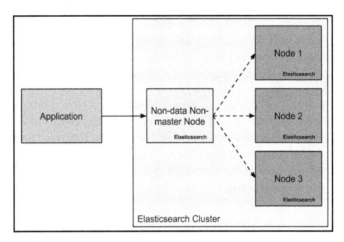

In the case of non-routing, Elasticsearch first needs to query all the index shards. If your index contains dozens of shards, the performance improvement will be significant as long as a single Elasticsearch instance can handle the shard size.

 Please remember that not every use case is eligible to use routing. To be able to use it, your data needs to be virtually divided so that it is spread across the shards. For example, it usually doesn't make sense to have dozens of very small shards and one massive one, because for the massive one, performance may not be decent.

Parallelize your queries

One thing that is usually forgotten is the need to parallelize queries. Imagine that you have a dozen nodes in your cluster, but your index is built of a single shard. If the index is large, your queries will perform worse than you would expect. Of course, you can increase the number of replicas, but that won't help; a single query will still go to a single shard in that index, because replicas are no more than the copies of the primary shard, and they contain the same data (or at least they should).

One thing that will actually help is dividing your index into multiple shards–the number of shards depends on the hardware and deployment. In general, it is advised to have the data evenly divided so that nodes are equally loaded. For example, if you have four Elasticsearch nodes and two indices, you may want to have four shards for each index, just like what is shown in the following figure:

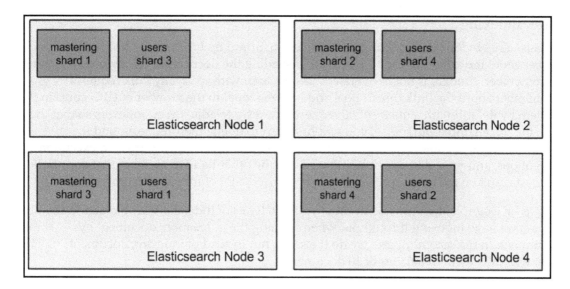

Keeping size and shard_size under control

When dealing with queries that use aggregations, for some of them, we have the possibility of using two properties: `size` and `shard_size`. The `size` parameter defines how many buckets should be returned by the final aggregation results; the node that aggregates the final results will get the top buckets from each shard that returns the result and will only return the top size of them to the client. The `shard_size` parameter tells Elasticsearch the same, but on the shard level. Increasing the value of the `shard_size` parameter will lead to more accurate aggregations (such as in the case of significant terms' aggregation) at the cost of network traffic and memory usage. Lowering this parameter will cause aggregation results to be less precise, but we will benefit from lower memory consumption and lower network traffic. If we see that the memory usage is too large, we can lower the `size` and `shard_size` properties of problematic queries and see whether the quality of the results is still acceptable.

High indexing throughput scenarios and Elasticsearch

In this section, we will discuss some optimizations that will allow us to concentrate on the indexing throughput and speed. Some use cases are highly dependent on the amount of data you can push to Elasticsearch every second, and the next few topics should cover some information regarding indexing.

Bulk indexing

This is very obvious advice, but you would be surprised by how many Elasticsearch users forget about indexing data in bulk instead of sending the documents one by one. The thing to remember, though, is not to overload Elasticsearch with too many bulk requests. Remember about the bulk thread pool and its size (equal to the number of CPU cores in the system by default with a queue of *50* requests), and try to adjust your indexers so that they don't to go beyond it otherwise, you will first start to queue their requests, and if Elasticsearch is not able to process them, you will quickly start seeing rejected execution exceptions, and your data won't be indexed. On the other hand, remember that your bulk requests can't be too large, or Elasticsearch will need a lot of memory to process them.

Just as an example, I would like to show you two types of indexing taking place. In the first figure, we have indexing throughput when running the indexation, document by document. In the second figure, we do the same, but instead of indexing documents one by one, we index them in batches of 10 documents:

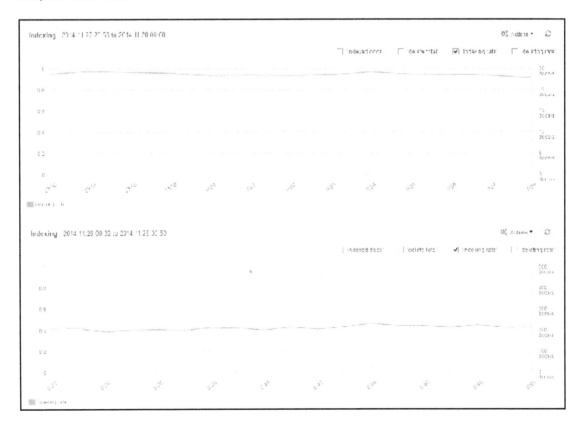

As you can see, when indexing documents one by one, we were able to index about *30* documents per second and it was stable. The situation changed with bulk indexing and batches of *10* documents. We were able to index slightly more than *200* documents per second, so the difference can be clearly seen.

Of course, this is a very basic comparison of indexing speed, and in order to show you the real difference, we should use dozens of threads and push Elasticsearch to its limits. However, the preceding comparison should give you a basic view of the indexing throughput gains when using bulk indexing.

Keeping your document fields under control

The amount of data you index makes the difference, which is understandable. However, this is not the only factor; the size of the documents and their analysis matters as well. With larger documents, you can expect not only your index to grow, but also to make the indexation slightly slower. This is why you may sometimes want to look at all the fields you are indexing and storing. Keep your stored fields to a minimum or don't use them at all; the only stored field you need in most cases is the _source field.

There is one more thing–apart from the _source field, Elasticsearch indexes the _all field by default. Let's remind you: the _all field is used by Elasticsearch to gather data from all the other textual fields. In most of the cases, this field is not used at all and because of that, it is nice to turn it off. Turning it off is simple, and the only thing to do is add the following entry to the type mappings:

```
"_all" : {"enabled" : false}
```

We can do this during the index creation, for example, like this:

```
curl -XPUT 'localhost:9200/disabling_all' -d '{
"mappings" : {
 "test_type" : {
  "_all" : { "enabled" : false },
  "properties" : {
   "name" : { "type" : "text" },
   "tag" : { "type" : "keyword" }
  }
 }
}
}'
```

The indexing should be slightly faster depending on the size of your documents and the number of textual fields in them.

There is an additional thing, which is good practice when disabling the _all field: setting a new default search field. We can do this by setting the index.query.default_field property. For example, in our case, we can set it in the elasticsearch.yml file and set it to the name field from our preceding mappings:

```
index.query.default_field: name
```

You can set the default field per index at the time of index creation in the following way:

```
curl -XPUT "http://localhost:9200/disabling_all" -d'
{
    "mappings": {
        "test_type": {
            "_all": {
                "enabled": false
            },
            "properties": {
                "name": {
                    "type": "text"
                },
                "tag": {
                    "type": "keyword"
                }
            }
        }
    },
    "settings": {
        "index.query.default_field": "name"
    }
}'
```

The index architecture and replication

When designing the index architecture, one of the things you need to think about is the number of shards and replicas that the index is built of. During that time, we also need to think about data distribution among Elasticsearch nodes, optimal performance, high availability, reliability, and so on. First of all, distributing primary shards of the index across all nodes we have, will parallelize indexing operations and make them faster.

The second thing is data replication. What we have to remember is that too many replicas will cause the indexation speed to drop. This is because of several reasons. First of all, you need to transfer the data between primary shards and replicas. The second thing is that, usually, replicas and primary shards may live on the same nodes (not primary shards and its replicas, of course, but replicas of other primaries). For example, take a look at what is shown in the following screenshot:

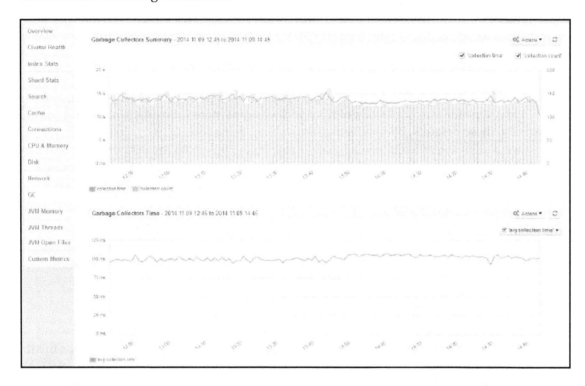

Because of this, Elasticsearch will need the data for both primary shards and replicas and, thus, it will use the disk. Depending on the cluster setup, the indexing throughput may drop in such cases (depending on the disks, number of documents indexed at the same time, and so on).

Tuning the write-ahead log

We have already talked about transaction logs in the *NRT, flush, refresh, and transaction log* section of `Chapter 7`, *Low-level Index Control*. Elasticsearch has an internal module called translog: (`http://www.elasticsearch.org/guide/en/elasticsearch/reference/current/index-modules-translog.html`). It is a per-shard structure that serves the purpose of write-ahead logging (`http://en.wikipedia.org/wiki/Write-ahead_logging`). Basically, it allows Elasticsearch to expose the newest updates for GET operations, ensure data durability, and optimize writing to Lucene indices.

By default, Elasticsearch keeps a maximum of *5000* operations in the transaction log with a maximum size of 512 MB. However, if we can pay the price of data not being available for search operations for longer periods of time and we want more indexing throughput, we can increase these defaults. By specifying the `index.translog.flush_threshold_ops` and `index.translog.flush_threshold_size` properties (both are set per index and can be updated in real time using the Elasticsearch API), we can set the maximum number of operations allowed to be stored in the transaction log and its maximum size. We've seen deployments with these property values set to five times the default values.

One thing to remember is that in case of failure, shard initialization will be slower–of course, on the ones that had large transaction logs. This is because Elasticsearch needs to process all the information from the transaction log before the shard is ready for use.

Thinking about storage

One of the crucial things when it comes to high indexing use cases is the storage type and its configuration. If your organization can afford **solid-state drive** (**SSD**) disks, go for them. They are superior in terms of speed compared to the traditional spinning disks, but of course, that comes at the cost of price. If you can't afford SSD drives, configure your spinning disks to work in RAID 0 (`http://en.wikipedia.org/wiki/RAID`) or point Elasticsearch to use multiple data paths.

What's more, don't use shared or remote filesystems for Elasticsearch indices; use local storage instead. Remote and shared filesystems are usually slower compared to local disk drives and will cause Elasticsearch to wait for read and write, and thus result in a general slowdown.

RAM buffer for indexing

Remember that the more the available RAM for the indexing buffer (the `indices.memory.index_buffer_size` property), the more documents Elasticsearch can hold in the memory, but of course, we don't want to occupy 100 percent of the available memory only for Elasticsearch. By default, this is set to 10 percent, but if you really need a high indexing rate, you can increase it. It is advisable to have approximately 512 MB of RAM for each active shard that takes part in the indexing process, but remember that the `indices.memory.index_buffer_size` property is per node and not per shard. So, if you have 20 GB of heap given to the Elasticsearch node and 10 shards active on the node, Elasticsearch will give each shard about 200 MB of RAM for indexing buffering (10 percent of 20 GB / 10 shards) by default.

Managing time-based indices efficiently using shrink and rollover APIs

Recently, we talked a lot about how to scale Elasticsearch clusters and some general guidelines to follow while going into production. In this section, we are going to talk about two new APIs introduced in Elasticsearch 5.0. The Shrink and Rollover APIs. Both of these APIs are specially designed for managing time series-based indices such as, daily-/weekly-/monthly-created indices for logs, or an index for each week or month of tweets.

We know these basic points related to shards of an index:

- We need to define the number of shards in advance at the time of index creation and we can't increase or decrease the number of shards for index once it is created.
- The greater the number of shards, the more indexing throughput, the lesser the search speed, and greater number of resources are needed.

Both of these problems may be an overkill for the performance and management of your cluster when the data size grows and scaling is needed. For example, suppose you create an index daily for each day of logs with five shards, each which will lead to creating 1,825 shards in a year. Also, you are not going to do indexing in older indices, therefore there is no benefit to keeping so many shards in the cluster. Similarly, if you perform a search on indices with too many shards, it will lead to poor response time.

Looking at these problems Elasticsearch has introduced these two new features which we are going to discuss in this section.

The shrink API

This API is exposed under the `_shrink` REST endpoint and allows you to shrink an existing index into a new index with fewer primary shards.

The shrinking process works as follows:

- First, it creates a new target index with the same definition as the source index, but with a smaller number of primary shards
- Then, it hard-links segments from the source index into the target index. (If the file system doesn't support hard-linking, then all segments are copied into the new index, which is a much more time consuming process)
- Finally, it recovers the target index as though it were a closed index which had just been re-opened

Requirements for indices to be shrunk

The following requirements must be met for an index to be shrunk:

- The target index must not exist in the cluster.
- During the shrinking request, the requested number of primary shards in the target index must be a factor of the number of shards in the source index. For example, an index with six primary shards can be shrunk into three, two, or one primary shard(s) or an index with 10 primary shards can be shrunk into five, two, or one.
- The source index must have more primary shards than the target index.
- The number of primary shards in the target index must be a factor of the number of primary shards in the source index.
- The source index must not contain more than 2,147,483,519 documents in total across all shards that will be shrunk into a single shard on the target index as this is the maximum number of docs that can fit into a single shard.
- The node handling the shrink process must have sufficient free disk space to accommodate a second copy of the existing index.

Shrinking an index

Lets create an index with name `source_index` to learn about index shrinking concept.

```
curl -XPUT "http://localhost:9200/source_index"
```

Once this index is created we will be shrinking this index to an index named `target_index`. But before that its important to know that to shrink an index, you have to take some more considerations into account, such as only read-only indices can be shrunk, all the primary shards must be allocated on a single node, and similarly all the replica shards must be allocated on a single node. These requirements can be achieved using a single command as follows:

```
curl -XPUT "http://localhost:9200/source_index/_settings" -d'
{
  "settings": {
    "index.routing.allocation.require._name": "shrink_node_name",
    "index.blocks.write": true
  }
}'
```

Please note that, `index.blocks.write` settings will block all the writes to this index.

Next, the index can be shrunk into a new index called `target_index` with the following command:

```
curl -XPOST 'localhost:9200/source_index/_shrink/target_index?pretty'
```

You can not specify mappings along with a shrink request, but you can add aliases at the time of the shrink request:

```
curl -XPUT "http://localhost:9200/source_index/_shrink/target_index"
-d'
{
  "settings": {
    "index.number_of_replicas": 1,
    "index.number_of_shards": 1
  },
  "aliases": {
    "search_index": {}
  }
}'
```

The shrinking progress can be monitored using the `cat` API, as mentioned in the following command:

```
curl -XGET localhost:9200/_cat/recovery
```

Rollover API

This API helps in creating a new index and rollover for an existing alias from an older index to the new index when the existing index is considered to be too large or too old.

This API request accepts a list of conditions and a single alias name. Please note that the alias name must be associated with only one index. If the existing index satisfies the specified conditions, then a new index is created and the alias is switched to point to the new index.

Using the rollover API

We are going to explain the working of this API using a step-by-step example as follows:

1. Create an index along with `aliases`:

   ```
   curl -XPUT "http://localhost:9200/myindex-000001" -d'
   {
     "aliases": {"index_alias": {}}
   }'
   ```

2. Index a document to test our rollover conditions:

   ```
   curl -XPUT "http://localhost:9200/myindex-000001/doc/1" -d'
   {"content":"testing rollover concepts"}'
   ```

3. Create a condition for rolling over the alias to a new index, which specifies creating a new index and adding the `index_alias` of `myindex-000001` to the newly created index, if `myindex-000001` becomes one day old or it has 1 document:

   ```
   curl -XPOST "http://localhost:9200/index_alias/_rollover" -d'
   {
     "conditions": {
       "max_age":    "1d",
       "max_docs":   1
     }
   }'
   ```

4. Now, when you check your indices lists using the _cat/indices API, you will find a newly created index, myindex-000002 and the alias should be automatically rolled over to the new index.

Passing additional settings with a rollover request

You can also pass the additional settings at the time of a rollover request as follows:

```
curl -XPOST "http://localhost:9200/index_alias/_rollover" -d'
{
  "conditions": {
    "max_docs": 1
  },
  "settings": {
    "index.number_of_shards": 2
  }
}'
```

Pattern for creating new index name

If the name of the existing index ends with – and a number–for example, logs-000001 – then the name of the new index will follow the same pattern, incrementing the number (logs-000002). The number is zero-padded with a length of six, regardless of the old index name.

If the old name doesn't match this pattern then you must specify the name for the new index as follows, but make sure you have created an alias in advance as these commands use an alias name, in our example the name of the alias is index_alias:

```
curl -XPOST
"http://localhost:9200/index_alias/_rollover/new_index_name" -d'
{
  "conditions": {
    "max_age":    "7d",
    "max_docs":   10000
  }
}'
```

Otherwise, you could just send a request like the following:

```
curl -XPOST "http://localhost:9200/index_alias/_rollover/" -d'
{
  "conditions": {
    "max_age":    "7d",
    "max_docs":   10000
  }
}'
```

 If you are interested, visit the URL:
https://www.elastic.co/blog/managing-time-based-indices-efficiently to get some more insight into shrinking and rollover concepts.

Summary

In this chapter, we primarily focused on improving the performance and scaling the clusters. We started with the concepts of validating queries to find out the bugs before actually executing them and then saw how to take advantage of query profiling to learn all the granular details of the overall query execution time. Next, we learned about hot threads to identify the issues in the cluster and then did a detailed coverage of how to scale the Elasticsearch clusters under different loads and requirements. We finally, ended the chapter after discussing two awesome features; index shrinking and rollover which are introduced in Elasticsearch version 5.0.

In the next chapter, we are going to learn about Elasticsearch plugins' development by showing and describing in-depth, how to write your own custom plugins in Java.

11
Developing Elasticsearch Plugins

In the last chapter, we saw how one can work on improving the performance and scaling of Elasticsearch clusters. We learned many useful concepts such as query validations and query profiling. We then read about hot threads to identify the issues in the cluster and then did a detailed coverage of how to scale the Elasticsearch clusters under different loads and requirements. We finally ended the chapter after discussing two awesome features, index shrinking and rollover, which are introduced in Elasticsearch version 5.0.

In this chapter, we are going to learn one of the most interesting things, and that is developing Elasticsearch custom plugins. By the end of this chapter, we will have covered the following topics:

- How to set up the **Apache Maven** project for Elasticsearch plugin development
- How to develop a custom REST action plugin
- How to develop a custom analysis plugin extending Elasticsearch analysis capabilities

Creating the Apache Maven project structure

Before we start with showing you how to develop a custom Elasticsearch plugin, we would like to discuss a way to package it so that it can be installed by Elasticsearch using the `plugin` command. In order to do that, we will use Apache Maven (http://maven.apache.org/), which is designed to simplify software project management. It aims to make your build process easier, provide a unifying build system, manage dependencies, and so on.

Please note that the chapter you are currently reading was written and tested using Elasticsearch 5.0.0.

Also remember that the book you are holding in your hands is not about Maven but Elasticsearch, and we will keep Maven-related information to the required minimum.

 Installing Apache Maven is a straightforward task; we assume that you already have it installed. However, if you have problems with it, please consult `http://maven.apache.org/` for more information.

Understanding the basics

The result of a Maven build process is an artifact. Each artifact is defined by its identifier, its group, and its version. This is crucial when working with Maven, because every dependency you'll use will need to be identified by these three mentioned properties.

The structure of the Maven Java project

The idea behind Maven is quite simple – you create a project structure that looks something like this:

```
▼ CustomRestActionPlugin
  ▼ src/main/java
    ▼ org.elasticsearch.customrest
      ▶ CustomRestAction.java
      ▶ CustomRestPlugin.java
  ▼ src/main/resources
      plugin-descriptor.properties
  ▶ JRE System Library [JavaSE-1.8]
  ▶ Maven Dependencies
  ▶ src
  ▶ target
  M pom.xml
```

You can see that the code is placed in the src folder – the code is in the main folder. Although you can change the default layout, Maven tends to work best with the default layout.

The idea of POM

In addition to the code, you can see a file named pom.xml that is located in the root directory in the previous image. This is a project object model (.pom) file that describes the project, its properties, and its dependencies. That's right – you don't need to manually download dependencies if they are present in one of the available Maven repositories – during its work, Maven will download them, put them in your local repository on your hard disk, and use them when needed. All you need to care about is writing an appropriate pom.xml section that will inform Maven which dependencies should be used.

For example, this is an example Maven pom.xml file:

```
<?xml version="1.0" encoding="UTF-8"?>
<project xmlns="http://maven.apache.org/POM/4.0.0"
xmlns:xsi="http://www.w3.org/2001/XMLSchema-instance"
  xsi:schemaLocation="http://maven.apache.org/POM/4.0.0
http://maven.apache.org/xsd/maven-4.0.0.xsd">
  <modelVersion>4.0.0</modelVersion>
  <groupId>bharvidixit.com.elasticsearch.customrestaction</groupId>
  <artifactId>CustomRestActionPlugin</artifactId>
  <version>5.0.0-SNAPSHOT</version>
  <name>Plugin: Custom Rest Action</name>
  <description>Custom Rest Action Plugin for elasticsearch</description>

  <properties>
    <elasticsearch.version>5.0.0</elasticsearch.version>
  </properties>

  <dependencies>
    <dependency>
      <groupId>org.elasticsearch</groupId>
      <artifactId>elasticsearch</artifactId>
      <version>${elasticsearch.version}</version>
      <scope>provided</scope>
    </dependency>
  </dependencies>
</project>
```

This is a simplified version of a `pom.xml` file that we will extend in the rest of the chapter. You can see that it starts with the root `project` tag and then defines the group identifier, the artifact identifier, the version, and the packaging method (in our case, the standard build command will create a JAR file). In addition to this, we've specified a single dependency – the Elasticsearch library version 5.0.0.

Running the build process

In order to run the build process, what we need to do is simply run the following command in the directory where the `pom.xml` file is present:

```
mvn clean package
```

It will result in running Maven. It will clean all the generated content in the working directory, and compile and package our code. Of course, if we have unit tests, they will have to pass in order for the package to be built. The built package will be written into the `target` directory created by Maven.

 If you want to learn more about the Maven life cycle, please refer to `http://maven.apache.org/guides/introduction/introduction-to-the-lifecycle.html`.

Introducing the assembly Maven plugin

In order to build the ZIP file that will contain our plugin code, we need to package it. By default, Maven doesn't support pure ZIP file packaging, so in order to make it all work, we will use the Maven Assembly plugin (you can find more about the plugin at `http://maven.apache.org/plugins/maven-assembly-plugin/`). In general, the described plugin allows us to aggregate the project output along with its dependencies, documentations, and configuration files into a single archive.

In order for the plugin to work, we need to add the `build` section to our `pom.xml` file that will contain information about the assembly plugin, the JAR plugin (which is responsible for creating the proper JAR), and the compiler plugin, because we want to be sure that the code will be readable by Java 8. In addition to this, let's assume that we want our archive to be put into the `target/release` directory of our project. The relevant section of the `pom.xml` file should look as follows:

```
<build>
<resources>
<resource>
```

```
<directory>src/main/resources</directory>
<filtering>false</filtering>
<excludes>
<exclude>*.properties</exclude>
</excludes>
</resource>
</resources>
<plugins>
<plugin>
<groupId>org.apache.maven.plugins</groupId>
<artifactId>maven-assembly-plugin</artifactId>
<version>2.6</version>
<configuration>
<appendAssemblyId>false</appendAssemblyId>
<outputDirectory>${project.build.directory}/releases/</outputDirectory>
<descriptors>
<descriptor>${basedir}/src/main/assembly/release.xml</descriptor>
</descriptors>
</configuration>
<executions>
<execution>
<phase>package</phase>
<goals>
<goal>single</goal>
</goals>
</execution>
</executions>
</plugin>
<plugin>
<groupId>org.apache.maven.plugins</groupId>
<artifactId>maven-compiler-plugin</artifactId>
<version>3.3</version>
<configuration>
<source>1.8</source>
<target>1.8</target>
</configuration>
</plugin>
</plugins>
</build>
```

If you look closely at the assembly plugin configuration, you'll notice that we specify the assembly descriptor called `release.xml` in the `assembly` directory. This file is responsible for specifying what kind of archive we want to have as the output. Let's put the following `release.xml` file in the `assembly` directory of our project:

```
<?xml version="1.0"?>
<assembly>
<id>plugin</id>
```

```
<formats>
<format>zip</format>
</formats>
<includeBaseDirectory>false</includeBaseDirectory>
<files>
<file>
<source>${project.basedir}/src/main/resources/plugin-
descriptor.properties</source>
<outputDirectory>elasticsearch</outputDirectory>
<filtered>true</filtered>
</file>
</files>
<dependencySets>
<dependencySet>
<outputDirectory>elasticsearch</outputDirectory>
<useProjectArtifact>true</useProjectArtifact>
<useTransitiveFiltering>true</useTransitiveFiltering>
</dependencySet>
</dependencySets>
</assembly>
```

Again, we don't need to know all the details; however, it is nice to understand what is going on, even on the general level. The preceding code file tells the Maven Assembly plugin that we want our archive to be packed with ZIP (`<format>zip</format>`), and we want the output to be generated inside the `elasticsearch` directory name, because according to the plugin structure conventions, all plugin files must be contained in a directory called `elasticsearch`.

Understanding the plugin descriptor file

According to Elasticsearch plugin development convention, it is mandatory that all plugins must contain a file called `plugin-descriptor.properties` and it must be assembled with your plugin artifact in the `elasticsearch` directory. You always need to create this file in the `src/main/resources` path of your project.

Also, it does not need to be added to the project classes but only packaged within the ZIP file. We need to define this condition inside the `release.xml` file. Please note that inside the `release.xml` file, we are filtering the `plugin-descriptor.properties` file, which means that at package time all Maven placeholders will be replaced by their needed values.

We don't want to add this file in our JAR so we have written following conditions inside `pom.xml`:

```
<build>
<resources>
```

```
<resource>
<directory>src/main/resources</directory>
<filtering>false</filtering>
<excludes>
<exclude>*.properties</exclude>
</excludes>
</resource>
</resources>
</build>
```

The following are the mandatory elements for plugins:

- `description`: A simple summary of the plugin.
- `version`: The plugin's version.
- `name`: The plugin's name.
- `classname`: The name of the class to load, fully qualified.
- `java.version`: The version of Java the code is built against. Use the system property `java.specification.version`. The version string must be a sequence of non-negative decimal integers separated by decimal points (.) and may have leading zeros.
- `elasticsearch.version`: The version of Elasticsearch compiled against.

> If you want to see the full project structure with the full `pom.xml` file and all the needed files, please look at the code provided with the book for `Chapter 11`, *Developing Elasticsearch Plugins*.

Creating a custom REST action

Let's start the journey of extending Elasticsearch by creating a custom REST action. We've chosen this as the first extension, because we wanted to take the simplest approach as the introduction to extending Elasticsearch.

> We assume that you already have a Java project created and that you are using Maven, just like we did in the *Creating the Apache Maven project structure* section at the beginning of this chapter. If you would like to use an already created and working example and start from there, please look at the code for `Chapter 11`, *Developing Elasticsearch Plugins* that is available with the book.

The assumptions

In order to illustrate how to develop a custom REST action, we need to have an idea of how it should work. Our REST action will be really simple – it should return names of all the nodes or names of the nodes that start with the given prefix if the `prefix` parameter is passed to it. In addition to that, it should only be available when using the HTTP `GET` method, so `POST` requests, for example, shouldn't be allowed.

Implementation details

We will need to develop two Java classes:

- A class that extends the `BaseRestHandler` Elasticsearch abstract class from the `org.elasticsearch.rest` package that will be responsible for handling the REST action code – we will call it `CustomRestAction`.
- A class that will be used by Elasticsearch to load the plugin – this class needs to extend the Elasticsearch `Plugin` class from the `org.elasticsearch.plugin` package – we will call it `CustomRestActionPlugin`. In addition, this class also needs to implement the `ActionPlugin` interface, which is an extension point available through the `org.elasticsearch.plugin.Plugin` class.

In addition to the preceding two, we will need a simple text file that we will discuss after implementing the two mentioned Java classes.

Using the REST action class

The most interesting class is the one that will be used to handle the user's requests – we will call it `CustomRestAction`. In order to work, it needs to extend the `BaseRestHandler` class from the `org.elasticsearch.rest` package – the base class for REST actions in Elasticsearch. In order to extend this class, we need to override the `prepareRequest` method in which we will process the user request and a three-argument constructor that will be used to initialize the base class and register the appropriate handler under which our REST action will be visible.

The whole code for the `CustomRestAction` class looks as follows:

```
public class CustomRestAction extends BaseRestHandler {
  @Inject
  public CustomRestAction(Settings settings, RestController controller) {
    super(settings);
```

```
    // Register your handlers here
    controller.registerHandler(GET, "/_mastering/nodes", this);
}

@Override
protected RestChannelConsumer prepareRequest(RestRequest restRequest,
NodeClient client) throws IOException {
    String prefix = restRequest.param("prefix","");
    return channel -> {
        XContentBuilder builder = channel.newBuilder();
        builder.startObject();
        List<String> nodes = new ArrayList<String>();
        NodesInfoResponse response =
client.admin().cluster().prepareNodesInfo().setThreadPool(true).get();
        for (NodeInfo nodeInfo : response.getNodes()) {
            String nodeName = nodeInfo.getNode().getName();
            if (prefix.isEmpty()) {
                nodes.add(nodeName);
            } else if (nodeName.startsWith(prefix)) {
                nodes.add(nodeName);
            }
        }
        builder.field("nodes", nodes);
        builder.endObject();

        channel.sendResponse(new BytesRestResponse(RestStatus.OK, builder));
    };
}
}
```

The constructor

For each custom REST class, Elasticsearch will pass two arguments when creating an object of such type: the `Settings` type object which holds the settings, and the `RestController` type object that we will use to bind our REST action to the REST endpoint. All of these arguments are also required by the superclass, so we invoke the base class constructor and pass them.

There is one more thing: the `@Inject` annotation. It allows us to inform Elasticsearch that it should put the objects in the constructor during the object creation. For more information about it, please refer to the Javadoc of the mentioned annotation, which is available at https://github.com/elastic/elasticsearch/blob/master/core/src/main/java/org/elasticsearch/common/inject/Inject.java.

Now, let's focus on the following code line:

```
controller.registerHandler(Method.GET, "/_mastering/nodes", this);
```

What it does is that it registers our custom REST action implementation and binds it to the endpoint of our choice. The first argument is the HTTP method type the REST action will be able to work with. As we said earlier, we only want to respond to GET requests. If we would like to respond to multiple types of HTTP methods, we should just include multiple registerHandler method invocations with each HTTP method. The second argument specifies the actual REST endpoint our custom action will be available at; in our case, it will available under the /_mastering/nodes endpoint. The third argument tells Elasticsearch which class should be responsible for handling the defined endpoint; in our case, this is the class we are developing, thus we are passing this.

Handling requests

Although the prepareRequest method is the longest one in our code, it is not complicated. As you can see, to process the request and create the response object, we need to pass two parameters to this method: RestRequest, which holds the request parameters, and the client type object, which is an Elasticsearch client and entry point for cooperation with it. We start by reading the request parameter with the following line of code:

```
String prefix = restRequest.param("prefix", "");
```

We store the prefix request parameter in the variable called prefix. By default, we want an empty String object to be assigned to the prefix variable if there is no prefix parameter passed to the request (the default value is defined by the second parameter of the param method of the restRequest object).

This code is using a lambda which creates our JSON document which will be returned in the response. Basically builder.startObject() and builder.endObject() create a JSON object {}.To fill this object, we have written the actual logic in which we have created a NodesInfoResponse object using the Elasticsearch client object and its abilities to run administrative commands. The NodesInfoResponse object will contain an array of NodeInfo objects, which we will use to get node names. What we need to do is return all the node names that start with a given prefix or all if the prefix parameter was not present in the request. In order to do this, we create a new array:

```
List<String> nodes = new ArrayList<String>();
```

We iterate over the available nodes using the following for loop:

```
for (NodeInfo nodeInfo : response.getNodes())
```

We get the node name using the `getName` method of the `DiscoveryNode` object, which is returned after invoking the `getNode` method of `NodeInfo`:

```
String nodeName = nodeInfo.getNode().getName();
```

If `prefix` is empty or if it starts with the given prefix, we add the name of the node to the array we've created. After we iterate through all the `NodeInfo` objects, we build the response which is sent through HTTP.

At the end, this code will produce something like the following:

```
{
"nodes" : [
"node-2"
]
}
```

Writing responses

The last thing regarding our `CustomRestAction` class is the response handling, which is the responsibility of the last part of the `sendResponse` method of the `channel` object. It automatically takes into consideration the `format` parameter used by the client in the call, so by default, we send the response in a proper JSON format just like Elasticsearch does and also take the YAML (`http://en.wikipedia.org/wiki/YAML`) format for free.

As you can see, we use the `builder` object we got to start the response object (using the `startObject` method) and start a `nodes` field (because the value of the field is a collection, it will automatically be formatted as an array). The `nodes` field is created inside the initial object, and we will use it to return matching node names. Finally, we close the object using the `endObject` method.

After we have our object ready to be sent as a response, we return the `BytesRestResponse` object. We do this in the following line:

```
channel.sendResponse(new BytesRestResponse(RestStatus.OK, builder));
```

The `RestStatus` class allows us to specify the response code, which is `RestStatus.OK` in our case, because everything went smoothly.

The plugin class

The `CustomRestActionPlugin` class will hold the code that is used by Elasticsearch to initialize the plugin itself. It extends the `Plugin` class from the `org.elasticsearch.plugin` package. In addition, we also need to implement the `ActionPlugin` interface which is an extension point of `Plugin` class. Similar to `ActionPlugin`, the `Plugin` class provides several extensions in the form of interfaces, as shown in the following screenshot, which has been taken from the source code documentation of the `Plugin` class:

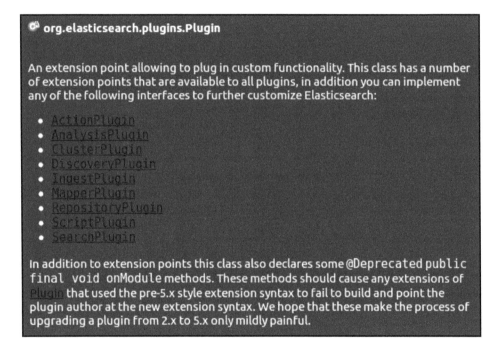

Because we are creating an extension, we are obliged to implement the `getRestHandlers` method in the `CustomRestActionPlugin` class, which is a REST handler added by this plugin.

The code of the whole class looks as follows. First we need to make necessary imports:

```
import java.util.Collections;
import java.util.List;
import org.elasticsearch.plugins.ActionPlugin;
import org.elasticsearch.plugins.Plugin;
import org.elasticsearch.rest.RestHandler;
```

Then we write the definition of the `CustomRestActionPlugin` class:

```
public class CustomRestActionPlugin extends Plugin implements ActionPlugin
{
    @Override
    public List<Class<? extends RestHandler>> getRestHandlers() {
      return Collections.singletonList(CustomRestAction.class);
    }
}
```

In the previous code, `Collections.singletonList` returns an immutable list containing only the specified object.

That's all when it comes to Java development!

Informing Elasticsearch about our REST action

We have our code ready, but we need one additional thing; we need to let Elasticsearch know what the class registering our plugin is – the one we've called `CustomRestActionPlugin`. In order to do this, we create a `plugin-descriptor.properties` file in the `src/main/resources` directory with the following content:

```
description=${project.description}.
version=${project.version}
name=${project.artifactId}
classname=org.elasticsearch.customrest.CustomRestActionPlugin
java.version=1.8
elasticsearch.version=${elasticsearch.version}
```

This file will be included in the JAR file that will be created during the build process and will be used by Elasticsearch during the plugin load process.

Time for testing

Of course, we could leave it now and say that we are done, but we won't. We would like to show you how to build each of the plugins, install it, and finally, test it to see whether it actually works. Let's start with building our plugin.

Building the REST action plugin

We start with the easiest part – building our plugin. In order to do this, we run a simple command from the project's home directory:

```
mvn compile package
```

We tell Maven that we want the code to be compiled and packaged. After the command finishes, we can find the archive with the plugin in the `target/release` directory (assuming you are using a project setup similar to the one we've described at the beginning of the chapter).

Installing the REST action plugin

In order to install the plugin, we will use the `plugin` command that is located in the `bin` directory of the Elasticsearch distributable package. Assuming that we have our plugin archive stored in the `/home/install/es/plugins` directory, we will run the following command (we run it from the Elasticsearch home directory):

```
bin/elasticsearch-plugin install
file:////home/install/es/plugins/CustomRestActionPlugin-5.0.0-SNAPSHOT.zip
```

We need to install the plugin on all the nodes in our cluster, because we want to be able to run our custom REST action on each Elasticsearch instance.

 In order to learn more about installing Elasticsearch plugins, please refer to the official Elasticsearch documentation at `https://www.elastic.co/guide/en/elasticsearch/plugins/master/ind ex.html`.

After we have the plugin installed, we need to restart our Elasticsearch instance we were making the installation on. After the restart, we should see something like this in the logs:

```
[2017-01-08T23:33:51,916][INFO ][o.e.p.PluginsService] [node-1] loaded
plugin [CustomRestActionPlugin]
```

As you can see, Elasticsearch informed us that the plugin named `CustomRestActionPlugin` was loaded.

Checking whether the REST action plugin works

We can finally check whether the plugin works. In order to do that, we will run the following command:

```
curl -XGET 'localhost:9200/_mastering/nodes?pretty'
```

As a result, we should get all the nodes in the cluster, because we didn't provide the `prefix` parameter and this is exactly what we've got from Elasticsearch:

```
{
"nodes" : [ "node-1" ]
}
```

Because we only had one node in our Elasticsearch cluster, we've got the `nodes` array with only a `single` entry.

Now, let's test what will happen if we add the `prefix=Nid` parameter to our request. The exact command we've used was as follows:

```
curl -XGET 'localhost:9200/_mastering/nodes?prefix=Nid&pretty'
```

The response from Elasticsearch was as follows:

```
{
"nodes" : [ ]
}
```

As you can see, the `nodes` array is empty, because we don't have any node in the cluster that would start with the `Nid` prefix. At the end, let's check another format of response:

```
curl -XGET 'localhost:9200/_mastering/nodes?pretty&format=yaml'
```

Now the response is not in a JSON format. Look at the example output for a cluster consisting of two nodes:

```
- -
nodes:
- "node-1"
```

As we can see, our REST plugin is not so complicated, but already has several features.

 You can find complete code for this custom REST action plugin inside the `CustomAnalyzerPlugin` directory of the code bundle of this chapter provided with the book.

Creating the custom analysis plugin

The last thing we want to discuss when it comes to custom Elasticsearch plugins is the analysis process extension. We've chosen to show how to develop a custom analysis plugin because this is sometimes very useful, for example, when you want to have the custom analysis process that you use in your company introduced, or when you want to use the Lucene analyzer or filter that is not present in Elasticsearch itself or as a plugin for it. Because creating an analysis extension is more complicated compared to what we've seen when developing a custom REST action, we decided to leave it until the end of the chapter.

Implementation details

Because developing a custom analysis plugin is the most complicated, at least from the Elasticsearch point of view and the number of classes we need to develop, we will have more things to do compared to previous examples. We will need to develop the following things:

- The `TokenFilter` class extension (from the `org.apache.lucene.analysis` package) implementation that will be responsible for handling token reversing; we will call it `CustomFilter`
- The `AbstractTokenFilterFactory` extension (from the `org.elasticsearch.index.analysis` package) that will be responsible for providing our `CustomFilter` instance to Elasticsearch; we will call it `CustomFilterFactory`
- The custom analyzer, which will extend the `org.apache.lucene.analysis.Analyzer` class and provide the Lucene analyzer functionality; we will call it `CustomAnalyzer`
- The analyzer provider, which we will call `CustomAnalyzerProvider`, which extends `AbstractIndexAnalyzerProvider` from the `org.elasticsearch.index.analysis` package, and which will be responsible for providing the analzyer instance to Elasticsearch
- Finally, the usual `plugin` extension (from the `org.elasticsearch.plugins` package) that will register our plugin; we will call it `CustomAnalyzerPlugin`

So let's start discussing the code.

Implementing TokenFilter

The funniest thing about the currently discussed plugin is that the whole analysis work is actually done on a Lucene level, and what we need to do is write the org.apache.lucene.analysis.TokenFilter extension, which we will call CustomFilter. In order to do this, we need to initialize the superclass and override the incrementToken method. Our class will be responsible for reversing the tokens, so that's the logic we want our analyzer and filter to have. The whole implementation of our CustomFilter class looks as follows:

```
public class CustomFilter extends TokenFilter {
private final CharTermAttribute termAttr =
addAttribute(CharTermAttribute.class);

protected CustomFilter(TokenStream input) {
super(input);
}

@Override
public boolean incrementToken() throws IOException {
if (input.incrementToken()) {
char[] originalTerm = termAttr.buffer();
if (originalTerm.length > 0) {
StringBuilder builder = new StringBuilder(new
String(originalTerm).trim()).reverse();
termAttr.setEmpty();
termAttr.append(builder.toString());
}
return true;
} else {
return false;
}
}
}
```

The first thing we see in the implementation is the following line:

```
private final CharTermAttribute termAttr =
addAttribute(CharTermAttribute.class);
```

It allows us to retrieve the text of the token we are currently processing. In order to get access to the other token information, we need to use other attributes. The list of attributes can be found by looking at the classes implementing Lucene's `org.apache.lucene.util.Attribute` interface (http://lucene.apache.org/core/6_2_0/core/org/apache/lucene/util/Attribute.html). What you need to know now is that by using the static `addAttribute` method, we can bind different attributes and use them during token processing.

Then we have the constructor, which is only used for superclass initialization, so we can skip discussing it.

Finally, there is the `incrementToken` method, which returns `true` when there is a token in the token stream left to be processed, and `false` if there is no token left to be processed. So, what we do first is we check whether there is a token to be processed by calling the `incrementToken` method of input, which is the `TokenStream` instance stored in the superclass. Then, we get the term text by calling the `buffer` method of the attribute we bind in the first line of our class. If there is text in the term (its length is higher than zero), we use a `StringBuilder` object to reverse the text, we clear the term buffer (by calling `setEmpty` on the attribute), and we append the reversed text to the already emptied term buffer (by calling the `append` method of the attribute). After this, we return `true`, because our token is ready to be processed further – on a token filter level, we don't know whether the token will be processed further or not, so we need to be sure we return the correct information, just in case.

Implementing the TokenFilter factory

The factory for our token filter implementation is one of the simplest classes in the case of the discussed plugins. What we need to do is create an `AbstractTokenFilterFactory` (from the `org.elasticsearch.index.analysis` package) extension that overrides a single `create` method in which we create our token filter. The code of this class looks as follows:

```
public class CustomFilterFactory extends AbstractTokenFilterFactory
implements TokenFilterFactory {
@Inject
public CustomFilterFactory(IndexSettings indexSettings, @Assisted String
name, @Assisted Settings settings) {
super(indexSettings, name, settings);
}

@Override
public TokenStream create(TokenStream tokenStream) {
```

```
return new CustomFilter(tokenStream);
    }
}
```

As you can see, the class is very simple. We start with the constructor, which is needed because we need to initialize the parent class. In addition to this, we have the `create` method, in which we create our `CustomFilter` class with the provided `TokenStream` object.

Before we go on, we would like to mention two more things: the `IndexSettings` object and `@Assisted` annotation. The first encapsulates all index-level settings and handles settings updates. It's created per index and available to all index-level classes and allows them to retrieve the latest updated settings instance. The `@Assisted keyword` results in the annotated parameter value to be injected from the argument of the factory method.

Implementing the class custom analyzer

We wanted to keep the example implementation as simple as possible and, because of that, we've decided not to complicate the analyzer implementation. To implement our analyzer, we need to extend an abstract `Analyzer` class from Lucene's `org.apache.lucene.analysis` package, and we did that. The whole code of our `CustomAnalyzer` class looks as follows:

```
public class CustomAnalyzer extends Analyzer {
public CustomAnalyzer() {
}

@Override
protected TokenStreamComponents createComponents(String field) {
final Tokenizer src = new WhitespaceTokenizer();
return new TokenStreamComponents(src, new CustomFilter(src));
    }
}
```

 If you want to see more complicated analyzer implementations, please look at the source code of Apache Lucene, Apache Solr, and Elasticsearch.

The createComponents method is the one we need to implement, and it should return a TokenStreamComponents object (from the org.apache.lucene.analysis package) for a given field name (the String type object – the argument of the method). What we do is create a Tokenizer object using the WhitespaceTokenizer class available in Lucene. This will result in the input data to be tokenized on whitespace characters. Then we create a Lucene TokenStreamComponents object, to which we give the source of tokens (our previously created Tokenizer object) and our CustomFilter object. This will result in our CustomFilter object being used by CustomAnalyzer.

Implementing the analyzer provider

Let's talk about another provider implementation in addition to the token filter factory we've created earlier. This time, we need to extend AbstractIndexAnalyzerProvider from the org.elasticsearch.index.analysis package in order for Elasticsearch to be able to create our analyzer. The implementation is very simple, as we only need to implement the get method in which we should return our analyzer. The CustomAnalyzerProvider class code looks as follows:

```
public class CustomAnalyzerProvider extends
AbstractIndexAnalyzerProvider<CustomAnalyzer> {
private final CustomAnalyzer analyzer;

@Inject
public CustomAnalyzerProvider(IndexSettings indexSettings, Environment env,
@Assisted String name, @Assisted Settings settings) {
super(indexSettings, name, settings);
analyzer = new CustomAnalyzer();
}

@Override
public CustomAnalyzer get() {
return this.analyzer;
}
}
```

As you can see, we've implemented the constructor in order to be able to initialize the superclass. In addition to that, we are creating a single instance of our analyzer, which we will return when Elasticsearch requests it. We do this because we don't want to create an analyzer every time Elasticsearch requests it; this is not efficient. We don't need to worry about multithreading because our analyzer is thread-safe and, thus, a single instance can be reused. In the get method, we are just returning our analyzer.

Implementing the analyzer plugin

Finally, we need to implement the plugin class so that Elasticsearch knows that there is a plugin to be loaded. It should extend the `AbstractPlugin` class from the `org.elasticsearch.plugins` package. In addition, we also need to implement the `AnalysisPlugin` interface which is an extension point of the `Plugin` class. This is similar to what we had implemented in our `CustomRestActionPlugin`. Because we are creating an extension, we are obliged to implement the `getAnalyzers` method, which is used to add additional analyzers.

The code of the whole class looks as follows:

```
public class CustomAnalyzerPlugin extends Plugin implements AnalysisPlugin
{
  @Override
public Map<String, AnalysisProvider<AnalyzerProvider<? extends Analyzer>>>
getAnalyzers() {
return singletonMap("mastering_analyzer", CustomAnalyzerProvider::new);
}
}
```

As you can see, we are binding our `CustomAnalyzerProvider` class inside the `getAnalyzers` method with the name `mastering_analyzer` and returning it as `singletonMap`.

Informing Elasticsearch about our custom analyzer

Once we have our code ready, we need to add one additional thing: we need to let Elasticsearch know what the class registering our plugin is – the one we've called `CustomAnalyzerPlugin`. In order to do that, we create a `plugin-descriptor.properties` file in the `src/main/resources` directory with the following content:

```
description=${project.description}.
version=${project.version}
name=${project.artifactId}
classname=org.elasticsearch.customanalyzer.CustomAnalyzerPlugin
java.version=1.8
elasticsearch.version=${elasticsearch.version}
```

Testing our custom analysis plugin

Now, we want to test our custom analysis plugin just to be sure that everything works. In order to do that, we need to build our plugin, install it on all nodes in our cluster, and finally, use the Admin Indices Analyze API to see how our analyzer works. Let's do that.

Building our custom analysis plugin

We start with the easiest part: building our plugin. In order to do that, we run a simple command:

```
mvn compile package
```

We tell Maven that we want the code to be compiled and packaged. After the command finishes, we can find the archive with the plugin in the `target/release` directory (assuming you are using a project setup similar to the one we've described at the beginning of the chapter in the *Creating the Apache Maven project* section).

Installing the custom analysis plugin

To install the plugin, we will use the `plugin` command, just like we did previously. Assuming that we have our plugin archive stored in the `/home/install/es/plugins` directory, we would run the following command (we run it from the Elasticsearch home directory):

```
bin/elasticsearch-plugin install
file:////home/install/es/plugins/custom-analyzer-5.0.0-SNAPSHOT.zip
```

We need to install the plugin on all the nodes in our cluster, because we want Elasticsearch to be able to find our analyzer and filter no matter on which node the analysis process is done. If we don't install the plugin on all nodes, we can be certain that we will run into issues.

After we have the plugin installed, we need to restart our Elasticsearch instance we were creating the installation on. After the restart, we should see something like this in the logs:

```
[2017-01-11T02:21:43,406][INFO ][o.e.p.PluginsService] [node-2] loaded
plugin [custom-analyzer]
```

With the preceding log line, Elasticsearch informs us that the plugin named `custom-analyzer` was successfully loaded.

Checking whether our analysis plugin works

We can finally check whether our custom analysis plugin works as it should. In order to do that, we start by creating an empty index called `analyzetest` (the index name doesn't matter). We do this by running the following command:

```
curl -XPUT 'localhost:9200/analyzetest/'
```

After this, we use the Admin Indices Analyze API (http://www.elasticsearch.org/guide/en/elasticsearch/reference/current/indices-analyze.html) to see how our analyzer works. We do that by running the following command:

```
curl -XGET
'localhost:9200/analyzetest/_analyze?analyzer=mastering_analyzer&pretty' -d
'mastering elasticsearch'
```

So, what we should see in response is two tokens: first is `gniretsam` which is reverse of `mastering` and second is `hcraescitsale` which is the reverse of `elasticsearch`. The response Elasticsearch returns looks as follows:

```
{
  "tokens" : [
    {
      "token" : "gniretsam",
      "start_offset" : 0,
      "end_offset" : 9,
      "type" : "word",
      "position" : 0
    },
    {
      "token" : "hcraescitsale",
      "start_offset" : 10,
      "end_offset" : 23,
      "type" : "word",
      "position" : 1
    }
  ]
}
```

As you can see, we've got exactly what we expected, so it seems that our custom analysis plugin works as intended.

You can find complete code for this custom analyzer plugin inside the `CustomAnalyzerPlugin` directory of the code bundle of this chapter.

Summary

In this chapter, we learned about developing custom plugins for Elasticsearch. We started with an overview of Apache Maven and its components and then created a custom REST action plugin for creating our own REST endpoints inside Elasticsearch. Finally, we created a custom analyzer plugin, and learned about various internal and useful classes of Elasticsearch and Lucene.

In the next chapter, we will go through the complete Elastic Stack and learn about how to work with Elasticsearch, Logstash, and Kibana together.

12
Introducing Elastic Stack 5.0

In the last chapter, we learned about developing custom plugins for Elasticsearch. We started with an overview of Apache Maven and its components and then created two plugins. The first plugin was a custom REST action plugin for creating our own REST endpoints inside Elasticsearch and the second plugin for creating a custom analyzer.

In this chapter, which is going to be the last chapter of this book, we are going to cover an overview of *Elastic Stack*. By the end of this chapter, we will have covered the following topics:

- Overview of Elastic Stack 5.0
- Installing and configuring Logstash, Beats, and Kibana
- Shipping data inside Elasticsearch with the help of Logstash
- Using Beats as lightweight data shippers
- Using Kibana for data exploration and visualization

Overview of Elastic Stack 5.0

Till now, we saw the awesomeness of Elasticsearch 5.0, but Elastic, as a company, offers more than only a search tool. In February 2016, Shay Banon, the creator of Elasticsearch, announced the renaming of ELK (Elasticsearch – Logstash – Kibana) Stack to Elastic Stack 5.0. According to Shay, this change had two main reasons. First, they had one more tool – Packetbeat was included in their stack of tools – and second, they wanted to use a unified version across all the products they offer.

The components of Elastic Stack are as follows:

- **Elasticsearch**: The REST- and JSON-based distributed full text open source search engine.
- **Logstash**: An open source tool for processing and ingesting data to Elasticsearch from a multitude of sources.
- **Kibana**: An open source tool for analytics and visualization of data residing inside Elasticsearch.
- **Beats**: Latest open source tool included in the Elastic Stack ,which are used as data shippers to Elasticsearch or Logstash. They need to be installed as agents on each of the servers from where data needs to be shipped.

Since there are multiple operating systems, Java versions, and browser versions are available, you must know the supported versions according to the version of Elastic Stack you are using. Please go to `https://www.elastic.co/support/matrix` to find out about the matrix of officially supported versions and their compatibilities.

Introducing Logstash, Beats, and Kibana

We have already seen how to install and configure Elasticsearch. So, we are not going to repeat it again. We will proceed with learning three more components of Elastic Stack: Logstash, Beats, and Kibana.

Working with Logstash

Logstash is one of the most popular tools for collecting, parsing, and enriching log-based data (usually, data which has a timestamp associated with it) from multiple sources such as log files, databases, Twitter, Amazon S3, Amazon CloudWatch, Apache Kafka, and many others. After processing and transforming the data through Logstash, you can send it to either Elasticsearch or many other data stores such as MongoDB, Amazon S3, and so on.

Logstash architecture

Logstash has plugin-based architecture. As shown in the following figure, there are three components of Logstash: **Input**, **Filter**, and **Output**:

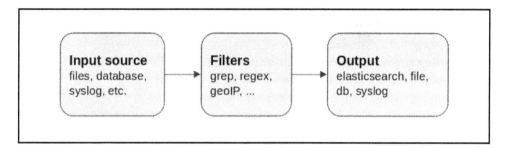

There are hundreds of input, filter, and output ready-made open source plugins available to be used and the best part is if you do not find a plugin available for your use case, you can easily write one for yourself.

The list of currently available plugins is so long that it is beyond the scope of this chapter to mention all the names. But you can have a look at the following URLs to learn all of them. We will be showing examples of how to use some of these plugins in this chapter:

- For input plugins:
  `https://www.elastic.co/guide/en/logstash/master/input-plugins.html`
- For output plugins:
  `https://www.elastic.co/guide/en/logstash/master/output-plugins.html`
- For filter plugins:
  `https://www.elastic.co/guide/en/logstash/master/filter-plugins.html`

Installing Logstash

Similar to Elasticsearch, Logstash can also be installed on different operating systems, including Microsoft Windows. We will cover the installation steps of Logstash on Linux servers in this section.

 Please never install Logstash into a directory path that contains a colon (`:`) character.

Installing Logstash from binaries

You can always visit `https://www.elastic.co/downloads/logstash` to download the binaries according to your supported platform. To get a list of past releases of Logstash, you need to visit `https://www.elastic.co/downloads/past-releases`.

Installing Logstash from APT repositories

To install Logstash on APT-based Linux distributions, you can follow these steps:

1. Install the `apt-transport-https` package on Debian if you do not have it installed already:

```
sudo
apt-get install apt-transport-https
```

2. Download and install the public signing key:

```
wget -qO - https://artifacts.elastic.co/GPG-KEY-elasticsearch | sudo
apt-key add -
```

3. Save the repository definition to `/etc/apt/sources.list.d/elastic-5.x.list`:

```
echo "deb https://artifacts.elastic.co/packages/5.x/apt stable main"
| sudo tee -a /etc/apt/sources.list.d/elastic-5.x.list
```

4. Run the `sudo apt-get update` command and the repository is ready for use. You can install it with the following command:

```
sudo apt-get update && sudo apt-get install logstash
```

Installing Logstash from YUM repositories

To install Logstash on YUM-based Linux distributions, you need to follow these steps:

1. Download and install the public signing key:

```
rpm --import https://artifacts.elastic.co/GPG-KEY-elasticsearch
```

2. Add the following to your `/etc/yum.repos.d/` directory in a file with a `.repo` suffix, for example, `logstash.repo`:

```
[logstash-5.x]
name=Elastic repository for 5.x packages
```

```
baseurl=https://artifacts.elastic.co/packages/5.x/yum
gpgcheck=1
gpgkey=https://artifacts.elastic.co/GPG-KEY-elasticsearch
enabled=1
autorefresh=1
type=rpm-md
```

3. After that, you can install Logstash with the following command:

```
sudo yum install logstash
```

 Please note that these repositories do not work with older RPM-based distributions that still use RPM v3, such as CentOS5.

Configuring Logstash

After installation, Logstash configuration has a similar directory structure to the one we have seen for Elasticsearch.

You can find the following configuration files inside the /etc/logstash/ directory:

- conf.d: A directory where you need to create all your processing pipeline configuration files.
- jvm.options: Used for JVM-related configurations. You can specify the min and max heap size to be used by Logstash using -Xms (defaults to 256 MB) and -Xmx (defaults to 1 GB).
- log4j2.properties: For configuration of log4j parameters.
- logstash.yml: This is the Logstash setting file in which you can configure the parameters to control Logstash execution. Apart from configuring the data path, log path, and pipeline configuration directory path, you can see many other configuration properties in this file. You can refer to the official documentation for details about more sophisticated parameters: https://www.elastic.co/guide/en/logstash/5.0/logstash-settings-file.html.
- startup.options: Contains settings which are only used by $LS_HOME/bin/system-install to create a custom startup script for Logstash. You don't really need to change anything in this file.

Logstash configuration file structure

A Logstash configuration file always has the following structure:

```
# You can add your comments here to describe about what this file does
# parts of your configuration.
input {
    ...
}

filter {
    ...
}

output {
    ...
}
```

As you can see, the input section contains the details about your input plugins. Input plugins specify where Logstash needs to fetch the data from. The filter section is where you need to include filter plugins and write all your processing logics for data transformation, and the output section contains the configuration of the output plugins. Output plugins specify where processed data needs to be sent. We will see examples in the upcoming sections on how to play around with these configurations.

Example – shipping system logs using Logstash

Syslogs are generated on every Linux system and they contain very important information about system events. In this example, we will create a configuration file to process our syslog data in real time through Logstash and will index them inside Elasticsearch.

Please note that when you install Logstash, a user and group is automatically created with the name `logstash`. So if you need to process a file using Logstash, you need to give access permission of that file to the `logstash` user. In the case of processing syslogs, you can do it using the following command:

`sudo usermod -a -G adm logstash`

In the above command, we are adding the `logstash` user to the `adm` group which has access to the syslog file. If the above command does not work for you, please check the group name of the syslog file and replace it with the correct one in the above command.

To do it, first of all let's create a configuration file inside the `/etc/logstash/conf.d` directory with the name `logstash_syslogs.conf` and add the following content inside that file:

```
input {
  file {
    path => [ "/var/log/syslog" ]
      type => "syslog"
  }
}

filter {
  if [type] == "syslog" {
    grok {
      match => { "message" => "%{SYSLOGTIMESTAMP:syslog_timestamp}
%{SYSLOGHOST:syslog_hostname}
%{DATA:syslog_program}(?:\[%{POSINT:syslog_pid}\])?:
%{GREEDYDATA:syslog_message}" }
      add_field => [ "received_at", "%{@timestamp}" ]
      add_field => [ "received_from", "%{host}" ]
    }
    date {
      match => [ "syslog_timestamp", "MMM  d HH:mm:ss", "MMM dd HH:mm:ss" ]
    }
  }
}

output {
  elasticsearch {
    hosts => ["localhost:9200"]
      index => "logstash-%{+YYYY.MM.dd}"
  }
}
```

You can see in the above code, we have three sections: `input`, `filter`, and `output`.

Inside the input section, we have used a file input plugin which contains the path and adds the type of the log name. This type automatically becomes the document type inside the Elasticsearch index for all the documents processed using this config file.

Inside the filter section, we have used two filters: `grok` and `date`. The first one, the `grok` filter, is one of the most widely used filter plugins of Logstash. The `grok` filter is used to parse unstructured data into meaningful structured and queryable content. Logstash is shipped with around 120 `grok` ready-to-use patterns which can be found here: `https://github.com/logstash-plugins/logstash-patterns-core/tree/master/patterns`.

In the above code, what we are doing using the `grok` filter is taking the content of the default message field and applying the regular expressions using the predefined `grok` patterns of Logstash.

We are also adding two extra fields, `received_at` and `received_from`, to enrich our final document.

And finally, we have formatted the timestamp in a standard format using a date filter. This means that we can take a syslog event which looks as follows:

```
Jan 21 01:46:33 bharvi-sentieo systemd[1]: Stopping logstash...
```

Then we can convert it into the following format:

```
{
  "syslog_pid": "1",
  "syslog_program": "systemd",
  "message": "Jan 21 01:44:11 bharvi-sentieo systemd[1]: Stopping
logstash...",
  "type": "syslog",
  "syslog_message": "Stopping logstash...",
  "path": "/var/log/syslog",
  "received_from": "bharvi-sentieo",
  "@timestamp": "2017-01-20T20:14:11.000Z",
  "syslog_hostname": "bharvi-sentieo",
  "syslog_timestamp": "Jan 21 01:44:11",
  "received_at": "2017-01-20T20:14:23.177Z",
  "@version": "1",
  "host": "bharvi-sentieo"
}
```

Finally, inside the output section, we have used an Elasticsearch output plugin to create the connection with local Elasticsearch and defined the index name pattern using `index =>` `"logstash-%{+YYYY.MM.dd}"` so that an index will be created for each day of the syslog.

Starting Logstash

To start Logstash, you simply have to use the following command and if all your configuration files are okay, which we have done in the previous example, then you can see an index will be automatically created in the format of `logstash-YYYY.MM.dd` and data indexing will be started.

```
sudo service logstash start
```

Introducing Beats as data shippers

Beats are lightweight tools for shipping data from hundreds or thousands of machines to Logstash or directly to Elasticsearch. The following figure, which has been taken from the Elastic website, explains the architecture of how Beats fit inside Elastic Stack:

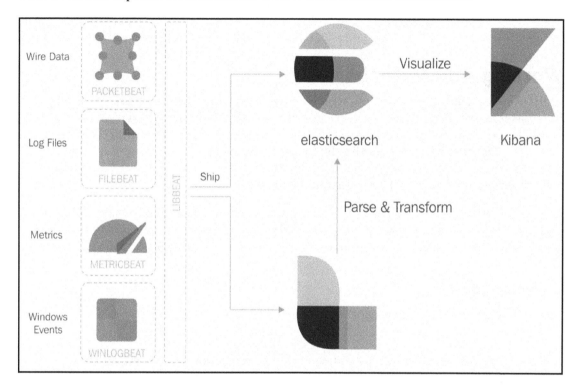

As you can see in this figure, Beats are available in different forms to capture different kinds of data. We have Packetbeat available for capturing packets moving across a network; Filebeat, for shipping data from log files; Metricbeat, which acts as a server monitoring agent and can be used for shipping metrics from an operating system or processes running on your system; and Winlogbeat, for capturing Windows event logs.

But the list of beats does not end here. Thanks to the open source communities, we have almost 40 other beats available, which are being maintained by community members. In addition, you can also develop your own beat according to your use case and make your contribution to the community. You can get the list of all the community beats here:
`https://www.elastic.co/guide/en/beats/libbeat/current/community-beats.html`.

Since this book is not dedicated to Elastic Stack or beats, it is beyond the scope of this book to discuss all the components. But in this chapter, we will be showing you an overview of how to work with Metricbeat. To learn more about working with beats in detail, or to learn how to develop a custom beat, please refer to following official documentation here: `https://www.elastic.co/guide/en/beats/libbeat/current/getting-st arted.html`.

Working with Metricbeat

In the *Working with Logstash* section, we saw what logs are and how to index system logs into Elasticsearch. But in this section, we are going to deal with metrics, which are different from logs. Similar to logs, metrics can also have a timestamp associated with them but unlike logs, metrics are sent periodically, for example, every 10 minutes or a specified interval, whereas logs are usually appended to the log file when something happens and they are indexed as soon as they appear in the log file.

Metrics are often used in the context of software or hardware health monitoring, such as; system resource utilization monitoring, like CPU usage and RAM usage; database execution metrics monitoring, such as performance metrics related to MongoDB, Redis, and so on.

Installing Metricbeat

Please download Metricbeat according to your operating system from `https://www.elastic.co/downloads/past-releases/metricbeat-5-0-0`.

For example, to download and install the Debian package, you can use the following commands.

To download the package, use this command:

```
    wget
https://artifacts.elastic.co/downloads/beats/metricbeat/metricbeat-5.0.0-am
d64.deb
```

To install the package, use this command:

```
    sudo dpkg -i metricbeat-5.0.0-amd64.deb
```

Configuring Metricbeat

Once you are done with the installation, you can find the configuration file inside the `/etc/metricbeat/` directory. Inside this directory, you can find the `metricbeat.yml` file which is used to store all the configuration of Metricbeat. This file is is composed of the following sections:

- **Modules**: This is the part where one specifies the modules that need to be used. By default, it comes preconfigured with the System module. You can configure more modules in this file. Apart from System, the currently supported modules are Apache, Docker, HAProxy, Kafka, MongoDB, MySQL, Nginx, PostgreSQL, Redis, and ZooKeeper. Please follow the official documentation (`https://www.elastic.co/guide/en/beats/metricbeat/current/metricbeat-modules.html`) to learn how to configure these modules.
- **General**: Here you can put the the shipper configuration, for example, its name.
- **Outputs**: In this section, you can specify whether you want to send the data to Logstash and/or Elasticsearch.
- **Metricbeat logging configuration**: To set the log level. The default is set to info.

 To get started with Metricbeat, you can leave the all these settings as they are. But if your Elasticsearch is running on some other server, do not forget to update the Elasticsearch host parameter. Also, if you are using the X-pack security plugin of Elasticsearch, you can set the username and password for Metricbeat in this file.

Running Metricbeat

To start Metricbeat, you can use the following command:

```
sudo service metricbeat start
```

Please keep in mind, as soon as you start Metricbeat, it will start indexing data to your Elasticsearch instance on an interval of 10 seconds.

Loading a sample Kibana dashboard into Elasticsearch

The Metricbeat package comes with a preconfigured dashboard which can be imported into Elasticsearch and used on Kibana. You can import these dashboards inside Elasticsearch using the following command and you will see dashboard getting downloaded and imported into Elasticsearch:

```
sudo /usr/share/metricbeat/scripts/import_dashboards
```

We will soon explore this dashboard on Kibana and will also learn how to create some custom visualizations.

Working with Kibana

We have already mentioned that Kibana is a tool which belongs to Elastic Stack and is used for visualization and exploration of data residing in Elasticsearch. If you have been using Kibana from its older version, you will notice that it has got a big transformation altogether in terms of functionality.

 This URL has all the breaking changes done in Kibana 5.0:
`https://www.elastic.co/guide/en/kibana/current/breaking-changes-5.0.html`.

Installing Kibana

Similar to other Elastic Stack tools, you can visit the following URL to download Kibana 5.0.0, as per your operating system distribution:

`https://www.elastic.co/downloads/past-releases/kibana-5-0-0`

I will show you here an example of downloading and installing Kibana from the Debian package.

First of all, download the package:

```
wget
https://artifacts.elastic.co/downloads/kibana/kibana-5.0.0-amd64.deb
```

Then install it using the following command:

```
sudo dpkg -i kibana-5.0.0-amd64.deb
```

Kibana configuration

Once installed, you can find the Kibana configuration file, `kibana.yml`, inside the `/etc/kibana/` directory. All the settings related to Kibana are done only in this file. There is a big list of configuration options available inside the Kibana settings which you can learn about here: `https://www.elastic.co/guide/en/kibana/current/settings.html`.

Starting Kibana

Kibana can be started using the following command and it will be started on port `5601` bounded on localhost by default:

```
sudo service kibana start
```

Exploring and visualizing data on Kibana

Now all the components of Elastic Stack are installed and configured, we can start exploring the awesomeness of Kibana visualizations.

Kibana 5.x is supported on almost all of the latest major web browsers, including Internet Explorer 11+.

To load Kibana, you just need to type `localhost:5601` in your web browser. You will see different options available in the left panel of the screen, as shown in following figure:

These different options are used for the following purposes:

- **Discover**: Used for data exploration where you get the access of each field along with a default time.
- **Visualize**: Used for creating visualizations of the data in your Elasticsearch indices. You can then build dashboards that display related visualizations.

- **Dashboard**: Used to display a collection of saved visualizations.
- **Timelion**: A time series data visualizer that enables you to combine totally independent data sources within a single visualization. It is based on simple expression language.
- **Management**: A place where you perform your runtime configuration of Kibana, including both the initial setup and ongoing configuration of index patterns, advanced settings that tweak the behaviors of Kibana itself and saved objects.
- **Dev Tools**: Contains the console which is based on the Sense plugin and allows you to write Elasticsearch commands in one tab and see the responses of those commands in the other tab.

Understanding the Kibana Management screen

The Management screen has three tabs available:

- **Index Patterns**: For selecting and configuring index names
- **Saved Objects**: Where all of your saved visualizations, searches, and dashboards are located
- **Advanced Settings**: Contains advanced settings of Kibana:

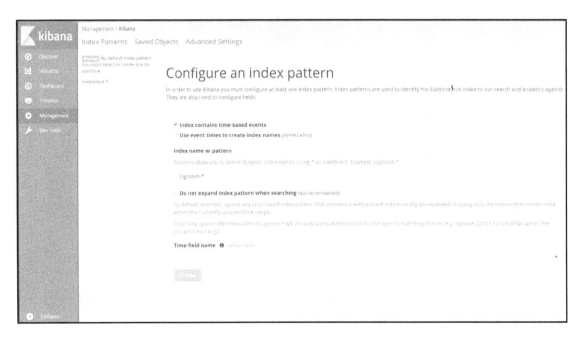

As you can see on the management screen, the very first tab is for **Index Patterns**. Kibana is asking you to configure an index pattern so that it can load all the mappings and settings from the defined index. It defaults to `logstash-*`; you can add as many index patterns or absolute index names as you want and can select them while creating the visualization. Since we do have an index already available with the `logstash-*` pattern, when you click on the **Time-field name** drop-down list, you will find that it will show you two fields, `@timestamp` and `received_at`, which are of the date type, as shown in following screenshot:

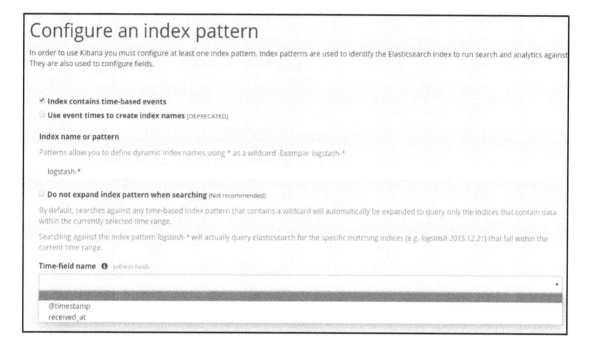

We will select the `@timestamp` field and hit the **Create** button. As soon as you do it, the following screen appears:

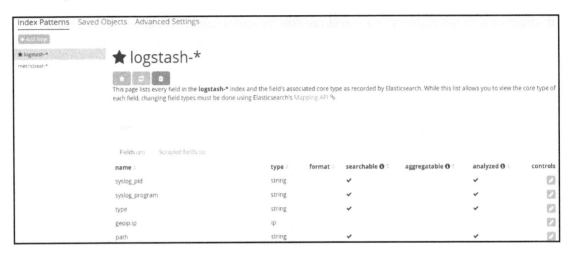

In the above screenshot, you can see that Kibana has loaded all the mappings from our Logstash index. In addition, you can see three labels in blue (for marking this index as the default), yellow (for reloading the mappings; this is needed if you have updated the mapping after selecting the index pattern), and red (for deleting this index pattern altogether from Kibana).

The second tab on the management screen is about saved objects, which contain all of your saved visualizations, searches, and dashboards as you can see in the following screenshot. Please note that you can see the imported dashboards and visualizations from Metricbeat here, which we have done a while ago.

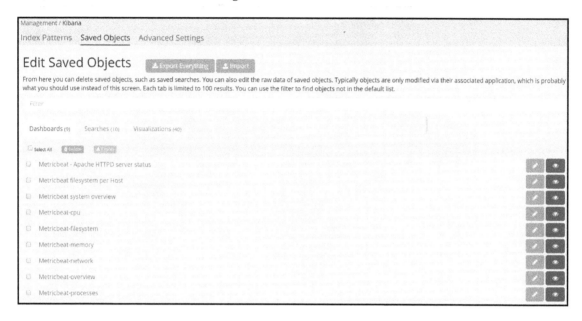

The third option is for **Advanced Settings** and you should not play with the settings shown on this page if you are not aware of the tweaking effects.

Discovering data on Kibana

When you move to the **Discover** page of Kibana, you will see a screen similar to the following:

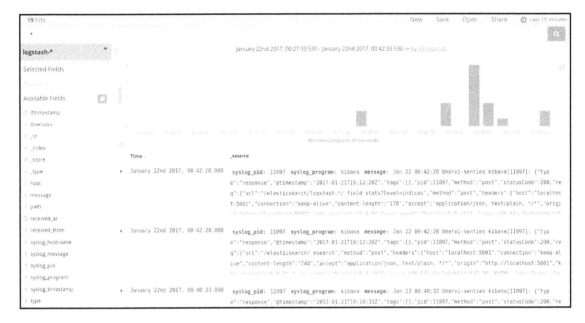

Setting the time range and auto-refresh interval

Please note that Kibana by default loads the data of the last 15 minutes, which you change by clicking on the clock sign which you can find in the top-right corner of the screen and selecting the desired time range. We have shown it in the following screenshot:

One more thing to take look out for is that, after clicking on this clock sign, apart from time-based settings, you will see one more option in the top corner with the name **Auto-refresh**. This setting tells Kibana how often it needs to query Elasticsearch. When you click on this setting, you will get the option to choose either to completely turn off the auto-refresh or select the desired time interval.

Adding fields for exploration and using the search panel

As you can see in the following screenshot, you have all your fields available inside your index. On the **Visualization** screen, by default Kibana shows the timestamp and _source field but you can add your selected fields from the left panel by just moving the cursor on them and then clicking **Add**. Similarly, if you want to remove the field from the column, just move the cursor to the field's name on the column heading and click on the cross icon.

In addition, Kibana also provides you with a search panel in which you can write queries. For example, in the following screenshot, I have searched for the logstash keyword inside the syslog_message field. When you hit the search button, the search text gets highlighted inside the rendered responses:

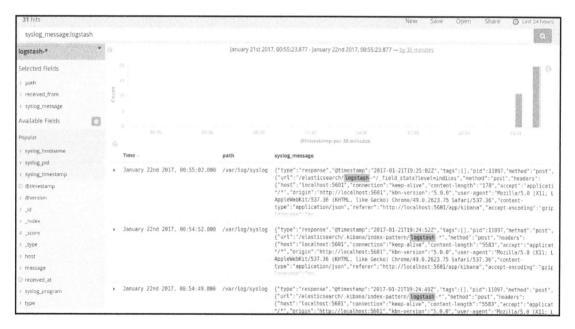

Exploring more options on the Visualization page

On Kibana, you will see lots of small arrow signs to open or collapse the sections/settings. You will see one of these arrows in the following image, in the bottom-left corner (I have also added a custom text on the image just beside the arrow):

When you click on this arrow, the time series histogram gets hidden and you get to see the following screen, which contains multiple properties such as **Table**, which contains the histogram data in tabular format; **Request**, which contains the actual JSON query sent to Elasticsearch; **Response**, which contains the JSON response returned from Elasticsearch; and **Statistics**, which shows the query execution time and number of hits matching the query:

Using the Dashboard screen to create/load dashboards

When you click on the **Dashboard** panel, you first get a blank screen with some options, such as **New** for creating a dashboard and **Open** to open an existing dashboard, along with some more options. If you are creating a dashboard from scratch, you will have to add the built visualizations onto it and then save it using some name. But since we already have a dashboard available which we imported using Metricbeat, we will click **Open** and you will see something similar to the following screenshot on your Kibana page:

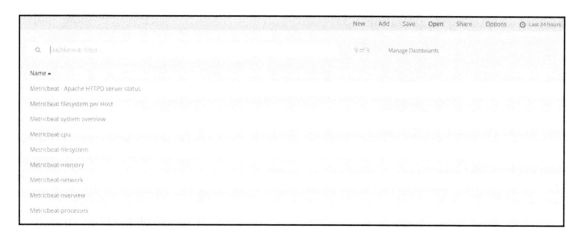

Please note that if you do not have Apache installed on your system, selecting the first option, **Metricbeat – Apache HTTPD server status**, will load a blank dashboard. You can select any other title; for example, if you select the second option, you will see a dashboard similar to the following:

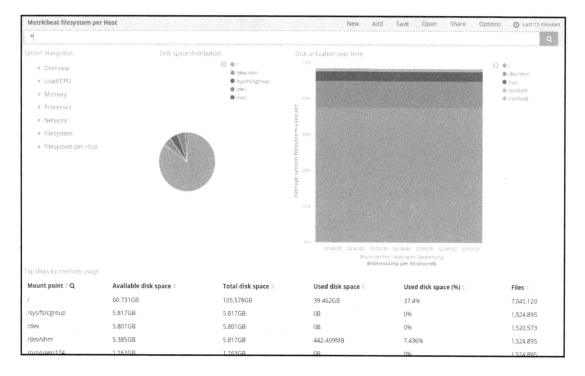

Editing an existing visualization

When you move the cursor on the visualizations presented on the dashboard, you will notice that a pencil sign appears, as shown in the following screenshot:

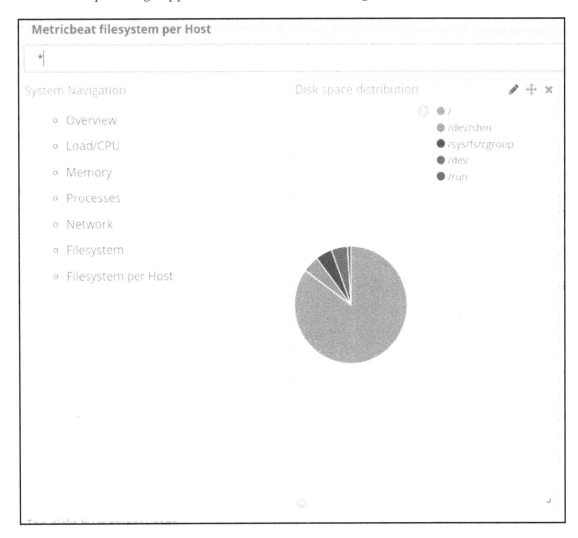

When you click on that pencil sign, it will open that particular visualization inside the visualization editor panel, as shown in the following screenshot. Here you can edit the properties and either override the same visualization or save it using some other name:

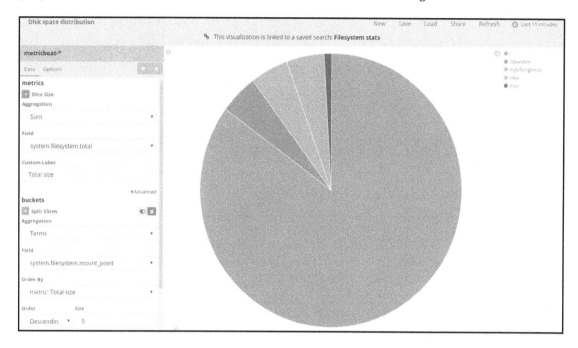

Please note that if you want to create a visualization from scratch, just click on the **Visualize** option on the left-hand side and it will guide you through the steps of creating the visualization. Kibana provides almost 10 types of visualizations. To get the details about working with each type of visualization, please follow the official documentation of Kibana on this link: https://www.elastic.co/guide/en/kibana/master/createvis.html.

Using Sense

Inside the **Dev-Tools** option, you can find the console for Kibana, which was previously known as Sense Editor. This is one of the most wonderful tools to help you speed up the learning curve of Elasticsearch since it provides auto-suggestions for all the endpoints and queries, as shown in the following screenshot:

You will see that the Kibana Console is divided into two parts; the left part is where you write your queries/requests, and after clicking the green arrow, the response from Elasticsearch is rendered inside the right-hand panel:

Summary

This chapter was written to give you an overview of the complete Elastic Stack, which contains Elasticsearch, Logstash, Kibana, and Beats as its components. We started with the overview and then covered how to do setup and configuration of Logstash, Beats, and Kibana. We also tried to explain the components of Kibana as much as the scope of this chapter allowed us.

And now we've reached the end of the book, and we wanted to write a small summary and say a few words to the brave reader who has managed to get to the end. We decided to write *Mastering Elasticsearch 5.x, Third Edition*, because the previous edition of this book was based on Elasticsearch version 1.4.x and since then so many things have been changed in this technology. We wanted to keep you updated with all the concepts around this awesome search server along with letting you know about the major changes which took place across major releases of Elasticsearch. Although you will see this book covers Elasticsearch 5.0.0 in the entire example, the concepts are the same across the 5.x versions. At the time of writing this final chapter, Elasticsearch 5.2.0 has been released and you can use the same concepts learned in this book on this version too.

Finally, we will say thank you for reading the book; we hope that you like it and that it brought you some knowledge that you were seeking, and that you'll be able to use it whether you use Elasticsearch professionally or just as a hobby. If you face any issue related to Elasticsearch, you can post your questions to the official user discussion group at `https://discuss.elastic.co` and we also suggest you keep visiting the official blog of Elasticsearch at `https://www.elastic.co/blog` to keep yourself updated with the latest and greatest news around this technology.

We wish you the best!

Index

www.ingramcontent.com/pod-product-compliance
Lightning Source LLC
Chambersburg PA
CBHW081501050326

40690CB00015B/2883